30
121
81
128
130
41
47

THE LEGEND OF THE FORMULA FORD FESTIVAL

THE LEGEND OF THE FORMULA FORD FESTIVAL

BEN EVANS

FIFTY YEARS OF MOTOR RACING ACTION

pitch

First published by Pitch Publishing, 2022

Pitch Publishing
9 Donnington Park,
85 Birdham Road,
Chichester,
West Sussex,
PO20 7AJ
www.pitchpublishing.co.uk
info@pitchpublishing.co.uk

A CIP catalogue record is available for this book from the British Library.

ISBN 978 1 80150 179 8

Typesetting and origination by Pitch Publishing

Printed and bound in India by Replika Press Pvt. Ltd.

Contents

To Brian Jones, without
whom none of this would
have been possible

Acknowledgements

THE LIST of thank yous could fill half a chapter, as everyone I've contacted has been uniformly generous with their time and help with the project.

There are a few that I can't not thank here. Maria, for pushing me to write this book and managing to maintain a complete disinterest in motorsport. My ongoing causes of writer's block, Alex and Sophie. Dad, for carting and funding me around the racing circuits of Britain for 20 years as a spectator and competitor, including regular trips to the Festival. Mum, for her constant encouragement for the book – I think she's just glad I'm not trying to get behind the wheel again.

To everyone who has spoken to me on and off the record for this book, I appreciate your time, insight and input, even if some of the best stories are unprintable. The same goes to everyone who has helped with fact checking and other material.

I wouldn't have been in a position to write this book without having enjoyed multiple opportunities within the sport. In no particular order, I'd like to thank Andy Storer, Ian Sowman, Brian Jones, David Addison, Nick Kennerley, David Willey, Caroline Sintes, Jesus Pareja, Brian Lavio, Peter McDonnell,

David Pottier, David Jensen, Keith Collantine and Nick Barnett for all giving me a leg-up during my time as competitor and commentator. I'd also like to thank everyone at Pitch Publishing for supporting this project.

Author's note

AS WITH any sport, motor racing is littered with jargon and abbreviations. Where the term may be unfamiliar I've tried to explain it, but there may well be some of the sport's lexicon that has slipped in.

I've taken some liberties with using shorthand, particularly when describing drivers' further careers. IndyCar is used as a broad-brush term for the top tier of US single-seater racing. During the period covered in this book, this was variously known as IndyCar, CART, IRL and ChampCar. Given there have been entire books written about the fragmentation of the US single-seater racing, I've tried to keep it simple – IndyCar is the most commonly used descriptor so I've stuck to that. Similarly 'touring cars' and 'sportscars' are applied as broad-brush terms. I recognise this could include any number of championships, but again for ease I've simplified.

There are two huge limitations in trying to cover 50 years of action in a few hundred pages. Firstly, there will be some mistakes, these are all my own and I apologise. Secondly, every single Festival had multiple subplots and stories and it sadly hasn't been possible to include them all.

Again, I apologise if your favourite moment or personality has been glossed over or omitted.

Introduction

I CAN'T remember exactly what it was that hooked me on Formula Ford, but I do remember sitting in one on my first visit to Brands Hatch. It was for the Free Race Day, one of the many initiatives run by the circuit to bring in new fans. By this point I'd watch any and all motorsport on BBC's *Grandstand*, but seeing the cars up close, meeting the drivers and, most importantly, experiencing the sheer visceral thrill of motorsport in person was enough to hook me for life.

Situated in a natural bowl just south of the M25 in Kent, Brands Hatch is one of those few motorsport venues – Monza and Spa are two others – that is alive. To sit in the grandstand or stand on the banking is to soak in the great races and racers of the past.

Since opening in 1950, Brands Hatch has hosted the highest-profile series (Formula 1, World Superbikes), the greatest drivers and some of the iconic motorsport moments. However, for a sizeable subset of the motorsport community, the circuit is best known for the category it founded and its longest-running event – Formula Ford and the Formula Ford Festival. Three generations of motorsport stars used Formula Ford to take their first steps in motorsport and it was at the Formula Ford Festival where many of them made their name. The intense late-October weekend has made dreams come true for some and effectively ended the Formula 1 hopes of others. It has introduced names such as Mark Webber, Johnny Herbert and Eddie Irvine to BBC tea-time audiences, whilst providing momentary career setbacks for Michael Schumacher and Mika Hakkinen to name but two.

The knockout format sees the tension build throughout the weekend from Saturday's heats into the sharp end of Sunday. Fortunes ebb and flow; drivers who qualified well may fade in the races, others will come good as the conditions change: season-long frontrunners may crack under the pressure and near-unknowns will suddenly shoot to prominence. It is a winner-takes-all weekend. For many in the sport, the only takeaway from a long season of competition is the name of the Formula Ford Festival winner.

If the atmosphere in the paddock is all business, in the grandstands and Kentagon bar the tone is decidedly social. Everyone who's anyone seems to be there, doing business for the following season, trading gossip and, where possible, starting rumours that may unsettle the opposition.

For 50 years the racing has been peerless. Formula Ford cars have no wings to provide downforce and spoil the airflow. This means the cars can run precariously close to each other and are not aerodynamically inhibited from overtaking. That doesn't make overtaking easy – far from it – but it does make it possible, and this is what gives the racing its edge.

During the Festival's heyday the best vantage point – the Paddock Hill Bend grandstand – was sold out; everyone crammed in to watch the cars hurtle through the intimidating, high-speed right-hander. It is a corner where fortune can favour the brave. The grandstand has always been populated by a knowing community; the applause, gasps and boos are driven by deep insider knowledge and insight.

For 40 years the ringmaster and narrator of the action was Brian Jones, whose rich tones remain the definitive soundtrack to the weekend. Beloved by competitors and spectators alike, Jones' commentary and disarmingly direct interview style made everyone present feel like they were insiders and part of the club.

After watching it on TV, pester power paid off and Dad took me to my first Formula Ford Festival in 1992. Although the extensive media coverage gave the Festival a high profile, the magic came from being there in person. Thinking back to that first visit, it was an all-senses experience: the sound of generators and engines warming up, the smells of oil and burger vans, spotting semi-famous motorsport people in the crowd and visiting the shops to see VHS videos (remember them) along with other goods that I could only dream of owning. The most important memories are of the racing – Formula Ford has always captured my imagination like nothing else – and a weekend of nothing but Formula Ford action couldn't be topped.

Since 1992, I've tried to go to the Festival every year (admittedly with a far from 100 per cent success rate) and I have been lucky enough to be there as a spectator, support-race competitor (thanks for asking – it ended in the wall, albeit not my fault – the crash is on YouTube) and five times as a commentator for the weekend alongside Brian Jones. But for Brian Jones' kindness I wouldn't be writing this book. After my driving 'career' petered out – both money and talent in short supply – and really coming to the understanding that I was first and foremost a fan and not a professional, I wanted to stay involved in the sport. After Ian Sowman kindly let me join in for a couple of races at Snetterton, I decided I wanted to try my hand at commentating. I wrote to all the organising clubs and commentators I could think of, and it was Brian who was the first to come back to me to offer advice and opportunities. With Brian's guidance, I was able to secure a few bookings to get started, whilst he was always on hand to gently, but perceptively, offer advice and pointers.

Brian had always talked about writing a book about the Festival, but as the years went by this seemed less and less likely. Tragically his passing in January 2021 meant his definitive story would never happen. But a book about the Festival still needed writing, and whilst this isn't a comprehensive history of the event (you won't find discourses on the differences between Reynard and Van Diemen's suspension in 1983 here), I hope it captures some of the essence of some truly magical weekends.

I came into the project expecting to write a celebratory romp though some entertaining races and rough-and-tumble moments, whilst highlighting the first steps into the spotlight of some great names. That is all there, but there is also an undertone of loss to the book.

Personally, I associate my early Festival visits with staying with my grandparents and days out with my dad, times that can never be recaptured. Even as an adult making solo trips, the nostalgia kicks in – getting absolutely soaked in 2006 but being so exhilarated by what I'd seen that the subsequent drive to Sheffield for a work commitment flew by in a sea of euphoria.

For the drivers, there is a different sort of loss. Whilst the Festival made names, it effectively ended the dreams of many more. Too many hopefuls to mention left Brands Hatch realising that they came up slightly short when pitted against the very best. For anyone this is difficult to come to terms with, but especially when you're in your late-teens or early-20s. Speaking to several former drivers for this book, all had a difficult period of adjustment when their careers came to an end, often falling short of achieving the ultimate dream.

For all the deeper themes, there is one underlying truth to this book; nothing, absolutely nothing, tops the feeling of sitting in the Paddock grandstand and watching the cars in the final come to grid at the end of their formation lap with 20 racing laps ahead to decide the winner of the Formula Ford Festival.

The origins of Formula Ford

MOTOR RACING is not a meritocracy. If football fans can point to the likes of Robin Friday as the greatest player you never saw, he at least made it to the football league. The greatest racing driver you never saw is most likely hurtling a taxi or delivery van around Swindon, Vilnius or Nairobi, having never set foot inside a racing circuit.

Unlike almost any other sport, a driver with bottomless resources and a reasonable level of competence can find themself on the grid for a world championship-level event, as the lower reaches of the entry list for the 24 Hours of Le Mans will testify.

Even Formula 1 is not immune and has established ever-escalating measures to prevent monied but out-of-their-depth drivers getting on the grid.

So how to identify the top emerging talents, test them against their peers, help the best rise to the top and do it without causing multiple bankruptcies? These are questions the sport has grappled with for generations. In Formula Ford, for the best part of 40 years, it found an answer.

Prior to the Second World War, being a racing driver was a pursuit reserved almost exclusively for the aristocracy and the very well monied. Those that became works drivers, as did Richard Seaman for Mercedes, had in many cases spent today's equivalent of millions of pounds to reach that level. The aspirant Grand Prix driver would generally get their start in a small-engined sportscar before working their way through more powerful machinery until they could secure a start in the biggest races. There was no formal ladder, and certainly very few opportunities for a driver without means to become a Grand Prix driver. The Brooklands tagline – 'the right crowd and no crowding' – neatly summarises the social standing of motorsport in the 1920s and 1930s.

As motorsport restarted after the war, Formula 1 remained the top class, particularly in Europe, with the various Grand Prix being organised into a formal World Championship launching at Silverstone in 1950. Many of the immediate post-war aces were drivers who had established themselves prior to the conflict.

For drivers starting out in their careers, there needed to be a clearer path to the top, one which better identified those with standout talent. The emergence of the 500cc class, officially adopted as Formula 3 by the FIA in 1950, provided just such a route. The slight chassis were powered by motorcycle engines, offering the necessary level of fuel economy imposed by enduring post-war petrol rationing. The plethora of marques, relative simplicity of the regulations and affordability proved a hit. Consequently, the category enjoyed extensive popularity, especially in the United Kingdom, throughout the 1950s. As a ubiquitous feature at almost every meeting, the aspirant driver had no shortage of opportunities to make their mark

In Britain the category was overseen by the 500 Club, which in 1954 changed its name to the British Racing and Sportscar Club (BRSCC), whose future would be intertwined with both Brands Hatch and the Formula Ford Festival.

The best-known graduate of 500cc racing was Stirling Moss, whose talent shone within the evenly matched competition. Moss was one of many drivers who were able to progress from this relatively humble start to Formula 1 within the space of a few years.

One of the best-known venues for Formula 3 racing was the newly opened Brands Hatch circuit in Kent. In 1926, cyclists from London had spotted some bowl-shaped fields that formed part of Brands Hatch Farm. Because the land was unsuitable for agricultural use and had been previously used by the army, the farmer – Bert Cornwall – was happy to let cyclists and cross-country runners use it for racing. A year later the first motorcycle races started with the venue serving two different types – summer grasstrack racing on the kidney-shaped circuit laid out in the fields and winter scrambling (motocross) races through the adjacent woodland.

The venue was certainly popular, drawing crowds of up to 30,000 (despite incredibly rudimentary facilities) during the 1930s to watch grasstrack action on the one-mile circuit. Brands Hatch even hosted the first motorcycle racing shown on British television, a meeting in 1947. However, it was the 500 Club that sparked the change in direction to four-wheeled racing on a properly tarmacked surface. During the winter of 1949/50, at a cost of £17,000 (approximately £600,000 today), the permanent surface was laid. On 16 April 1950, Brands Hatch hosted its first car racing meeting.

Brands Hatch proved to be the perfect venue for 500cc cars. The machinery itself wasn't too quick for the relatively short circuit, whose flowing kidney shape allowed for close competition. Speaking to Chas Parker for his history of the circuit, Moss recalled, 'You could go around corners side by side, more or less, and Brands lent itself quite well to it.' Initially running anticlockwise into a long left-hander at Clearways and a short blast along the Bottom Straight before an uphill left-hand climb at Paddock Hill Bend, the circuit experienced a number of serious incidents involving drivers and spectators.

Safety concerns resulted in two big changes ahead of the 1954 season. Firstly, following the lead taken by motorcycle competitors in 1952, all races would be held in a clockwise direction, turning the left handers into right handers. Secondly, the track was extended uphill from the bottom of Paddock Hill Bend, cutting slightly into the woodland for the Druids hairpin, before running back downhill to reconnect via a swooping left-hand turn into the Bottom Straight. Further developments came in the form of safety banking to protect spectators and ongoing upgrading of the circuit's infrastructure.

The track's proximity to London ensured healthy support from both drivers and spectators, with 500cc meetings during the early 1950s frequently attracting four heats of cars to be whittled down for the main race of the day – presaging the format that would make the Festival such a hit. Likewise, being just a short drive from London, both the BBC and ITV would frequently broadcast meetings live, ensuring the venue enjoyed a high public profile.

By the mid-1950s the 500cc cars had started to be overtaken by technology, with Formula Junior emerging as the entry-level category of choice, a position that was all but confirmed by the end of the decade when the Boxing Day Formula Junior races were shown live on BBC television. Founded by Count Giovanni Lurani, arguably as a reaction to Italy's limited success in the 500cc class – which was dominated by British marques – Formula Junior was based on the principle of a racing chassis propelled by production car components. The category boomed, and by the early 1960s there were over five hundred manufacturers worldwide producing Formula Junior cars.

Despite the humble intentions of the category, as its popularity boomed it faced two major challenges. Firstly, aspiring frontrunners required the latest equipment, specially tuned engines and other trick parts, pushing up the costs of competition. Secondly, Formula Junior, running as an international category below Formula 1, catered to a huge breadth of experience from absolute beginners to those on the cusp of a Formula 1 opportunity. In time this led to the more uniform establishment of the Formula 3 and Formula 2 ladder that remains today, but it did still leave a hole for drivers looking to take their first steps in motorsport.

Brands Hatch had always been pioneering in offering on-track opportunities to the public, with the Cooper Car Company opening a racing school in February 1957, and Motor Racing Stables from 1958, both of which offered instruction and track time to aspiring drivers. Initially utilising 500cc cars, by the mid-1960s Motor Racing Stables' fleet was predominantly Formula Juniors.

By this point, Brands Hatch was part of the Motor Circuits Development group under the ownership of Grovewood Securities that also included the Mallory Park, Oulton Park and Snetterton circuits. The operation was run on a day-to-day basis by John Webb. Since taking over the circuit at the end of 1960, Webb had already demonstrated a flair for promotion, bringing big races (both Grand Prix and non-championship Formula 1) to the circuit, whilst steadily supplying the papers with photos of spectacular mishaps. Underpinning Webb's approach was the desire to make motorsport more inclusive. This included ongoing investment in competitor and spectator facilities alongside promotions to get as many people as possible through the gates.

Working alongside Motor Racing Stables owner Geoff Clarke, Webb was keen that this would include opportunities to get on track. Clarke started to experiment with the fleet of school cars to create something that was affordable, punchy to drive and offered parity between the aspirant competitors. Transplanting the Ford Cortina GT 1498cc 'Kent' engine into a Lotus Formula Junior or Formula 3 chassis seemed a good starting point.

With positive feedback from the drivers, Webb and Clarke progressed the idea through the winter of 1966 into 1967. Not only would a category on these lines produce an ideal race school car, it also had the potential to be the perfect entry-level category. Betting that calling the category 'Formula Ford' would attract some backing from the manufacturer, the pair got to work. Henry Taylor, Ford's competition manager, was soon on board, offering several engines for below retail price. The next challenge was finding constructors to build chassis. After initial rejections from both Brabham and McLaren, it was Lotus and Alexis who made up the first field of cars.

Solider Ray Allen (who was subsequently bought out of the army to pursue a motorsport career) has the distinction of winning the first Formula Ford race held, fittingly, at Brands Hatch on 2 July 1967. As a precursor to the close racing the category would become known for, the entire field in that opening race was covered by just 31 seconds. The formula was an immediate success, with a plethora of manufacturers entering the fray for its second season in 1968. The combination of regulations that drove parity but allowed engineering creativity was a huge hit, as was the relative affordability.

Within years of its launch, Formula Ford was a motorsport industry success story, attracting a deep talent pool of drivers who knew they needed to win at this level to progress and a vibrant manufacturer community that continued to drive innovation within the tightly specified regulations, all at a price level that gave the young aspirant realistic dreams of going all the way to F1.

Added to the mix were immediate driver success stories. 1970 saw two Formula Ford graduates make their Formula 1 debuts: Tim Schenken having competed in the 1968 season and, more impressively, 1969's star driver Emerson Fittipaldi, who by the end of 1970 was a Grand Prix winner. Although no one could have known at the time, it would turn out that Fittipaldi's mechanic, Ralph Firman, would have a far greater impact on Formula Ford than the two-time Formula 1 champion.

The technical side of the category was appealing too, as a generation of designers and engineers learned their craft in Formula Ford. The combination of tightly regulated mechanicals (engines, gearboxes and tyres), along with a degree of chassis freedom, leant itself to innovation. The multi-marque competition was integral to the category's growth, ensuring technical development and rivalry for those going for national honours, whilst guaranteeing obsolete gear (if year-old machinery could be described that way) was available to clubmen at low cost. By 1992, at least 160 different Formula Ford marques had taken to the grid.

Formula Fords are immediately distinctive, essentially looking like miniature Formula 1 cars without the front and rear wings. The narrow body of the car houses the driver, engine and gearbox; four wheels stick out at the corners. Even from the earliest days, within this template, each marque's contender had their own distinctive appearance – a 1989 Van Diemen is appreciably different from a Reynard of the same vintage, despite clearly being within the same category.

By the turn of the 1970s, whatever the meeting at Brands Hatch, or indeed any other circuit in the UK, Formula Ford was almost always a feature. With multiple national and regional championships, nearly any given meeting was oversubscribed with the need for heats or qualification races to form the grid for the main event.

The category's popularity wasn't just confined to the participants. Spectators loved Formula Ford. Equal cars, which seemed to just have a tiny bit more power than grip, and hard-charging competitors resulted in a heady cocktail. The racing was rarely anything less than intense, often just on or beyond the line of what was acceptable. Meanwhile the cars entered and exited every corner at all sorts of angles, sliding as they scrambled for grip – the tyres of the day not offering much in the way of traction.

By the time the category reached its fifth anniversary there were some perennial contenders, but the bulk of the field, particularly in the main championships, were predominantly drivers looking to use Formula Ford as a springboard to greater things. The talent pool was increasingly global too and included Brazilians looking to follow in Fittipaldi's wheel tracks, European drivers who recognised they needed to succeed in the British series to make a name for themselves and several Americans looking to plot a path to Formula 1.

The ladder onward from Formula Ford was also clear: graduation to Formula 3, where results and circumstances permitting, there would be Formula 2 and Formula 1 opportunities. Given its entry-level status, Formula Ford was rarely the headline event at most race meetings, often featuring alongside saloons and homebrewed GT cars in support of Formula 5000, Formula 3 or sportscars. Thus the idea of building a race meeting around Formula Fords – even as a club event, let alone a headline meeting – felt like a step into uncharted territory. But that would change in the autumn of 1972.

Early days at Snetterton

THE FIRST Formula Ford Festival was held at Snetterton on 6 November 1972, a chilly and damp Norfolk Sunday.

Throughout 1972 Formula Ford had experienced a challenging year. On the surface, the category continued to thrive, with the UK scene regarded as the place to be for any young driver with serious Formula 1 aspirations. Dig a bit deeper and it had been a fractious season, the contemporary view of the category being far from rosy – rumours of trick engines and other dodgy components abounded (this was to become a near-annual theme). On track, drivers were increasingly frustrated with the number, and cost, of accidents.

Reflecting on the expense of a season's Formula Ford racing in *Autosport*, Gordon Kirby concluded, 'In many ways Formula Ford has become a distasteful business, a class of racing that a driver commits himself to only because he has no alternative, either financially or in terms of experience.'

To offer balance, Kirby then went on to say, 'In England it [Formula Ford] offers extremely valuable experience that cannot be equalled in any other class of racing anywhere in the world.'

To give some context, Kirby reported the cost of a frontrunning season was about £6,000 (equivalent to the average 1972 house price and worth about £70,000 today), including the purchase of a complete car and engine package, along with a towing vehicle. Breaking down the budget, Kirby highlighted accident damage being by far the largest drain on budget – drivers assumed six or so incidents through the course of the season. Only season standouts, such as Ian Taylor, were able to turn a profit from the campaign, benefitting from sponsorship, payment in kind and prize money.

For today's drivers, other expenses seem ludicrously cheap, particularly entry fees and testing costs. By way of comparison, a driver today would do well to compete in a season of British Formula 4 (the grandchild of Formula Ford) for less than £250,000.

Despite the rising cost of competition, professionalism in the paddock was still nascent, sleek transporters and awnings over a decade away. Away from the track there was a strong sense of camaraderie among the competitors and an overwhelming appetite to go racing as much as possible.

In that context, there was a clear gap in the calendar for a symbolic season-closing meeting to provide a full stop to the year. To date the year had wound down as various championships concluded, albeit with some winter series and Boxing Day racing (which would continue until the mid-2000s) available for those that fancied it.

This led to the announcement by the BRSCC of the inaugural Formula Ford Festival, to be run at Snetterton in November 1972. Sitting somewhere between an end-of-season bash and a showpiece event, the Formula Ford Festival was a welcome addition to the calendar, applauded as much as anything for its pioneering format. The Snetterton meeting wasn't the only attempt in 1972 at creating a blue riband event for the category. A 'World Cup' race earlier in the season at Brands Hatch, claimed by Johnny Gerber, had been less than thrilling, leading to *Autosport* stating that the Festival should take on the 'World Cup' mantle.

Reflecting the informal nature of the event, the BRSCC dispensed with timekeepers for the weekend, with grids for the heats being formed from past performances, championship positions and 'unofficial' lap times from practice. The money not spent on timekeepers was used to boost the prize pot, with £250 (the equivalent of just under £3,000 in 2022) up for grabs for the winner – a not-insignificant sum in the context of the season's expenditure.

For an event synonymous with Brands, it is sometimes easy to forget that the first four editions were held at Snetterton. The Norfolk circuit was within the Motor Circuit Developments portfolio and stewardship of John Webb, with many events being organised by the East Anglian arm of the BRSCC. Situated between Thetford and Norwich, the pancake-flat circuit was opened in 1951 and, like so many tracks of its generation, started life as a Second World War airbase.

Whilst never having the same cachet as Brands Hatch or Silverstone, in its 1972 layout Snetterton was a high-speed challenge that allowed drivers to enjoy the type of slipstreaming (trains of cars towing each other and fanning out under braking) battles that became synonymous with Silverstone. A regular test venue for the local Lotus Formula 1 team, and host to the Formula 5000 Championship along with several prestigious sportscar races, it was an ideal venue to try out the new event.

Snetterton in 1972 enjoyed a very different layout from the twisty contemporary circuit. Fully utilising the former runways and perimeter roads, the 2.7-mile lap was fast, challenging and unforgiving with several high-speed corners abutted by unforgiving earth banks. From the starting grid the field would approach the fast right-hander at Riches, followed by a short straight to the slightly tighter right at Sear. The exit from Sear was all important as the road ran through a left-hand kink before heading on to the Norwich Straight running parallel to the A11. The Hairpin that followed always produced plenty of action as cars scrabbled on the brakes to make the tight right-hander, before another lengthy straight – Home Straight – fed the cars into the left-right of the Esses. Then followed another fast right at Coram curve before the high-speed Russell bend completed the lap. Packs of cars towing along the straights and unleashing heroics on the brakes was the expected order of business.

Whatever the paddock dissatisfaction with the state of the formula (history is yet to record a satisfied paddock), it certainly didn't adversely impact the entries in either strength or depth. Eighty-five cars made the trip to Norfolk with most of the season's frontrunners in the field. Taylor was arguably the pre-event favourite, having won both the Grovewood Award and BP Superman of the Year on top of the BRDC (British Racing Drivers' Club) and BRSCC (British Racing and Sports Car Club) Formula Ford Championships. There was also a multinational flavour with American Danny Sullivan, Australian Larry Perkins and Belgian Patrick Neve featuring alongside British and other global talent.

Nestled in the entry list was a driver who would become a pivotal character in the Festival over the next 20 years: Rick Morris. 'I was in an old Hawke DL2B, having scraped together the money. I'd never seen the circuit before; it was amazing, very fast. My main memory of the old track was the run to the Hairpin and that as you slowed down there was this little grandstand facing you.'

Peter Browning, the BRSCC executive director, devised the format for the weekend. The cars would be split into four 21- or 22-car heats run over seven laps, from which the top 15 finishers would progress to the semi-finals. From the semi-finals (this time ten lappers), once more it would be the top 15 in each race who progressed to the 25-lap final.

The duration of the final caused some consternation. Being far longer than the usual encounters, there would be problems in making the fuel last the distance with many tanks simply not being large enough to cover a 67-mile race. Despite some bids to shorten the race, the organisers ultimately decided to keep to 25 laps as planned, their decision swayed by the fact that several competitors had already made modifications to ensure they made it to the flag, whilst others fitted auxiliary fuel tanks.

Following Saturday's untimed practice, the serious business got under way on Sunday morning with the four heats. Not unsurprisingly for November, and in keeping with the years to follow, proceedings got off to a wet start, with all four heats and both semi-finals taking place on a damp track. Given the size of entry and event format, staying out of trouble would be the order of the day in the heats before things got more serious thereafter.

The Titan-equipped Derek Lawrence had the honour of being the first Festival race winner, comfortably winning heat one with most of the action focused on those behind. Heat two was a similarly one-sided affair with Taylor in a Dulon taking an easy win from Sullivan (running unusual bodywork on his Elden ahead of a trip to Daytona). Finishing just off the podium was future *Top Gear* presenter Tiff Needell in the Lotus 49 he'd won as part of an *Autosport* competition. Another name of the future in the field was Adrian Reynard, who within a decade would see the cars bearing his name fighting for Festival glory. Heat three was the first truly exciting fight for the lead, settled in Robert Arnott's favour following a precarious three-wide move at Riches. David Loring won the last of the heats, making it two in succession for the Merlyn marque, working hard for the spoils in a race peppered by spins from his main challengers.

After the lunchbreak and more rain, the top 30 drivers from the opening brace of heats assembled for the first semi-final. It was a classic, with Robert Fearnall's *Autosport* report introducing the race thus, 'This ten-lapper was one of the most fraught Formula Ford races ever.' At the front it was a five-car dogfight with Taylor, Sullivan, Perkins (Elfin, his top gear restored after problems in the heat), Lawrence and Mike Young (Hawke) all squabbling for the win. With multiple place changes on every lap the leaders never got away, and by the closing stages five had become seven – with Needell and stunt driver from the film *Grand Prix*, Buzz Buzaglo (Elden), joining the train.

On lap nine, the mayhem started. Young was the first casualty; attempting to outbrake five cars into the Hairpin, it (not unsurprisingly) went wrong. Young clipped a marshal post to the inside of the corner, launched off a kerb and ended in the middle of the track, ultimately retiring. Young's drama served to slightly split the leading pack, with Lawrence taking over the lead. This order didn't last long into the final lap as Perkins punted Lawrence off into the bank (amazingly Lawrence continued without bodywork to finish fifth), the Australian Perkins also spinning in the incident. This elevated Sullivan to the lead where he took the spoils ahead of Buzaglo and Taylor.

The battle in the second semi-final wasn't quite as fraught, but was still entertaining with a three-way fight between Arnott, Loring and Richard Sterne. The lead places were swapped regularly but interspersed with periods of relative stability amongst the lead group. It all closed up again for the penultimate lap, enabling Loring to strike and demote Arnott from his once comfortable lead. Arnott made a last-lap bid at Sear but ran wide into the grass, allowing Loring to take the win from Sterne, Arnott coming home a distant third. Behind the leading trio, the racing was robust, with several competitors either flinging themselves at, or being squeezed into, the scenery. *Autosport*'s Fearnall summarised, 'There were numerous other spinners in this race, and off the track the action continued with a punch or two.'

By the time repairs had been effected and the grid sorted out, the weather had improved sufficiently for the track to dry out. The three-car front row comprised Sullivan in pole from Loring and Buzaglo – the cars lining up in a three-by-two formation, the drivers on each row alongside each other. Amazingly, the 30-car field got off the line safely before the accidents started at Riches, with a brace of cars left stranded in the trackside ditch. At the front, it was Loring who had taken the early advantage as part of a quintet, also including Sullivan, Taylor, Sterne and Lawrence, which broke clear of the field early on.

With a lengthy race ahead, the frenzy of the semi-finals was set aside for a more tactical affair, the leaders using the slipstream to tow themselves away from the pack. Sterne was the first to fall by the wayside due to failed distributor points. By mid-race it was Taylor and Lawrence who were emerging as the frontrunners, although the leading quartet were changing places on every lap. Eventually, Sullivan and Loring were definitively demoted as Taylor and Lawrence attempted to break clear.

Loring was the next to falter, slowing with an oil splattered visor which he eventually discarded (given the risk to eyesight such a move today would result in an immediate black flag), forcing him to a distant fourth. Sullivan was in the mix until the 21st lap when a spin at Sear dropped him down to sixth. This paved the way for Taylor and Lawrence to sort out victory between themselves.

Taylor was content to let Lawrence lead the way until the final lap, when he squeezed past, under braking at the Esses. Moments later, they crossed the line, with Taylor claiming victory in the first Formula Ford Festival by the tiniest of margins from Lawrence – although with no event timing the actual time differential is lost to history. Third place went to Perkins, who had enjoyed a race-long tussle with Neve, the Australian being the beneficiary of the problems striking Sullivan and Loring.

Of the frontrunning drivers from the weekend, three of the top six in the final would go on to race in Formula 1: Neve and Perkins briefly in the mid-1970s and Sullivan for a solitary season with Tyrrell in 1983. However, both Perkins and Sullivan would go on to have extraordinary careers in their homelands, Perkins becoming a six-time winner in Australia's most prestigious race, the Bathurst 1000, whilst Sullivan's success at the 1985 Indianapolis 500 attained legendary status due to his recovery from a high-speed spin en route to victory. Luck never quite propelled Taylor to Formula 1, but alongside running Thruxton's racing school, he was one of Britain's top national drivers throughout the 1970s and 1980s. Tragically, he was killed racing in the Rover 216 GTi Challenge at Spa in 1992.

It had been a fine inaugural event – the format and racing being acclaimed in the motorsport media – ensuring the Festival was on course, at the very least, to return the following year. Morris recalls, 'It had a great atmosphere, already people were coming from all over, we knew it would continue.' Almost exactly 12 months later on 4 November 1973, 140 competitors (near double the field of the initial event) made the trip to Snetterton.

The event would follow the pattern of the preceding event, although the less fortunate would get fewer laps for their money – the heats being run over just five laps. The four heats would once more form the grid for a brace of ten-lap semi-finals and a scheduled 25-lap final.

It is worth briefly comparing the track time available to drivers in the 1970s with that of current competitors. In the 1970s, race meetings comprised six to eight races, which for Formula Ford were almost certainly run over ten or fewer laps. Given the popularity of the category and oversubscribed entries, following the brief 15-minute practice session there would be either a shorter qualification or consolation race for the slower runners. The Formula Fords would have the opportunity to race every weekend through the season, with drivers entering 25 to 30 meetings as a result. By way of further compensation, testing in the 1970s was unrestricted and at a comparatively lower cost than today. This enabled drivers (funds permitting) to do far more practice laps than today's competitors on the Formula 1 ladder, who will do much of their practice on simulators as testing is limited to just a handful of days a year.

In comparison, most championships in the 2021 season had an eight- to ten-round calendar, with each race meeting featuring two or three races. Today's races are often run over a set time to provide parity between categories (a sports prototype completes ten laps of Brands Hatch a lot faster than a Mini 7). This means that a contemporary Formula Ford driver, whilst only competing ten times a season, can expect 80 minutes or so on track each weekend. In 1973, meanwhile, an unsuccessful competitor in the heats at the Festival could be on their way back down the A11 after just nine minutes of racing.

During the season the main championships had fallen into different hands, with Don MacLeod taking the BRSCC title – the only one of the main championships to visit Snetterton – American Ted Wentz the BARC (British Automobile Racing Club) crown and Derek Lawrence the largely Silverstone-based BRDC series. Wentz would be the only driver of the trio to skip the meeting, where MacLeod and Lawrence would be pushed by the likes of Syd Fox and a returning Robert Arnott.

Once more organised by the BRSCC's East Anglian Centre, Saturday was given over to untimed practice, which would be used, alongside other divinations (performance during the season was another consideration) to form the grids for the four heats. The BARC dinner dance had been held the preceding evening and many drivers took to the circuit nursing sore heads.

Future Formula 1 circuit commentator Bob Constanduros was *Autosport*'s correspondent at the meeting, noting of practice, 'On unofficial timing, conversation seemed to revolve around

Richard Sterne … equally however conversation reflected that few people expected the South African to last 43 laps (heat, semi-final and final) without spinning.' Constanduros also reports 'a steady stream of damaged cars eliminated themselves from the running'.

With official timing instated for the races themselves, it is possible to get a sense of just how quick the 'old' Snetterton was compared to the current Brands Hatch layout. The average speed for the final winner was 93.09mph, a good 2mph quicker than a pole position lap time at the height of the Duratec era.

Although escaping the inclement weather of the previous year, the track remained largely damp throughout race day, with a dry line only really emerging for the final. Unlike the glory days of the 1980s, the early editions of the Festival were squarely aimed at the drivers, with Constanduros noting 'only a handful of spectators turned out to watch mainly excellent racing'.

Heat one got the day's proceedings off to a lively start with a frenetic opener. MacLeod, in the locally produced Van Diemen, and Roger Manning were at the sharp end, with future Formula 1 racer Hans Binder, Peter White and Graham Cuthbert. It was Manning who eventually prevailed, just, from Cuthbert, as MacLeod got delayed late on by a spinning White. The second heat was similarly competitive, with the early running made by Lawrence and two returnees from 1972, Patrick Neve (Lola) and Tiff Needell (Elden), both in uprated machinery. It was the latter who got the victory after Lawrence botched a last-lap effort at Riches and almost spun at Russell.

Entertainment value dipped a bit in the penultimate heat. Practice pacesetter Sterne built a substantial early advantage over Arnott. As the race wore on, Arnott was able to use the slipstream to great effect, towing up to and passing Sterne as they raced to the line, taking the flag almost side by side. The much-fancied Stephen South got a lightning start to heat four but couldn't hold the advantage. This time it was Fox who would reel in the leader, taking the lead at Riches and moving clear to take the win.

For the frontrunners, the heats had served their purpose, with the favourites all safely through and ready to challenge in the longer semi-finals run over ten laps. The first semi-final was the better of the races. The opening five laps provided some spectacular racing featuring the top drivers from the first heat – Lawrence, Manning, Needell and MacLeod – who would all be expected to challenge.

The start jumbled the order with Needell making a terrible getaway, whilst Manning promptly lost first gear, slowing the field behind (the grid once more formed in the three-by-two formation). This brought Neve and Robert Joubert into play and the duo fought for the lead early on with Lawrence and Cuthbert. By mid-race, Lawrence had worked up to the front before building an immediate advantage. Lawrence was aided by Cuthbert having a moment that delayed both him and Neve. Neve, however, held second. Third went to Joubert, ahead of MacLeod, who had climbed from 15th on the first lap.

The second semi-final was less exciting as South once more took an immediate lead. This time he held on, although he was caught late on by a charging Fox, who'd had his work cut out climbing through the pack. Third went to John Bicht after a tough race dicing up through the pack from seventh.

At this point the organisational drama started to kick in. The instigator was Manning. Without first gear and little time to repair or replace his gearbox he'd likely be a non-starter for the final. Showing the camaraderie of the sport, another competitor offered Manning use of his Elden-Piper (a slightly older model than Manning's car, but still familiar enough for Manning to jump into). The BRSCC, opting to play by the rule book, felt they had to get the consent of the other competitors for the car swap. As this was done on an individual basis, and with 30 cars on the grid, it was a time-consuming process – a risky move on an inclement November afternoon (the previous day a meeting at Brands Hatch had been abandoned due to the weather). The net result was that the organisers had no option but to shorten the final by five laps.

Still, 20 laps of Snetterton would be no small challenge, representing a race duration of just shy of 35 minutes, more in line with Formula 3 than Formula Ford. The front row comprised South, Lawrence and Fox. Contemporary reports don't record exactly how the grid was formed, but with South starting from pole despite having won the slower semi-final, the race time of the semi-finals clearly wasn't the deciding factor it later became.

South led away into Riches for the first time, chased by Lawrence and Fox. By Sear, Lawrence was into a lead he would hold until the flag. South was initially the foremost of the chasers but was soon forced into retirement with electrical issues.

Constanduros summarised the state of play for *Autosport* saying, 'it was really now down to who was going to be second', as Lawrence had already opened a handy lead. Fortunately for the hardy souls on the banking, there was a great battle for second with Joubert, MacLeod, Fox and Cuthbert among others in the mix. The dynamic of the race was becoming clear. Either the pack fighting for second would continue to squabble, allowing Lawrence to romp further into the distance, or someone would break free and set about reeling in the leader, the slipstream effect at Snetterton making this easier than in future years at Brands Hatch.

In the event it was the former, a classic Formula Ford battle, with drivers falling by the wayside as the pressure ramped up. By lap 18, they'd all gone except for MacLeod and Fox, the latter having consistently been the pacesetter of the group. This left the duo no time to do anything about Lawrence, but they still had to sort out second, which went the way of MacLeod after a move at the Esses on the last lap. At the flag, it was the win for Lawrence, then MacLeod and Fox, with Arnott the best of the rest in fourth.

Constanduros recorded, 'The competitors adjourned to make merry, receive some prizes from Tarmac and Wella (all provisionally).' The last comment was either auspicious or benefitted from some insider signposting. The top seven cars were all weighed and the engines from Lawrence and MacLeod's cars were taken to Boreham for further eligibility testing.

The outcome of the tests was Lawrence's disqualification. Peter Browning from the BRSCC commented at the time, 'Lawrence's winning engine was found to be illegal on no fewer than four counts – length of valve springs, rockers ground, inlet and exhaust valves polished and pistons machined round the top – and having been found illegal at an eligibility check only a few weeks previously, we consider this a case of blatant cheating.'

Thus history records Don MacLeod as the winner of the second Formula Ford Festival, despite him not winning a race and leading only a few hundred metres all day. Looking back at some of the images of the day, a picture of a garlanded Lawrence printed in *Autosport* tells the story. Instead of the euphoria of future Festival winners, Lawrence offers half a smile. His expression and eyes suggest that he knows everything may unravel in the post-race checks.

Were Lawrence's actions totally out of kilter with the 1970s, and indeed the contemporary racing scene? As Gordon Kirby reported in 1972, the Formula Ford paddock was full of acrimony and rumour of eligibility lines being blurred and rules bent – and this was far from a unique case.

At all levels of motorsport, rumours abound regarding one team or another cheating, or at least interpreting the rules in alternative ways. Paddock rumour and internet gossip swell with the Formula 1 championship-winning car that ran an illegal launch control system, touring cars with painted (hollow) exhaust pipes instead of a weighty roll cage, and on, and on. That said, systematic cheating on the level alleged against Lawrence – or at least being caught – was unusual. There are instances, the Toyota World Rally Championship incident being a good example, in which the car's turbo was cleverly, but indefensibly, modified to give the cars an extra 50bhp. Upon discovery at the 1995 Rally Catalunya, despite the company's clout, Toyota were expelled from the remainder of the 1995 campaign and entire 1996 season. All told, it was a sour note on which to end the season.

But, once more, 1974 saw Formula Ford as the pre-eminent junior category in Britain, with Richard Morgan (BARC), Patrick Neve (BRDC) and Syd Fox (BRSCC) taking the main titles. Whilst most of the frontrunners from the season would make the trip to Snetterton, neither Neve nor the notoriously disqualified Lawrence would be in Norfolk, having opted instead to travel to Venezuela for the self-described 'richest ever' Formula Ford race.

Nonetheless it was still a competitive field that returned to Norfolk for another wintry day of competition on 10 November. Don MacLeod, the 1973 winner, returned to defend his crown having had a frustrating year attempting, and failing, to graduate to Formula 2. MacLeod would be in contention, as would Tiff Needell, returning to try and improve on his previous efforts. Needell was the source of much paddock amusement, having secured sponsorship from Durex for the weekend. Motorsport sponsorship was still in a relatively nascent state and the RAC, scrabbling for a reaction, dictated these particular logos could only be a certain size. Durex certainly weren't put off by the experience, going on to sponsor the Surtees Formula 1 team. This in turn led to a British TV blackout of much of the 1976 Formula 1 season, with the BBC, in particular, unprepared to show the Durex-branded cars – an inauspicious decision given James Hunt's run to the title.

The other main source of discussion in the paddock was the various innovations being shown off by the chassis manufacturers and engine tuners. The Festival was already being established as the place to show off next year's model. Arguably driving this trend was local marque Van Diemen, who had overturned expectations with a strong showing the previous year and were now instigating an enduring tradition of using the Festival to unveil new equipment.

Heading into the event, the topic vexing *Autosport,* although (to their ire) not the drivers, was the future of the tyres for category – and the wider implications for policing the series. A spectacularly grumpy editorial in the week of the Festival served to capture all the controversies surrounding the category in a tone that could easily have been narrated by a John Cleese headmaster.

Today an entry-level category would give anything for that level of media attention, even if it is a stern telling-off.

The gripes are laid bare. The category isn't properly governed, resulting in cheating and competitors having an insufficient voice in decision making. In turn this leads to competitors being short-changed by regulation changes necessitating new cars, or bits for cars, and ever-shorter races. Whatever the concerns, the competitors couldn't muster the enthusiasm to form a drivers' association or attend key meetings en masse to determine the future of the formula. Despite the organisational apathy, they were voting with their feet with a smaller than usual entry presenting at Snetterton for the Festival, so clearly the concerns were filtering through.

For those who did enter there was a change of circuit layout. The run down the Norwich Straight to the Hairpin had been removed, the cars instead had a shorter run out of Riches to a newly reprofiled Sear, before heading down the Revett straight to the Esses, now a fast-flowing left-right sequence. This served to reduce the lap time as the circuit was shorter but the track was still very fast – the winner's average speed in the final being 92.75mph as opposed to a (subsequently disqualified) 93.09mph the preceding year.

As with previous years, the grids for the heats were set by a combination of past record, untimed practice and other (undisclosed) factors taken into account by the organisers. This made the five 20-minute sessions on the Saturday semi-irrelevant, resulting in a number of grumbles from the drivers frustrated at the miserly running time, given that the circuit was otherwise silent. The field would again be split into four heats, albeit increased from five to eight laps from 1973. The leading finishers would then progress to the ten-lap semi-finals and 20-lap final.

Race day itself got off to a troubled start when Mike Keegan from British Air Ferries (a strong supporter of the category) pulled down powerlines when landing at the circuit, meaning that early proceedings would be run from a generator. Fortunately, the day was bright and sunny, escaping the wet and damp conditions of previous editions.

Morgan claimed the first heat, having made some bold overtaking moves to climb up from his initial third position. Second place went to Peter White and third to Fred Sigafoos, whilst fourth was claimed by Rupert Keegan, son of Mike and a future Formula 1 competitor, after a good scrap. Heat two was better, both as a result of some good dicing and late drama after oil was dropped at the Esses. Frank Hopper took the win, having cleared early traffic to take the lead on lap three and managing his advantage through to the flag.

The third heat saw the first mention of many in despatches for Rick Morris. This time though, Morris had to settle for third after a fantastic four-way scrap for the final two podium places. At the front, perennial pacesetter Fox was able to build an early lead. Further back was one of the Festival's first monster shunts. Alistair Cameron was fortunate to walk away after rolling into the spectator area at Russell. There was plenty of strength in depth in the final heat, where Needell, Tim Brise and Mike Young enjoyed a fine dice. Late on, Brise was able to make the decisive break before Young pipped Needell for second on the final lap.

The race of the day was indisputably the first semi-final and the superb dice between Morgan and Hopper. Summarising for

Autosport, Bob Constanduros commented, 'It was exactly what Formula Ford racing should be, with the two fighting for every one of the ten laps and providing really exciting, clean and close racing … it was superb stuff.' In the final equation, Morgan won by a nose cone, but the pair had traded the lead on nearly every lap, with third position going the way of Roy Klomfass. Behind the racing was just as close but more ragged, with the inevitable consequences – Roger Orgee having a huge accident at Russell and ending up entangled with a public address loudspeaker pole.

The second semi-final was more controversial. Fox took a runaway win, but only with assistance that, to some, contravened the rules. Whatever the opinion, Fox blasted into second from the third row and was shortly after into an unchallenged lead. There was another fierce battle for the remaining places, with Jim Walsh eventually prevailing in second from Needell. Pacesetter in the battle for second, Brise, spun late on and was collected by MacLeod, eliminating them both.

The final itself proved to be something of an anti-climax. Morgan, Fox and Hopper had been the class of the field throughout, but there wasn't to be a repeat of the semi-final dicing. Fox initially got the jump from Morgan but would only last a lap before pump failure eliminated the Hawke. Already the pair had built a bit of a buffer over the field, thus giving Morgan an immediate advantage over Hopper. Also in the mix was Klomfass, who had his work cut out throughout to eventually finish in third position.

It wasn't the most thrilling of finals. Morgan ever so slightly extended his lead each time through, eventually building an eight-second buffer by the flag. Likewise, Hopper in second had a near ten-second advantage over Klomfass by the end. Crossing the line in tenth position was Eddie Jordan, the Irish competitor still entered as a driver at this point. Few would have predicted that 17 years in the future Jordan would be taking his team into Formula 1.

It had been a good, if not vintage, Festival, the semi-final battle between Morgan and Hopper being the highlight of the day. Winner Morgan would progress into Formula Atlantic the following season before his career stalled and he drifted away from the sport. Overall, this was reflective of the 1974 season. It had been a solid year of competition, but didn't feature the type of golden generation that had come before or would come after.

After the handwringing of the previous winter, 1975 proved to be a much stronger season for Formula Ford. Whether or not behind-the-scenes activity had boosted the category, the on-track class of 1975 was a strong one. Unlike the previous year, many of the class of 1975 would make it all the way to the top of the sport and the likes of Derek Warwick, Derek Daly and David Kennedy would compete in Formula 1, as would the runaway star of the season, Geoff Lees. Winning the BARC, BRDC and BRSCC championships, Lees enjoyed a standout year.

Since the inception of the Festival in 1972, the technical side of the sport had appreciably advanced. The multi-marque nature of the formula was still one of its strengths, with Crosslé, Royale, Van Diemen and many more all fighting at the front. The cars had evolved, with much more streamlined, compact designs to the fore. Likewise there was fierce competition in the engine department, as tuners such as Minister and Scholar emerged as essential contributors to successful campaigns.

After the challenge laid down by *Autosport* the previous autumn, there appeared to be a step-up in professionalisation throughout the category. This was certainly the case for the Festival. The entire meeting would now be run over a single day, with grids for the heats being set from timed practice. The heats (eight laps), semi-finals (ten laps) and final (15 laps) format remained, but added to the programme was a ten-lap consolation race for the drivers eliminated from the heats.

For the first time, the Festival was also a bit more of a draw for spectators with banking appreciably fuller, despite the 9 November race day. Once more the *Autosport* editorial was a step ahead, imploring circuits to do more to accommodate spectators and give them better value for money – something that John Webb would fully take on board at Brands Hatch the following year. On track, it was a bumper entry, with 114 cars entered for the day, encompassing most of the British Championship frontrunners bolstered by a strong Irish entry (almost all equipped with Crosslés), although the Scottish scene was barely represented.

With the cars lining up in three-by-two formation, as they would until 1985, a decent practice time wasn't the be-all and end-all, but history should record that Mike Blanchet was the fastest in qualifying, a good 0.4s clear of any rivals. The track was running a little slow, with only 11 drivers getting under the 1m 15s barrier (the lap record being 1m 13.4s). At least it was dry, if a little grey.

Blanchet duly took his qualifying pace into the first heat, taking the win after working his way to the front during the opening laps, before pulling clear in the second half of the race. *Autosport* summarised the second heat as '[it] didn't look like the put-up job it was', before clarifying that Rad Dougall and Tiff Needell's close running and constant place swapping was both outwardly entertaining as well as being highly effective in pulling clear of the pack. Dougall just edged the win, although both were awarded the same race time. Timing to 0.001s was to come in later years.

Heat three followed a not dissimilar pattern, this time with Rod Bremner and Jim Walsh breaking clear of the pack – Bremner taking victory by 0.2s. The final heat was the first Festival race to be halted and re-run. This followed an incident at Russell where Barnaby Holland-Martin crashed, mildly injuring a marshal, necessitating a stoppage to provide assistance. In this era, stopping a race to respond to an incident was still a rarity. The restarted race followed the expected form, with Lees taking a runaway victory and finishing some seven seconds clear of Matthew Argenti.

Overall, the heats were a step-up from prior editions, reflecting the strength in depth throughout the field, the quality of racing at the front and a paucity of unnecessary incidents among the frontrunners.

The first semi-final promised to be a good one, with Blanchet pitted against Dougall and Needell, who'd dominated the second encounter. The race initially followed the pattern of the second heat, with Dougall and Needell repeating their trick of towing away from the field. This worked well initially for the pair, but then Needell got a stone through his radiator – initially a distraction, but then taking the edge off his engine (and it ultimately took him out of contention in the final). This gave Dougall the victory and, late on, Needell fell into the clutches of Blanchet, who slipped through into second, edging Needell by 0.2s on the line.

The second semi-final was arguably the race of the day, a thriller throughout the whole ten laps. The first half of the race was frantic but well-judged pack racing before, at mid-distance, the trio of Daly, Bremner and Lees opened a gap on the rest of the field. The timekeepers had Daly and Lees as the lap leaders, but on track Bremner headed the pack more than once. Constanduros summarised, 'It was very good stuff, and the three were covered by just a second at the end.' After ten laps, it was Lees who prevailed from Bremner in second and Daly in third.

Run as a curtain-raiser for the final, the consolation race was taken in dominant fashion by Rob Orford. The slicker organisation and shorter final did allow for the extra race to be run, but it meant that by the time the cars assembled for the main event it was amid gathering gloom.

It had been a day where the cream had risen to the top, giving a front row of Lees, Bremner and Daly, ahead of Dougall and Blanchet. Individual race times from the semi-final were used to set the grid positions.

As was still tradition, the field were released by flag drop as opposed to lights, but Bremner appeared to over-anticipate the start and was headed into Riches by Daly, with Lees in hot pursuit. Daly then hit technical trouble and dropped back down the pack as Lees moved to the front at the Esses. By the end of lap two, Lees and Bremner were already beginning to pull clear when a sign was held over the pit wall notifying Bremner that ten seconds would be added to his race time for jumping the start.

Whether or not Lees was aware of the penalty would be a matter of conjecture until after the race, for whilst the cars were on track, he and Bremner engaged in a thrilling dice, the cars swapping places lap after lap. Behind, after the usual early squabbles, a similar pattern emerged, with Blanchet and Dougall engaging in a similarly entertaining contest.

The last lap would settle everything. In the leading dice, Lees seemed to suddenly back off, trailing Bremner by 0.4s over the line, which in the context of contemporary Formula 1 doesn't seem like much, but in the context of the race was an eternity. Bremner duly took the flag, but with his ten-second penalty hanging over him, a spot on the podium was dependent on others. Ultimately, the fight for third (on the road) was too close to the leading duo, demoting Bremner to fourth. On adjusted times Lees took the win, with Blanchet squeaking second from Dougall, the pair being credited with identical times by the race officials.

The immediate focus turned to why Lees had backed off on the final lap. Had he seen the penalty and decided he'd had his fun? No, despite the November gloom, Lees had opted for a tinted visor, which, as the race and sunset unfolded, gave him diminishing visibility. It transpired that in his visually impaired state Lees had no knowledge of Bremner's penalty and had backed off, unaware it was the final lap, because he couldn't see where he was going.

For the second time in three years, the Festival winner wasn't the first driver to take the chequered flag. Even so, it had been a great Festival, with a notable step-up in professionalism and prestige. These developments had not escaped the attention of John Webb. For 1976, it was decided that the Festival had outgrown Snetterton and would move to what would become its spiritual home, Brands Hatch.

The Snetterton meetings have become something of a footnote in Festival history. Fading memories and the remodelling of Snetterton mean that the 1970s events are increasingly lost to time and the surroundings. The first four years of the event provided some hugely entertaining racing, enjoyed great competitor support and crucially started to build the prestige of the meeting from an end-of-season run-out to something overall more worthwhile.

Early Brands Hatch years

FOR 1976 and every edition since, the Formula Ford Festival moved from Snetterton to Brands Hatch. Whatever the merits of the Norfolk circuit in terms of the racing proffered, the Kent venue had two huge advantages: proximity to London and Dover, and spectator viewing being largely unsurpassed with almost the entire circuit being visible from any given vantage point.

In late 1975, behind-the-scenes changes were made that would have a big impact on the event. In September, John Webb was appointed managing director of Brands Hatch, Snetterton and Mallory Park by circuit owners Grovewood. This move gave Webb a more strategic hand in allocating meetings across the three circuits (as well as Oulton Park, where he was appointed vice chairman). With Webb's flair for promotion and the growing prominence of the Festival (which enjoyed the front cover of *Autosport* in 1975), it was inevitable that the circuit switch, mooted since the inaugural meeting, would finally happen.

Ahead of the 1976 season, Brands Hatch had the benefit of a major facilities upgrade. A dedicated Formula 1 pit and paddock was constructed in the centre of the track, eradicating a steep slope adjacent to the pit lane that made for miserable working conditions for the mechanics. The circuit was slightly altered too; in a nod to safety, the notorious Paddock Hill Bend was slightly tightened, the old track being left as run-off, whilst Cooper Straight (formerly Bottom Straight) was resurfaced. As could have been expected, the developments didn't run totally smoothly, but once the season was in full swing everything was complete.

By 1976, Brands Hatch was established, alongside Silverstone, among the best-known and pre-eminent motorsport venues. Unlike the aloof atmosphere that could sometimes be found at the BRDC-run Silverstone, Brands Hatch prided itself on being accessible and welcoming. The two venues alternated the honour of hosting the British Grand Prix.

Unlike flat Silverstone, Brands Hatch was a spectator's dream, with the grandstands and elevated spectator banking offering views of almost the entire circuit. Not yet christened the 'Indy circuit' (this would follow in 1978 after the visit of the American IndyCars), the short 1.2 mile-layout provided no respite for the drivers. Unlike Snetterton, where lengthy straights preceded heavy-braking zones, the lap at Brands Hatch was all action. From a tactical point of view, this meant that drivers had to be both opportunistic and patient, taking immediate advantage of a rival's error, whilst also plotting moves several laps ahead.

The layout was barely altered from the mid-1950s. The lap started on the undulating, gently rightward-curving Brabham Straight before feeding into the right-hander at Paddock, the road plummeting downhill just as the drivers hit the apex. From there, the road rose steeply into the right-hand hairpin at Druids before falling once more into the swooping, downhill left-hander at Graham Hill Bend. Fed on to the short Cooper Straight, the drivers then hit Surtees, a left-right combination taken at speed, before the never-ending right-hander of Clearways and Clark Curve that fed drivers back on to the Brabham Straight to complete the lap.

Integral to the Brands Hatch experience in the mid-1970s and for the 40 years that followed was Brian Jones. Alongside day-to-day management duties at the Brands Hatch Racing School, Jones was the 'voice of Brands Hatch'. His wonderfully rich, expressive tones became a fixture for decades. Combining a love of, and deep insider's knowledge about the sport with a warm and irrepressible personality, Jones's unique skill was making everyone present feel part of the club. The booming catchphrases such as 'high, wide and handsome' were as much a part of a day out at Brands Hatch as anything that might happen on the track.

The highlight of the 1976 season was the British Grand Prix, where a 77,000-strong crowd came to acclaim James Hunt. In a race infamously not televised live due to a row with the BBC about which sponsors logos could be shown, a first-corner incident at Paddock almost decided the outcome of the championship. The two Ferraris of Lauda and Regazzoni collided, with Hunt being tipped into the air by a spinning Regazzoni. With cars scattered and Hunt having sustained damage, the race was stopped. Jones, commentating from Westfield on the Grand Prix loop, then began inadvertently whipping the crowd into a frenzy, with tens of thousands of spectators collectively insisting that Hunt be allowed to join the restarted race. This was permitted and Hunt took victory before being disqualified two months after the event when it was judged that he shouldn't have joined the restarted race.

In a title fight that went down to the final round in Fuji, Hunt claimed the Formula 1 championship in monsoon-like conditions after Lauda withdrew. Hunt was now a fully fledged national hero and household name in millions of homes.

Never one to miss a trick, Webb hastily rebranded the Festival meeting as the Tribute to James. A Shellsport 5000 race was hastily added to the timetable to provide the crowds with some Formula 1 and Formula 5000 machinery, supplementing the Formula Ford action. Hunt himself was on hand to demonstrate his title-winning McLaren, sign autographs and present trophies, and, incredibly, so too was Lauda. Even at the time this was remarkable, although Hunt and Lauda did have a strong personal relationship, but in the present day would be near impossible – imagine Max Verstappen attending a celebration event in honour of Lewis Hamilton or vice versa. *Autosport*'s post-event editorial takes aim at the lack of respect shown to Lauda, who was neither interviewed over the public address nor able to undertake planned demonstration laps in a Ferrari Berlinetta. Throughout 1976 Lauda had shown incredible dignity and bravery, his day out at Brands Hatch being another such example.

For the Formula Ford competitors, after four years of ending their season in front of a handful of enthusiasts, their 1976 day in the spotlight would be played out in front of 11,000 spectators. The season had been a good one, with strongly contested championships and, according to contemporary reports, the greatest strength in depth the category had ever seen with the combination of returning drivers and newcomers providing a heady mix.

Stars of the season included BARC champion Rod Bremner (who'd come so close to winning the Festival the previous year),

David Kennedy (leader of the BRSCC title hunt), along with Jim Walsh (BRDC champion) and Derek Warwick, who had consistently been at the front end. They were all among the favourites heading to Brands Hatch along with 1973 winner Don MacLeod and Derek Daly, who had funded his racing by working as a miner in Australia.

Once more running as a two-day meeting, the event was expanded to eight seven-lap heats to be run on Saturday. In 1976's horrendous weather, this was only just over seven minutes of racing time, and in the dry would be closer to six and half minutes. On Sunday, these would be followed by four ten-lap quarter-finals, a brace of 12-lap semi-finals and a 15-lap final. The combination of elevated prestige and booming interest in the category led to an incredible 183 entries being received, although pre-event and practice attrition meant that 139 cars took part in the heats, a still very respectable 17 cars per race.

A particular quirk to the event (abandoned the following year) was that the first heat doubled as the final round of the Star of Tomorrow Formula Ford Championship and the final itself similarly doubled as the final round of the BRSCC championship. The Star of Tomorrow drivers (all first-year competitors) being grouped together led to a somewhat lopsided draw.

The conditions for Saturday's heats were atrocious, with torrential rain for most of the day. The subplot for the opening heat was that Sean Walker had to stay clear of future BTCC (British Touring Car Championship) star David Leslie in order to take the Star of Tomorrow title. An early spin at Surtees delayed Walker, allowing Leslie and Ian Bell to dispute the lead. Despite his early setback, Walker caught the leading duo on the final lap, just pipping Leslie for second to claim the title, whilst Bell took the win.

The second heat was less entertaining as Bremner quickly recovered from a poor start, and from mid-race was installed at the front. Treacherous conditions at Surtees decided the outcome of heat three where initial leader Daly had a moment, elevating John Poxen to a substantial lead. Minutes later, Poxen also got caught out at Surtees, allowing Daly to pounce, taking victory by eight seconds.

Rotations at Surtees were also the order of the day in heat four, where Rick Morris claimed the spoils. Morris was the first of the frontrunners to spin at Surtees before Rob Wicken did the same a lap later. This left Mike Blanchet in the lead, but Morris's pace proved decisive, reeling in and passing Blanchet to take the flag with a four-second margin.

By the time the fifth heat got under way, track conditions had improved somewhat – a combination of the rain easing off, and the big Shellsport 5000 cars clearing a dry line. Whether or not the track changes made a difference, Kenny Gray put in an excellent performance to win by over ten seconds, a huge margin for a seven-lap race on a short circuit. It was an even bigger gap from the victor to the rest in the following heat, where Kennedy built up a 14-second margin over his rivals, a rate of some two seconds per lap. This feat was undertaken in rapidly worsening conditions, failing light and a new downpour made the race time some 40 seconds slower than the one that preceded it.

More rain greeted the drivers for penultimate heat, from which 1973 winner MacLeod took victory, once more over ten seconds clear of second-place driver Walsh. Never looking comfortable on the sodden circuit, Walsh had been fortunate to inherit second as others fell by the wayside. In near darkness, it was hardly surprising that the final heat wasn't a thriller – Warwick leading home a fairly stable upper order.

The weather cleared overnight and fine conditions greeted the drivers on Sunday morning. This was the point of proceedings where things started to get serious – although not so much in the first quarter-final. The Star of Tomorrow novices made things a bit easier for some of the veterans who joined the field from the second heat. Bremner was the principal beneficiary, although both Walker and Leslie gave him a run for his money. The fight for fourth had most of the action, a large squabbling group covered by just 1.4s at the line.

A red flag for a blocked track following a four-car pile-up at Paddock Hill Bend meant the second quarter-final got off to a false start. Once running properly, Daly and Morris were the class of the field. Both equipped with Hawkes, it was Morris who had the initial running, but Daly, sporting a prototype chassis, was able to jump clear and build a slight buffer. Morris then became entangled with Blanchet and Poxen but managed to ease clear once more to take second, some six seconds back from Daly.

On paper the third quarter-final promised to be the best yet, with Gray and Kennedy both in contention for the BRSCC championship that would be decided as part of the final. Unfortunately it was a bit of a damp squib – Gray made a superb start, whilst Kennedy was delayed by wheel-to-wheel contact with David Heale. The incident enabled Gray to build an immediate gap, and with slight damage Kennedy was unable to do too much about reeling him in, Gray once more taking the victory by over ten seconds.

With bad weather effectively washing out their heats as meaningful contests, the competitors in the concluding quarter-final hadn't yet really shown their hands. Past form, however, suggested it would a highly competitive race. And so it proved with a fantastic three-car fight emerging at the front between MacLeod, Warwick and Dutch competitor Michael Bleekemolen. All this happened with a large portion of the circuit covered by yellow flags after Rob Ellis crashed into the bank at Surtees, breaking his leg and ankle. A similar incident today would result in an immediate red flag, but in 1976 the race continued around the rescuers as they tried to free the trapped Ellis. After ten frantic laps, MacLeod claimed the honours from Bleekemolen and Warwick, the trio covered by just 0.4s.

The weather started to turn inclement again for the first of the semi-finals, which once more was a Daly-Morris Hawke benefit. For Daly, the entire 12 laps were comfortable, having taken a decent lead at the start. Initially it was Walker who gave chase, but he was quickly passed by Morris before eventually fading to fifth. Daly and Morris didn't quite fly in formation – the gap between the pair was just over four seconds, but they were comfortably the class of the field. After a busy race, Blanchet finished in a rather distant third.

The second half of the draw continued to be blighted by bad weather. Once more the conditions were worsening and continued to deteriorate over the 12 laps. It was both a thrilling and ultimately attritional race. Initially, the crowd was entertained by multi-car dice with Gray, Kennedy, Warwick, MacLeod and Bleekemolen all in the mix. By mid-distance it was Gray who had the lead, as Warwick became the first to falter with engine trouble. Fortunately Warwick's issue wasn't terminal and the wet track somewhat mitigated his disadvantage.

With Gray pulling clear, MacLeod made his move, passing Kennedy for second. Kennedy then began to drop down the order as his visor misted up, eventually finishing in fifth, behind both Bleekemolen and Warwick. By the final laps MacLeod had steadily worked his way on to Gray's tail and, heading to Druids for the final time, he was close enough to challenge. Gray made the traditional defensive move of covering the inside line but was caught out by the slippier surface and understeered off the track. This elevated MacLeod to take the win with Warwick also able to dart ahead of the recovering Gray to pip fractionally him for second.

This set the scene for a tantalising final. Daly and Morris had been the class of the field in the first semi-final and Daly had not really been challenged throughout the meeting. Those progressing from the second semi-final had needed their street-smarts about them, having to get their elbows out for the result.

For the crowd, the anticipation built throughout the day, everyone picking out favourites and monitoring progress. But, as with any sporting event, despite the build-up, the final could still be pot luck – in years to come some wonderful finals would redeem otherwise largely unexciting meetings; equally thrilling qualification races would be somewhat forgotten in the wake of a dull final. Other years would go exactly as the form book predicted, but what would keep a hardcore returning to the Brands Hatch banking for the best part of 50 years would be the hope of an end-to-end classic Festival capped by a thrilling final.

Morris's memories of the weekend are mixed: 'The move to Brands worked out brilliantly for me as it was my home circuit. 1976 was a great year, I was part of a semi-works Hawke team alongside Devaney, Warwick and Daly. The summer had been so dry and that suited the car perfectly. Ultimately, I made the wrong decision for the Festival. I'd been testing the [new] DL17 and hated it; it flexed too much and didn't give me the feel I wanted. Derek [Daly] decided to use it for the Festival and it worked perfectly in the wet.'

The build-up to the 1976 final wasn't auspicious as rain continued to pelt the circuit and darkness descended. This meant that five laps were lopped off the race distance, reducing it to just ten laps – although given the adventures on a sodden track throughout the weekend, this would be challenge enough.

The front row of Daly, MacLeod and Warwick left the line as one, but it was Daly who swept into Paddock in the lead. Quickly a four-car leading group emerged with the front-row trio joined by a charging MacLeod. It was only really MacLeod who was able to give Daly a fright, forcing him into a small error at Druids, piling on the pressure. A moment at Surtees on the sixth lap effectively ended MacLeod's charge, the trip over the grass filling his visor with mud, causing a spin. MacLeod would eventually recover to finish in seventh position.

This gave Daly a slender buffer as, at the same moment, Warwick moved ahead of Morris into second position, establishing the order through to the chequered flag. The closing laps were played out in ever-more challenging conditions, but the frontrunners held their nerve, Daly winning the first Brands Hatch edition of the Festival by just under two and half seconds. Other business was taken care of elsewhere in the top ten as Kennedy's sixth place finish gave him the BRSCC championship. Finishing in tenth position was another driver who would cross paths with Kennedy and Daly in Formula 1 a couple of years later. Dutchman Jan Lammers had not had a spectacular weekend and underperformed according to some observers, but this was a small blip in a career that would see him start 41 Grand Prix and win the 1988 24 Hours of Le Mans.

Daly would make his Formula 1 debut within two years of his Festival triumph. His Grand Prix career never quite fulfilled his junior formula potential, although he came within a few hundred metres of winning the 1982 Monaco Grand Prix. Daly is instead almost better known for his post-racing career as a broadcaster on American television following a successful transition to IndyCar and as an expert on the business of motorsport, having written the excellent *Drive to Win* on the subject.

Formula Ford continued to go from strength to strength in 1977. Dud Candler, writing in the 1987 event programme, reflected, 'Some years in Formula Ford 1600 are classics, 1977 was such a year.' In the era of multiple championships, there was no single dominant driver throughout the season but rather a quartet of favourites descending on Kent to battle it out: namely Van Diemen's BRSCC title-winning Brazilian hotshot Chico Serra, the national champion (this title not yet having its later prestige), South African Trevor van Rooyen in a Royale, the similarly chassised David Leslie (BARC Champion) and BRDC champion Nigel Mansell in the Crosslé. Mansell had endured a challenging year, sustaining a serious neck injury in an incident early in the season at Brands Hatch, an accident that came weeks after he'd resigned from his job to concentrate on racing.

Hindsight would record 1977 as one of the better Festivals, with entertaining racing throughout the day as the six heats, three semi-finals and final provided plenty of action. As Candler commented in 1987, 'The Formula Ford Festival, the last chance, no championships at stake, just a lot of pride.' It was another packed entry, with over 120 cars to be whittled down over the course of the single day of racing held on 6 November (the grids had been determined by timed practice on Saturday).

The first of the ten-lap heats got under way promptly at 10.30, immediately bringing one of the frontrunners – Serra – into the fray. The Brazilian leapt to the front at the start, maintaining a largely comfortable lead until forced on to the grass late on by a backmarker. This gave Mike Blanchet a brief spell in the lead before Serra came back through to win. Other action was provided by Suzuki motorcycle star Pat Hennen, who showed great pace early on before crashing into retirement.

Mansell was the star attraction of heat two, but his day proved to be short lived. Initially jumping into the lead, Mansell had a wayward first lap and dropped to sixth before his Festival ended on the fourth lap after a collision with Ted Whitbourn. This left Yves Sarazin to take the win in a high-quality field from James Weaver and Kenny Acheson.

1973 winner Don MacLeod and fellow Scot Leslie contested the honours in heat three, the pair working past initial leader Bernard Devaney in the early stages. MacLeod put his wiles to good use and there was no way past for Leslie, the timekeepers separating them by just two-tenths of a second. Van Rooyen had it easier in the fourth heat, taking a comfortable victory – his 33rd race win of the season – to make it safely through to the semi-finals. Mansell's upset aside, the expected favourites had all made it through their heats without too much drama.

The penultimate heat threw up the first surprise of the day when Irish challenger Colin Lees was able to get the better of perennial frontrunner Rick Morris. Morris, in the new and unraced Saracen, was able to stay with Lees throughout, but couldn't find a way past. Last seen attempting to qualify for the Dutch Grand Prix (and returning to Formula 1 the following season, when he did make it on to the grid for the US Grand Prix), Michael Bleekemolen was the star turn of the final heat, running out a comfortable three seconds clear of local challenger Roger Pedrick.

The first semi-final had Sarazin and Serra as the star draws with Weaver completing the front row, in one of the less-entertaining races of the day. Leading away, Serra was soon able to break away from Sarazin and made short work of the opposition to win by six seconds. Sarazin took a solid second although Blanchet, in third, applied some pressure late on. For Weaver it was disappointment as he spun away his chances early on.

If the first race had been relatively polite, there were no such manners in the second semi-final, where MacLeod, Leslie and van Rooyen came up against some wild driving from Devaney. Leslie was the first to decisively clear Devaney for the lead, with MacLeod not far behind. As the pair tried to move clear, van Rooyen needed all his nerve to consolidate third. Pushed on to the grass at Paddock by a power-depleted Devaney, van Rooyen held on despite suspension damage from earlier contact.

Roger Pedrick was the star of the last of the semi-finals, impressing onlookers as he hurtled around in his Crosslé. However, Bleekemolen took the honours, moving into the lead on the fourth lap before building a decisive cushion through to the flag.

A largely incident-free trio of races meant the 21-car field for the final was packed with prospective winners, Mansell being the day's only casualty of substance. Starting from pole position, Serra once more led into Paddock and thereafter controlled the race, albeit with attention throughout from Leslie. The main action was for third, with Sarazin, Blanchet and van Rooyen all in the mix. Eventually, van Rooyen claimed the position, helped somewhat by Sarazin overdoing it at Paddock and ending his race in the barrier. Fifth meanwhile went to MacLeod, who'd had to work back up through the field following a poor start.

Festival success helped propel Serra up the ladder and within four years he would be in Formula 1 with the then-declining Fittipaldi team. After making 18 starts from 33 entries, including a solitary point at the 1982 Belgian Grand Prix, Serra returned to Brazil and become a star in the national stock car series.

Leslie had an even more diverse career, also making it to Formula 1 (albeit the British series) in 1979. After his single-seater career petered out in the early 1980s, Leslie became synonymous with the Ecurie Ecosse team, firstly in the World Sportscar Championship, then BTCC. One of the top drivers of the super-touring era, Leslie's best season came in 1999 when he finished runner-up for Nissan. Also, while running a successful Formula Ford squad in the late 1980s, Leslie introduced Allan McNish and David Coulthard amongst others to the sport. Tragically, he was killed alongside sportscar team owner Richard Lloyd in a private jet accident near Biggin Hill airport at the start of 2008.

The class of 1977's biggest star never made it through

his heat. Nigel Mansell had a far from straightforward path to Formula 1, but by the summer of 1980 had made his debut for Team Lotus at the Austrian Grand Prix. After moving to Williams for the 1985 season, he scored his debut victory at Brands Hatch at the European Grand Prix later that season. By the time he returned to Kent to win the British Grand Prix in 1986, Mansell-mania was sweeping the country and he was a national hero when he finally won the F1 championship in 1992, before taking the 1993 IndyCar crown.

After the success of the previous year, the 1978 Festival was expanded to fill the whole weekend with Formula Ford action and accommodate the overflowing entries. Consolidating the format for the weekend into a new guise that would run until 1992, Saturday's action compromised eight heats before the quarter-finals, semi-finals and final on the Sunday.

With grids limited to just 20 cars (by the early 1980s, this would be increased to 28), the equation for the drivers was simple – finish in the top ten or the weekend was over. However, with an entry of 174 drivers for 160 starting slots, an unfortunate 14 competitors wouldn't progress beyond qualifying. The most significant of those to miss out was Jonathan Palmer. The future Brands Hatch owner set a decent enough time in qualifying but got involved in someone else's accident and couldn't get his car repaired in time to race.

Kenny Acheson had been the season's dominant driver, taking the national, BRSCC and BARC titles as well as the Grovewood award. He would be one of the favourites for the weekend as part of a field that was a combination of class stalwarts (Morris, MacLeod), returnees (Devaney, Weaver) and promising newcomers (Tommy Byrne and Mike Thackwell).

Also considered as possible winners by the pundits were Michael Roe, who had been fast all year but luckless in terms of results, and the Belgian champion Thierry Boutsen.

Former karting and hot rod racer Terry Gray made the early running in the first heat before engine issues saw him passed by both MacLeod and Colin Lees. MacLeod was giving his homebuilt Sark chassis a successful debut outing. A poor start from pole position in heat two ultimately failed to deter Weaver, who charged back to reclaim the lead at Paddock on the sixth lap. Peter Morgan took second, reflecting to *Autosport*, 'I could see he was in a determined mood' by way of explanation for conceding the lead. The works Van Diemen of Carlos Abdala took third.

Roe and Devaney were drawn together for the third heat, but, instead of battling it out, the pair decided to work together to ensure safe passage and a decent race time. This they achieved, the heat being the fastest of the day. Roe had the measure of Devaney, leading throughout except when his engine briefly faltered at Paddock, but he was soon back in front. Third went the way of future Formula 3000 team principal David Sears, who prevailed in a multi-car dice. Heat four delivered the first frontrunning casualties of the weekend, when Thierry Tassin's overexuberance removed himself and David McClelland from proceedings whilst battling for the lead. This promoted Italian novice Almo Coppelli to win from Marc Duez.

A superb three-car battle for the lead between Boutsen, Roberto Guerrero and Cameron Binnies entertained the crowd during heat five. *Autosport* reported, 'Such was the intensity of the battle that one could be forgiven for thinking this was the final.' The decisive moment, almost inevitably, came at Paddock when Boutsen tried to outbrake Guerrero, followed by inevitable contact. Although both somehow avoided a monster shunt, Guerrero would suffer a slow puncture that dropped him to fourth. Boutsen was able to hold on to the flag, with Binnie second.

Qualifying had suggested heat six would be one of the closest, with Irish driver Tommy Byrne and Trevor Templeton very evenly matched. Byrne's car might not have been one of the most elegantly turned out, but it was fast. The race seemed Byrne's to take, but late on he left a slight gap into Paddock, an invitation that Templeton was loath to refuse. Byrne's best efforts to fight back came to naught as Templeton took the honours, rounding out the podium in a not too distant third was John Village.

The impressive 17-year-old Thackwell was a decisive winner of the penultimate heat, his racecraft belying his experience and age. His getaway was somewhat aided by the dice for second where Peter Argetsinger had the edge over Didier Theys (one of several strong Belgian drivers in this year's entry). A lightning start for Jim Walsh was enough to propel him to victory in the final heat from Acheson and Rob Zurrer – the latter noseless for much of the race after an early chop from Walsh. The Royale driver's win gave five different marques success during the heats: Sark (McLeod), Van Diemen (Weaver, Roe, Templeton and Thackwell), Tiga (Coppelli), Crosslé (Boutsen) and Royale (Walsh).

A damp track greeted the drivers the following morning, with a shower shortly before the first quarter-final, making for tricky conditions. MacLeod put his experience to good use, making a clean start before building a six-second gap over the rest of the field. Terry Gray likewise was a reasonably comfortable second but couldn't close down MacLeod. The fight for third was a bit livelier, particularly in the opening laps. By one-third distance, Weaver had made the place his and was content to settle thereafter, although Abdala chased him all the way.

Roe and Devaney were once more the class of their race, finishing ten seconds clear of the rest. Whilst they had it their own way to sort themselves out, it was a far firmer battle than the shadowboxing of the day before. The pair swapped places throughout, neither quite content to settle for second. It came down to the final lap, when Roe braked as deeply as he dared at Paddock, demoting Devaney, and holding on for the final mile. Van Diemen team principal Ralph Firman was less amused, giving an unfussed Roe a dressing-down for pushing so hard in the quarter-final.

It was initially a four-way battle in the third quarter-final until Binnie and Byrne collided at Druids. Byrne recovered to scrape into the semi-finals, whilst another spin put Binnie out. This left Templeton and Boutsen to dispute the win. Templeton had to work all the way and Boutsen was cheered on from the pits by Jacky Ickx, but Templeton scraped home 0.2s clear.

To complete the symmetry of the quarter-finals – two close races sandwiched by runaway wins – Walsh was comfortable in adding to his heat win from the previous day, his Royale RP24 seeming to have the edge over Acheson's newer RP26 model. Third went to Thackwell, who once more showed a knack for maturity in a category not renowned for that trait.

The first semi-final proved to be one of the best races of the weekend, with Roe and Devaney's ongoing battle joined by a charging Weaver. Initially the race followed the prior pattern with the Irish duo breaking clear. Meanwhile, Weaver was busy moving through the traffic and, once into clear air, was able to chase down the leaders. He was aided in this task by Roe taking a defensive approach, slowing the leading pair. Devaney could see Weaver coming and darted past Roe at Druids on lap 13. For Roe, there was more pain as Weaver repeated the move a lap later to confirm the order. All three had put on a great race and would surely be in the mix in the final. Gray and MacLeod came in a far from distant fourth and fifth.

The second semi-final was less about the racing and more about survival. A first-lap accident at Druids stopped the race, eliminating six from the running including Acheson and Byrne. After such an impressive season, this had been a frustrating weekend for Acheson. Once the race restarted, Templeton and Walsh disputed the lead, the latter's persistent pressure eventually paying off. Meanwhile Boutsen clattered into Argetsinger at Druids, taking both out of the running. All of this allowed Thackwell to move up into third position, despite a broken rear anti-roll bar. Walsh was enjoying a perfect Festival – three wins from three races – but it would be the final where it mattered.

With 20 laps ahead, a good start wasn't everything, but it would be helpful. Devaney claimed the lead, which initially kept him clear of the carnage. A multi-car incident eliminated Coppelli and Adbala amongst others. At the front Devaney was joined by Walsh, and the pair were the established leaders fighting hard for the honours – too hard as it turned out. Heading into Paddock for the second time, Walsh challenged to the outside, Deveney was unprepared to give ground and the inevitable consequence was a sizeable accident which also took out Templeton and Village as they tried to take evasive action. Fortunately the comparatively low speed of the Formula Fords meant that most accidents, no matter how spectacular, resulted in little more than bumps and bruises – Walsh and Deveney being a case in point.

Roe was the big winner as he squeezed through and into the lead, Weaver chasing him all the way. Others were in the chase – Gray, Thackwell, Greenan – but the race became about the leading pair. Having fallen victim to a late challenge from Weaver in the semi-final, Roe wasn't about to be twice bitten, easily absorbing the pressure. Weaver did briefly take the lead on lap 16, but Roe was back through within a couple of corners and thereafter was never troubled.

Roe was a popular winner, loudly cheered from the grandstands as he took the chequered flag, just a tenth of a second up the road from Weaver. Third position went to Gray who was only just behind, with MacLeod in fourth from Morgan, whilst impressive teenager Thackwell finished seventh. It had been a superb weekend of racing, albeit one played out in front of a smaller than hoped-for crowd. Despite his disappointment, Abdala summed the weekend up nicely: 'This is real racing; in Brazil it's just playing around.'

After introducing new names over the past few seasons, the 1979 Festival was arguably the year of the veteran, with both 1973 and 1974 winners Don MacLeod and Richard Morgan featuring prominently. MacLeod, equipped with the latest iteration of his Sark chassis, had developed the car into a contender capable of engaging the more established marques, particularly Royale and Van Diemen.

The pre-event rumour mill pegged Terry Gray, third-place finisher from the previous year, as the driver to beat. Gray had claimed the BRSCC Formula Ford title, showing particularly strongly at Brands Hatch, including two late-season wins. Of the drivers emerging to prominence during the season, heat podium finisher the previous year David Sears had been the most impressive, taking the national and BARC crowns.

Festival week once more saw Brands Hatch in the motorsport headlines, but unusually not for Formula Ford-related matters. Instead, circuit proprietors MCD were busy launching what could evolve into a competitor category: Formula Talbot. The Formula Talbot cars were to be powered by methanol marking a step away from fossil fuels. Whilst similar in appearance (and sharing a chassis) with Formula Ford, the Talbot cars would run on slick tyres, with *Autosport* slightly breathlessly reporting, 'These new single-seaters will be markedly quicker than Formula Ford, more difficult to control and consequently considerably more exciting for the spectator.' The category would represent the first serious contender to Formula Ford's crown since its launch. As it turned out, Formula Talbot didn't mount the anticipated threat. The methanol technology was ahead of its time making the cars tricky to prepare and run. Despite producing some good racing, grids rarely rose into double figures and the series was quietly wound up in the early 1980s

Whilst Formula Talbot was an existential cloud for the Formula Ford community, it was physical clouds that promised to put a damper on the whole weekend. The weather was atrocious for both days of competition, but despite this there were surprisingly few serious incidents during the weekend. From a promotional perspective, after the smaller than hoped for crowd the previous year, a washout in 1979 would further deter spectators.

The eight heats would be contested over just seven laps, leaving very little scope for recovery for those who overstepped the line – although, as in 1976, this would be challenge enough for some. 1974 winner Morgan ran out the comfortable winner of a processional opening heat, from Ashley Ward and Mark Smith. The latter had to work for his podium, seeing off the attentions of Martin Boyle. The margin of victory was even larger in heat two, where Robert Gibbs came home five seconds ahead of a tussling duo, Bob Higgins and Russell Edmunds.

Uneven seeding resulted in a very strong heat three, with Sears up against Rick Morris, Silverstone star Jim Walsh, rapid Didier Theys and returning 1978 sensation Tommy Byrne. Sears laid down a marker to the rest, easing his Royale to a comfortable victory after passing Morris early on. Walsh, meanwhile, was having fun climbing to second until a spin and stall on lap six. By this point, the gap in the field was such that Walsh was able to re-join and finish in tenth, ensuring his progression to Sunday's quarter-finals. This left the way clear for Morris to take second and Theys to complete the podium.

Brazilian Carlos Abdala took victory in heat four. It was comfortable eventually but he had adventures along the way, almost crashing out as he tried to overhaul early leader John Davis. Once through Abdala was in control, Davis just over a second behind at the flag and Ian Shaw in third.

Next into the fray was MacLeod, who showed the potency of his self-built Sark chassis by taking an impressive win in heat five from Roberto Moreno and Dave Knapp. With an opportunity to show off his form, Gray was similarly dominant in heat six. Leading the Van Diemen charge for the weekend with Abdala, Gray took victory by over six seconds from the similar car of Fernando Ribeiro.

David Griffin, winner of the Irish Festival, was the moral victor of the penultimate heat, but a late steering failure pitched him into retirement. Peter Argetsinger duly took over at the front, crossing the line fractions of a second clear of Willie Moore – the two Royales some way ahead of the rest. The closing heat also saw the retirement of a long-time leader. In this instance, it was Bolivar de Sordi who crashed out at McLaren whilst holding a seemingly unassailable advantage. Cameron Binnie gladly accepted the gift to win from John Village.

Overnight and ongoing rain meant that the drivers were greeted by a waterlogged track on Sunday morning. Despite the conditions, the opening quarter-final, pitting the best of heats one and two, produced better racing than could reasonably have been expected. Gibbs and Higgins made the better starts, but it was the experienced Morgan whose racecraft came to the fore. Making his forward progress mid-race, he cleared Higgins and Gibbs on successive laps (demoting the latter around the outside at Paddock), before holding on for a close victory.

In a repeat of their heat, Sears was once more impressive in his quarter-final, besting Morris by the same margin as Saturday, 4.5s. Byrne was the other standout performer, a pugnacious performance earning him third.

The penultimate quarter-final was arguably the best of all, with Ribeiro, MacLeod, Gray and Moreno doing battle. Ribeiro got his elbows out to retain the lead as MacLeod and Gray took turns to challenge whilst constantly swapping places. After ten laps of stout defence, Ribeiro took the victory, followed swiftly by a trip to the stewards to be reprimanded for his defensive driving. Some late jostling was enough to give Moreno second from Gray and MacLeod. Binnie was the class of the field in the closing quarter-final, taking a relatively comfortable three-second victory over John Village with Argetsinger having do the most dicing en route to third.

The first semi-final was packed with quality, with Morgan, Morris and Sears among those at the front. For the latter it was a frustrating race. An early spin saw Sears drop down to thirteenth, before a fine recovery to seventh. Instead, it was Morris who came to the fore with a bravura performance to keep the rest at arm's-length. Morgan, some three seconds back, in turn finished a couple of seconds clear of Byrne.

Dominance was the order of the day in the second semi-final, with MacLeod enjoying victory by a sizeable margin. The Sark pilot didn't have it all his own way, but once he'd cleared Gray and Moreno he was off into the distance. It was nail-bitingly close for second, with Gray taking the place by a nose in a sprint to the line, whilst Binnie was nearby in fourth.

A remarkably incident-free day meant that the final got away well ahead of schedule – just as well given the fading light. Perhaps unsurprisingly given the conditions the race wasn't a thriller but there was plenty happening throughout the field. Gray got the better start, benefitting from the outside slot and a slightly drier line, to lead MacLeod and Morris into Paddock. MacLeod was immediately on the attack, the Sark slithering through at Graham Hill Bend on the second lap. Thereafter, he romped into the distance, whilst Grey had enough to hold off Morris to complete the podium.

The most impressive performance came from Sears who steadily climbed through the field to take a superb fourth – but for the semi-final spin, a podium if not more would surely have been on the cards. Morgan and Gibbs completed the top six. The race was married by an incident at the midway point which saw Dave Knapp's Van Diemen upside-down at the entry to Paddock, whilst Argetsinger was fired off into the Armco barrier. Fortunately, all escaped without injury, and overall the weekend had seen far fewer incidents than normal.

Despite its dominant performance, the Festival didn't prove to be a springboard for the Sark and it quietly disappeared over the next couple of years. Instead, the event proved to be something of a swansong for MacLeod – although his record as a double winner would stand until the Festival became a club event in the early 2010s. Gray graduated to Formula 3 the following year before his career petered out. Morris, meanwhile, still had a starring role in future Festivals, as in the following year would Moreno. Sears would progress up the motorsport ladder before running the successful Super Nova team in Formula 3000, propelling Juan Pablo Mon toya, Mark Webber and Sebastian Bourdais, among others, up the motorsport ladder.

Formula Ford finished the 1970s in a not dissimilar position to where the category had been at the launch of the Festival – hugely successful and dominant as the entry-level formula but surrounded by much handwringing around costs and the suggestion that there were better answers out there.

To many, the 1970s were the glory decade for Formula Ford. Almost every race meeting featured multiple heats, a final and possibly a consolation race. The relative technical equivalence of the cars kept the competition close, and never again would it be possible to compete with future Formula 1 stars for such relatively little outlay. Whilst every year featured a crop of well-funded drivers, they could be more than matched by those with the talent or technical wiles. The possibly of a strong result, even for those with only the budget for petrol money, explained why over 90 cars would turn up each weekend, at least a third of those harbouring hopes of victory. The 1980s would continue to produce fantastic racing, a conveyor belt of Formula 1 drivers and some enthralling competition between manufacturers. However, it would also see national-level Formula Ford move into a professional era, severing the link to the category's unload-the-trailer-and-go-racing past.

Glory days

THE 1980s were the apogee for the Formula Ford Festival, the decade when the event crossed over from being a gathering of the motorsport tribes, to being shown to millions of viewers on *Grandstand*. Throughout the 1980s, the stands around Brands Hatch, but particularly Paddock Hill Bend, were sold out as tens of thousands of spectators crammed in for finals Sunday.

Whether serendipity or inevitability, this was also the era when almost all aspiring Formula 1 drivers spent at least some time in Formula Ford. After growing through the 1970s, and with some nudging by Ford, the category became near ubiquitous throughout Europe (albeit with some countries being firmer strongholds than others) and, crucially, there were few serious rival series trying to lure drivers away.

The once humble end-of-season Brands Hatch meeting emerged as the crucible where the finest emerging talents from around the world could go wheel to wheel and forge their reputations. Of the Festival winners during the decade, six would race in Formula 1 (and one other would unsuccessfully attempt to qualify, and another would regularly be a demonstration driver for Jordan), as would dozens more from throughout the field.

The procession of talent through Formula Ford during the 1980s was phenomenal, as was the speed of their ascent after graduating from the category. Ayrton Senna dominated the British scene in 1981 but didn't race at the Festival. Others did – Damon Hill, Michael Schumacher and Mika Hakkinen all graced the entry list with varying degrees of success. All but two of the Formula 1 world titles from 1992 to 2004 were claimed by Formula Ford Festival alumni.

The beauty of Formula Ford in this era wasn't just that it was a stairway to stardom, the emerging names battling among themselves. The category was home to seasoned veterans who would push the rising stars to prove their mettle, Rick Morris and Dave Coyne being the two best examples. If a wet Tuesday night in Stoke is the footballing analogy, fending off Coyne over a Brands Hatch ten-lapper is the motorsport equivalent

It was also a decade that saw huge technical innovation within the confines of the formula as the sideways, tyre-squealing style and wide-nosed cars of the early 1980s were gradually replaced by more streamlined machinery, the compact packaging concealing some sophisticated engineering.

From a manufacturer perspective, Van Diemen was the ever-present frontrunner of the 1980s. Having come to prominence during the 1970s, the Norfolk marque always seemed to produce the most rounded and competitive package. Whilst occasionally borrowing heavily from others both stylistically and technically, the Van Diemens were always driveable, fast and popular – the latter being an important factor when pooling data and developing the car.

There were aberrations. Neither the 1983 or 1984 cars had a step on the field (and nor were they all that pretty), whilst in other years the Van Diemen was ubiquitous but ultimately unsuccessful in the Festival.

In the early part of the 1980s, it was Lola and Reynard who laid down the challenge. The Lola was technically advanced, sleek and potent on single-lap pace but let down by fragility and a tricksy reputation among drivers. Throughout the 1980s, Reynard largely produced cars that handled brilliantly and were beloved by drivers, but only secured one Festival win. The marque did well to bounce back from a period in the doldrums after a disastrous 1985 challenge. Then there were the smaller marques of whom Quest and Laser were the most successful, the former being part of the Festival's greatest fairy tale.

Throughout, there were constant concerns about the costs and career-ladder positioning of Formula Ford. The cost of all those technical innovations were largely borne by the drivers. During much of the 1980s, it was at least a two-year category for all barring the most exceptional talents, and the success of Formula First on its launch in 1987 suggested that many drivers wanted to take their first steps in motorsport without the costs of a full-blown Formula Ford campaign. The British recession of the early 1980s hurt sponsorship and the category had to consolidate. In 1980, there were four main national championships, but after some challenging seasons (1983 in particular), for 1985 the calendar was reorganised to focus on a sole British Championship and national junior championship, although the largely Silverstone-centric BRDC championship would run a while longer.

A glance through Festival entry lists as the 1980s progressed also shows a sharpening of the protagonists to national series runners, top European talent and Brands Hatch circuit specialists who knew enough tricks to spring a surprise. The clubmen and regional frontrunners, who had filled out the entry throughout the 1970s, gradually drifted away knowing they didn't have the means to be competitive – especially when up against works cars running some of next year's parts.

The racing, though, did get closer. Runaway wins (in any of the races) had all but disappeared by 1986. By 1988, victory by three seconds would be seen as a comfortable gap, compared to the frequent ten-second-plus heat wins of the late 1970s. Whilst there were always efforts to gain a competitive advantage, the contributors interviewed for this book were all adamant that cheating wasn't widespread. The competition was simply too close and evenly matched for anyone to gain a clear advantage without there being protests.

Although always a marquee event, the Festival didn't necessarily reflect wider trends in the sport. At the turn of the 1980s, the entry was capped at 20 cars per heat, before expanding to reflect demand. There were fallow years from 1983 where the heats were almost irrelevant with all but a handful of cars guaranteed to progress. The boom years came in the late 1980s, when an ill-timed spin in a heat would be enough to end the weekend of a favourite.

Politics is an ever-present in any motorsport paddock, and given the extent to which reputations could be earned and lost in Formula Ford, it is not surprising the news sections of *Autosport* and *Motoring News* throughout the period were full of intrigue and complaint. The Festivals of the late 1980s were somewhat marred by penalties, largely awarded for minor technical infringements spotted after qualifying, which, barring miracles (of which there were some), were largely unrecoverable. By 1988, the paddock atmosphere reflected the prestige and importance of the Festival, almost unrecognisable to the drivers who had turned out hungover to practice at Snetterton 15 years earlier.

The Festival went mainstream too. Brands Hatch had long been a favourite for television sports producers given its geography and topography – the track was a short drive from London headquarters and the track's undulations meant it could be covered by fewer cameras (therefore at lower cost) than the pancake-flat Silverstone. After Brian Kriesky's Videovision pioneered filming the event in 1981, the BBC first brought their cameras to the meeting in 1984, where they would remain until 1992. The quality of the coverage would vary – from just the final with a handful of cameras to in-depth action, including on-board cameras from the quarter-finals onward. It brought the action to millions of households. Once combined with multi-round coverage of the British Formula 3 championship from 1988 (though individual races were shown throughout the 1980s), it was possible to follow the progress of the likes of Mika Hakkinen or David Coulthard long before they became superstars.

What is undeniable is that for ten years, over 150 (often closer to 200) drivers arrived at Brands Hatch in October seeking victory in the Formula Ford Festival and all the spoils that would bring. It almost goes without saying that the racing was phenomenal. Full grids and a knockout format gave the action an intensity that lives on for drivers and spectators alike.

Formula Ford in 1980 was in strong health. The British scene was indisputably the place for challengers from around the world to stake their claim on the pathway to Formula 1. With a plethora of regional and national championships to aim for, several drivers could all point to a strong season: Tommy Byrne (national and BARC champion), Jim Walsh (once more taking the BARC title) and Roberto Moreno (BRSCC champion) had all starred. Moreno's Brazilian compatriot Raul Boesel had finished the year well with wins at Brands Hatch, whilst Rick Morris remained a perpetual frontrunner and the newly qualified doctor, Jonathan Palmer, was marking his territory as a future prospect.

The frontrunning chassis of the 1980 season had been the streamlined and tidy Van Diemen RF80, a car that won every round of the year's BRSCC championship. Morris and Walsh in their Royales had been the only drivers on the national scene to regularly break the Van Diemen hegemony. Heading into the Festival, pundits could comfortably point to at least ten drivers who would be in with a reasonable chance of victory.

Morris's first year in a Royale was 1980 after he moved across from PRS. As he explained, 'Tommy had tested a Royale and said "It's a f***ing fantastic car, you've got to get one." I'd already seen how quick they were when I diced with John Village in one on the Nordschlife. I did a deal on an RP26 for 1980. Pat Symonds had been employed at the end of 1979 to design for them and he needed a road car – so I sorted out a Ford estate for him, and he supplied me a Formula Ford.'

Symonds was one of many designers and engineers who cut their teeth in Formula Ford before moving on. Currently serving as Formula 1's chief technical officer, he spent much of his time in Formula 1 at the team variously known as Toleman/Benetton/Renault, where he was Michael Schumacher's race engineer when the German won the World Championship in 1994 and 1995, ultimately leaving the team in the wake of the 2008 Singapore controversy.

The Festival format was the now familiar: eight seven-lap heats, four ten-lap quarter-finals, 12-lap semi-finals and the 15-lap grand final. Such was the esteem in which the event was now held, that drivers now tested extensively in the week beforehand (a tradition that still continues), pounding round lap after lap in hope of that elusive hundredth of a second. As ever, the heat draw spread the expected frontrunners throughout the entry, and the strength of the field would ensure no one would get an effortless run through to the final. With just 20 cars starting each heat, the entry was fully subscribed with reserves on hand in case anyone hit trouble in practice.

Despite the efforts to spread the favourites evenly, the draw still threw up quirks. In this instance, none of the expected contenders would feature in the first heat. It was a race that had more in the way of drama than excitement, oil patches on the circuit leading to attrition at the front, with four leaders falling off over the seven laps. Denmark's Jesper Villumsen won but only after his predecessors had spun out of contention or into retirement. It was the slowest of the heats by some margin – the race time a good 15 seconds slower than some of those that would follow.

Heat two started to bring the favourites into the fray, with Dave Coyne and Raul Boesel the expected frontrunners. Boesel maintained his run of form to pass Coyne at Surtees on the first lap, before taking a comfortable win ahead of Mexican Alfonso Toledano. Robert Gibbs was the comfortable winner of heat three, the best battle being for third until it ended in tears at Druids.

Favourite Moreno was drawn in heat four alongside Walsh, who would provide a good yardstick for the Brazilian. It was no contest. Moreno ran away from the field, setting a new lap record in the process. Only Walsh could stay anywhere near Moreno's pace. The result was taken after six laps when the race was stopped because local driver Martin Holman was trapped in his Ray following an accident at Paddock Hill Bend. Heat five wasn't quite of that calibre, but Andrew Gilbert-Scott raced well to fend off local specialist Andy Ackerley. Castle Combe champion Steve Lincoln was the reasonably comfortable winner of heat six, Lincoln benefitting from those behind tripping themselves up.

The closing pair of heats brought more expected challengers into the mix. Palmer, with his sights already set on Formula 3, was initially headed by Warren Briggs before taking an unheaded lead on lap two. Runner-up was 1979 winner MacLeod, benefitting from a final corner collision between Briggs and Peter Argetsinger. The heats were rounded out with a win for Morris, who finished some way clear of Tommy Byrne.

With survival and a quarter-final grid position the primary aim, the heats only occasionally provided thrilling racing, but did serve to whittle down the field. Moreno was the fastest of all, with Morris on pace emerging as his main challenger.

On Sunday, the conditions were again clear and sunny but bitingly cold as the first quarter-final got under way. Gibbs got the best start to build an immediate gap before a plethora of red-mist induced accidents forced a stoppage – Colin Lees being trapped in his car at Druids was the decisive factor in the race being halted. Not that it mattered too much to Gibbs, who once more drove clear of the pack to lead Bo Martinsson home in a repeat of their heat. The fight for third, meanwhile, produced the type of action that drew the crowds – Chris Hackman passing two cars in a single move around the outside of Paddock to definitively claim the position. This was a brave move at the best of times, but in the circumstances even more so given the aggression of the later rounds of the Festival.

The second quarter-final featured many of the favourites. Despite a good start, Walsh couldn't edge out Moreno into Paddock, allowing the latter to once more romp off into the distance. Boesel also snuck past Walsh before crashing out – the first of the frontrunners to exit the fray. The fight for second was still a good one as Walsh and Coyne battled, experience eventually winning out as Coyne couldn't find a way through. Moreno again was dominant, setting another lap record and comfortably the fastest race pace of the quarter-finals.

The third encounter was pretty static among the frontrunners, with Palmer taking a comfortable win from Briggs, Gilbert-Scott and MacLeod, all of whom didn't have to fight too hard for their placings. The last of the quarter-finals was probably the most entertaining with Morris and Byrne enjoying a good scrap for the honours – Morris sneaking through mid-race after Byrne had taken an initial lead. Behind, the dicing was similarly close, Lincoln working hard for his third place.

As the cars started to assemble for the semi-finals, the grandstand pundits once more debated overall winners. From the opening rounds Moreno was the one to beat, but he'd been clear out front – could he replicate his pace in a pack? Morris and Palmer were the other form men, whilst Byrne was getting quicker with each appearance.

If progression had been key until now, a good finishing position was crucial for an elevated grid slot in the final. In the first, Palmer once more continued his clean sweep of the weekend, aided by a huge spin in front of the pack by Briggs at

Paddock early on, scattering the chasers. Second went to Gibbs, with Gilbert-Scott once more in third. Briggs did recover until a snapped throttle cable put him out of the event.

Moreno's semi-final was the race of the weekend, although not for the Brazilian who once more departed over the horizon, completing the 12 laps some eight seconds faster than Palmer. Instead, it was the fight for second that kept the crowd captivated, with Walsh keeping the pack behind him. Unlike Silverstone or Snetterton where those behind can slipstream past, at Brands Hatch track position trumps all and it is possible to defend a place throughout the race. However, this tactic is not without its risks as the pressure from behind builds inexorably.

In the pressure cooker of the semi-finals, events came to a head. Byrne darted past Walsh at Paddock, with Morris then making it three-wide trying to overtake the pair around the outside. A demoted Walsh subsequently spun out of contention at Clearways on lap eight and, with so much of the pack queuing up behind him, wouldn't qualify for the final. Eventually, Byrne came home second ahead of Morris.

The scene was set for the 15-lap final, the challengers knowing that for any hope of victory they had to get ahead of Moreno at the start. Despite excellent getaways from both Palmer and Byrne, neither could chop ahead of Moreno on the run to Paddock, the Brazilian holding tight to the inside line.

It was immediately clear that no one could match Moreno's pace, although Byrne would emerge as the nearest challenger after passing Palmer early on. Byrne, who'd finally cured a persistent understeer problem, was now showing his true speed, as he chased off after Moreno, the pair of them pulling away from the field. The only battle for the podium placings was the one for third, which turned into a tooth and nail dice between Palmer and Morris. Affectionately recalling the battle at the Festival's 40th Anniversary Dinner in 2010, Palmer's reminiscences mainly focused on just how wide Morris was able to make his car. It was certainly to good effect as Morris came home just half a car length clear of Palmer to take third.

For Moreno, it had been the perfect weekend as he'd dominated all four races. It was a performance that helped to propel him into Formula 1. Offered a Lotus testing contract on the strength of his Formula Ford form, Moreno would secure his first Formula 1 entry at the 1982 Dutch Grand Prix, although he'd ultimately fail to qualify. Thereafter, the incredibly likeable Brazilian established dual careers in Formula 1 and IndyCar, often as a 'super-sub'. Winning the 1988 Formula 3000 championship re-set Moreno's career, but it was the 1991 full-season deal with Benetton that ought to have brought him regular Formula 1 success. Despite several points finishes, he was unceremoniously booted out of his seat late in the year to make way for Michael Schumacher. Regrouping in 1992, he managed to qualify the hopeless Andrea Moda at Monaco, before, after a final, fruitless year with Forti Corse, he returned to IndyCar and finished third in the 2000 campaign.

Moreno returned to the circuit in 2010 on the 30th anniversary of his victory, reminiscing with Brian Jones at the Saturday night Festival Forum. A decade later, in 2021, he returned once more, this time to be reunited with his 1980 Van Diemen – unfortunately, he didn't progress beyond his heat. On the Saturday evening of the 2010 Festival when I was commentating, I gave Moreno a lift to the local railway station. We mainly discussed the merits of the NHS as opposed to the American healthcare system, as the ex-Formula 1 podium finisher put a brave face on being chauffeured in a battered Vauxhall Corsa.

Another of the graduating class of 1980 would go on to have a huge impact on future Festivals. After a racing career that saw him take the 1981 British Formula 3 championship, 1983 Formula 2 title and a six-year stint in Formula 1, Jonathan Palmer would purchase Brands Hatch in 2004 as part of the Motorsport Vision group. Best known to the wider public as Murray Walker's BBC Formula 1 co-commentator from 1993 to 1996, Palmer's business acumen and intuitive understanding of how a motorsport venue should operate have been crucial in Brands Hatch remaining a motorsport venue and not becoming another housing development.

If 1980 had been all about the Brazilian who swept all before him, the major story of the 1981 Festival was of the Brazilian who wasn't there: Ayrton (Senna) da Silva. Senna, as he would become universally known, had dominated the British season, winning two of the major championships in a works Van Diemen.

Facing marriage difficulties with wife Lilliane (who shockingly wasn't so fond of Norfolk in March), and the need to raise sponsorship for the following season, Senna returned to Brazil immediately after the final BRSCC championship round in late September. This left a big question to be pondered among his team, rivals and journalists as to whether he'd return for the October season finale.

Setting aside speculation, this put Van Diemen principal Ralph Firman in a bind – his other works drivers Quique Mansilla and Alfonso Toledano were quick, but not on a par with Senna and unlikely on pace alone to win the Festival. Firman turned to Byrne, his Formula Ford star of the previous year, who had been campaigning Firman's Formula Ford 2000, offering him Senna's car for the weekend. Meanwhile Senna had told Firman he would give him an answer by 18 October.

Recounting events to Tony Dodgins for the excellent *Ayrton Senna: All His Races*, Firman recalled, 'On the very day of the 18th Ayrton phoned and said, "Ralph, I'm at the airport, I'll be in tomorrow." I said, "Ayrton, I haven't got a car for you … I'm sorry, but that's it." It was totally my fault, all down to me. He was absolutely correct. So I must be the only bloke on the planet who ever refused him a drive. He just said, "OK, Ralph, I understand."'

With Senna out of the equation, the field was opened up, albeit controversially. Of the Formula Ford class of 1981, only Morris and Mansilla had bettered Senna when they'd gone head to head, Mansilla's win coming early in the year whilst Senna was still finding his feet. Morris had enjoyed some good scraps with Senna, most memorably coming out on top in a fiercely contested June race at Silverstone. Given the one-sided nature of the season, the class of '81 contemporaneously wasn't regarded as a vintage one.

Morris's retains sharp memories of the season, 'It was a fraught year, Ralph [Firman] had a really strong roster of drivers and split them between the various championships. That meant I didn't get Senna all the time. Apart from Senna it would have been a brilliant year [for me].'

This perception was bolstered somewhat by the number of drivers 'dropping down' to Formula Ford for the weekend. A couple of major factors were at play. Firstly, alongside the prestige of victory, there was a prize Formula 3 drive on offer in the end-of-season televised meeting at Thruxton. Secondly, within the Formula Ford community, the Festival was increasingly a showcase for the following year's kit – this meant the manufacturers would engage trusted fast-men to show off their new machinery in the best possible light.

Of those returning to the category for the weekend, Byrne was an obvious favourite. He'd shone the previous year and was fully familiar with Van Diemen machinery, having taken their Formula Ford 2000 model to British and European title success. Also in the mix would be James Weaver, entrusted with the 1982 specification Reynard after a financially afflicted Formula 3 campaign, and German Formula 3 runner-up Stefan Bellof. Others under consideration at the Kentagon included the up-and-coming Julian Bailey, along with returning 1980 sensation, Andrew Gilbert-Scott.

Throughout the entry, strength in depth was the order of the day, with over 180 cars entered for the weekend. The format for the weekend was much the same as the previous year, eight seven-lap heats forming the grid for ten-lap quarter-finals, 12-lap semi-finals and a 15-lap grand final. The only substantial change was that the grid capacity was expanded from 20 to 24 cars, boosting the entry and giving a handful more drivers the hope of progression. After a 1980 event which, in terms of on-track action, was intriguing rather than spectacular, the hope was that 1981 would elevate the entertainment levels.

The first heat went to 34-year-old David Wheeler, a category frontrunner for the previous five seasons, who saw off a spirited challenge from Bailey as most behind, including Bellof, settled for survival and progression. The second heat also saw a close contest for the honours, with Gilbert-Scott spectacularly fending off Danish star Jesper Villumsen – the brief seven-lap heats still feeling more than long enough if you were doggedly clinging to position. Heat three saw the first dominant performance of the weekend, with Byrne finishing a comfortable four seconds clear of runner-up John Village and 13 seconds up the road from third-placed Kevin Haddock. Byrne's performance was comfortably the quickest of the heats, a good four seconds faster than the other races at an average speed of 84.65mph.

Byrne's Van Diemen stablemate, Mansilla, was victorious in heat four. 'Quique' found a way past Warren Briggs and perennial frontrunner Dave Coyne, who finished second and third respectively. The knowing eyes were drawn to Weaver in fourth place who put in a very solid performance in his first racing laps in the Reynard.

Heat five brought the first stoppage of the weekend, with entangled cars blocking the track. Robert Gibbs benefitted at the restart, taking victory from Jeremy Plunkett and the unique Martlet chassis, and local star Andy Ackerley, whose enthusiasm had been tempered by contact prior to the stoppage. The following heat was the first not to feature much in the way of positional changes amongst the frontrunners, with future sportscar star Cor Euser taking the victory from Anthony Reid – the Scot making his only race appearance of the year.

Another stoppage punctuated heat seven, with four cars becoming entangled at Paddock. Among these was then *Autosport* writer Jeremy Shaw – his reporting duties over the weekend becoming much easier once relieved of his driving commitments. At the restart, somewhat predictably, Morris pulled clear. Behind, there was a good scrap for second, with local driver Mike Thompson in the Quest using circuit knowledge to fend off the highly rated Mario Hytten. The final heat was a Van Diemen benefit, with Toledano in the works RF81 having enough in hand to keep Steve Lincoln at bay in the customer-prepared version of the car.

Whilst Saturday's running had, at least for the racing, been dry, overnight rain made for tricky conditions on the Sunday morning. The circuit was at its most treacherous for the first quarter-final, where Byrne and Village were expected to make the running. Recognising that the midfield could be somewhat precarious in such slippery conditions, Byrne was a little too keen to break clear, incurring a ten-second penalty for jumping the start. As he and Village immediately gapped the rest of the pack, Byrne's quick-witted pit crew signalled the penalty. Thus inspired, Byrne was almost six seconds clear at the end of lap four. His Van Diemen was ideally suited to the drying track and Byrne found traction where others struggled. This allowed the Irishman to edge out Village by just 0.5s on adjusted time, but in reality, he was ten seconds up the road, having blown the field apart. The podium was completed by Village, with heat one winner Wheeler in third. Further back, the hotly tipped Bellof found himself being black-flagged after two incidents. The first removed Bailey and Haddock from proceedings at Paddock, before a further collision with Ted Whitbourne sufficiently enraged officialdom to see him excluded from the event (from sixth on the road).

The second quarter-final was more of a contest with Briggs, Gilbert-Scott and Mansilla all taking their turns at the front. Despite dogged defence, Briggs was shuffled down to third late on. It was Mansilla who took the flag, having only taken the lead on the penultimate lap, crossing the line just 0.2s clear of Gilbert-Scott. Running with the leaders had been Coyne and Weaver, the latter finishing fifth despite a late spin in the Reynard, where he was somehow avoided by Coyne.

Morris was the expected frontrunner in the third quarter-final and duly took the win by six seconds. It wasn't without challenge, as Thompson initially took the advantage. Morris was soon through and not long after Thompson wrenched a wishbone loose after attacking the bumpy kerbs at Surtees a bit too aggressively, pitching the Quest into the barriers. The battle for what became second was decent, with Hytten and Gibbs switching places, eventually in Gibbs's favour.

Following Morris's triumph in the Royale with a comfortable win in the fourth quarter-final, Toledano returned the form book to Van Diemen, meaning three of the four quarter-final victories went to the Norfolk marque. This was the most pedestrian of the quarter-finals. The leading trio of Toledano, Euser and Lincoln were covered by over seven seconds, with neither close battles nor penalties to add jeopardy. The main story was down in fourth place, where Reid was consistently impressing.

If the drivers had largely exercised caution during the quarter-finals, the semi-finals would see a shift in tone. The draw produced two fascinating races on paper. The first placed the two quickest drivers of the weekend, Byrne and Morris, head to head. The second would see Mansilla and Toledano revive their fiery season-long rivalry.

Semi-final one was a fantastic race, with Byrne and Morris barely separated by a car length throughout. Byrne made the better start, using track position and camber to keep Morris behind as they traversed Paddock Hill Bend. Thereafter, it was a thrilling tactical battle with both drivers exploiting circuit knowledge and the strengths of their cars to maximum effect. Byrne's Van Diemen had the traction through – and crucially on the exit of – the slower corners, whilst Morris's Royale had the pace at the quicker turns.

On the Brands Hatch Indy layout, the most clear-cut overtaking opportunity has always been to get to a better exit from the slow right-hander at Clearways and ease alongside or ahead of your rival before the braking zone at Paddock Hill Bend. However, with Byrne being quicker on the exit of Clearways, this took away Morris's most obvious opportunity to pass, particularly as a driver of Byrne's calibre would be able to keep the car tight to the inside line elsewhere. As the pair romped clear of the rest of the field (third-placed Gibbs was eight seconds back), there was no way through for Morris. After 12 laps, they were eventually separated by 0.7s.

Long-in-the-tooth motorsport fans will often complain about the death of multi-marque racing in junior single-seaters, and this race serves as a strong argument for the prosecution. Contemporary junior racing is now almost always regulated so that all competitors must run a specified chassis, engine and all other control components.

Broadcaster and motorsport insider Tom Gaymor, who raced in Formula Ford 20 years later, best articulates the challenge: 'Today's drivers don't get the engineering side. Although the Formula Fords weren't hugely complex, every change you made on the car had an impact. I really learnt how to understand and adjust my equipment. Today a lot of the championships are single make, and the cars come out of the factory with a base setup, which means the only things the drivers can really play with is tyre wear and tyre temperature. In my opinion, that doesn't give them a good grounding for Formula 1, where they have to develop all technical aspects of the car.' Back in 1981 – with a multitude of differing chassis and tuned engines on the grid – drivers had to learn to drive around their cars' strengths and weaknesses, providing an extra tactical dimension to the racing.

If the first semi-final was a prime example of thoughtful Formula Ford racing, the second was an exhibition in the overexuberance that made the category so notorious. Toledano v Mansilla was the hotly touted battle, but early on Euser was in the mix and frustrating Mansilla whilst Toledano tried to break clear. By the third lap Mansilla was up to second, and for the following three tours he and Toledano circulated as one.

At mid-race Mansilla decided to make his move, challenging to the outside at Paddock Hill Bend. Neither driver gave the other quite enough space, resulting in the inevitable locking of wheels. For a fraction of a second, it looked as if they might get away with it, but both cars rotated off into the catch fencing, which lined the circuit. Brian Kreisky's cameras caught the incident and it was characteristic of so many Formula Ford accidents – the interlocking wheels and tell-tale tyre smoke could only lead to one outcome, but the relatively low speed avoided any major contact with the scenery. Neither driver was injured, but both were visibly furious as they stalked away.

This left Euser in the lead but being rapidly chased down by Weaver, Coyne and Gilbert-Scott – the latter being lucky to continue after he and Briggs had got entangled at Paddock, leaving an unharmed Briggs deep in the catch fencing. To the audible delight of the grandstands, the race finally went to Weaver after he had been able to pass both Coyne and

Euser. Coyne claimed second after also finding a way past the Dutchman. In turn, Euser finished third, fractions of a second clear of Gilbert-Scott.

The semi-finals had given the faithful exactly what they'd come for – two thoroughly entertaining and varied races. They also set the scene perfectly for the final. On pure pace, it was hard to see past Byrne and Morris, but neither had been embroiled in the wild racing seen elsewhere. Meanwhile, Weaver had been working wonders in the new Reynard but was yet to really have his chance in clear air.

With anticipation building and the Formula 3 prize drive on the line, the cars lined up in three-by-two formation. As the lights changed, Byrne held his nerve making a perfect getaway and taking the lead into Paddock. As in the semi-final Morris immediately slotted in behind him, with the rest of the pack dicing behind. For the leading duo, it was a near full replay of their earlier encounter, running nose to tail for the full 15 laps. Byrne continued to use his superior exit to Clearways to full effect, meaning there was no way past for Morris, who was once more a podium bridesmaid: 'I just couldn't get past, I didn't quite have the edge to make the pass. If you don't want someone to get through, at Brands you can make it very difficult, and Tommy did that.'

After passing Coyne early on, Weaver ran a lonely third, albeit the best part of ten seconds behind the leaders. For Coyne, it was a rather rougher 15 laps, initially spinning in collision with Gilbert-Scott, before engaging in a wild battle with Gianfranco Cane for 11th. This gave Gibbs fourth ahead of Wheeler. Rounding out the top ten was Reid, who given his limited means and experience impressed throughout the weekend.

For Byrne and Van Diemen the spoils, and for observers two great what-ifs. Would Senna have added his name to the Festival roll of honour? And who would have prevailed in a Byrne v Senna head to head? The answer to the former is, barring mechanical or backmarker disaster, almost certainly a yes. Senna had dominated throughout 1981 and there was no reason to suggest that run of form wouldn't have continued into the Festival, particularly given how well this generation of Van Diemens worked at Brands Hatch.

The second doesn't lend itself too easily to a snap answer. Off the track, Senna and Byrne couldn't have been more different. The Brazilian from an affluent and urbane background was everything a racing driver 'should be'. In contrast, Byrne had no backing to his name and had fought for every drive. He had an off-track reputation for partying and was rarely anyone's idea of a sponsor's dream. However, once on the circuit, both were devastatingly quick and, whatever the backstory, clearly generational talents. Differing views on who would have prevailed are readily available, but either way it would have been one hell of a race.

In the 12 months following his Festival triumph, Byrne's star burned extraordinarily brightly, winning the 1982 British Formula 3 championship as well as starting and ending his Formula 1 career with the Theodore team. Entering five races, qualifying for two of them, but not making the finish in either, Byrne was out of Formula 1 before he'd even got going. His image, coupled with his being unable to bring sponsorship, meant that no teams were willing or able him a drive, despite some blistering pace in testing. An adventure-filled career in the USA and Mexico followed along with an autobiography and feature film documentary – Byrne truly is one of the sport's great characters.

Other stars of the year didn't quite hit the heights of Formula 1 but enjoyed solid careers. Weaver starred in the BTCC, before moving on to a hugely successful sportscar career, whilst Reid was another who became a BTCC frontrunner right at the peak of the series' super-touring era.

By the time the 1982 Festival rolled around, the previous year's winner had already graduated to and left Formula 1. Many of the 1981s emerging talents remained in Formula Ford, with Julian Bailey, Rick Morris and Gianfranco Cane all claiming titles over the course of the season. Of the newcomers, it was another Brazilian, Mauricio Gugelmin, who shone in taking the national title. Gugelmin, the 1981 Brazilian Formula Fiat champion, was a close friend of his predecessor in the works Van Diemen and shared a house with Senna from 1982 until 1987. The now un-retired Senna was at Brands Hatch over the weekend to cheer Gugelmin on, commenting to *Autosport*, 'It is a very good and important meeting'.

Throughout the year, the pre-eminent rivalry had been between Bailey and Gugelmin, the pair of them doing the bulk of the winning alongside known quantity Morris. Indeed, the tensions between Bailey and Gugelmin had spilled over. An acrimonious incident in the final national championship round had given Gugelmin the title, with Bailey feeling the Brazilian had punted him off.

The past two Festival winners, Moreno and Byrne, had both been in Van Diemens propelled by the same Minister-tuned engine – the increasingly legendarily Patch, so named due to the prominent patch on the engine casing. For 1982, the combination was split, Gugelmin in the latest Van Diemen, but with an Auriga-prepared engine, whilst Patch was transplanted into Bailey's Lola chassis.

As so often the case, come late October, Formula Ford seemed to be in both fine health but also a cause for concern. With 174 competitors in practice spread across 24 different marques (albeit with 73 drivers equipped by Van Diemen), it was hard to make a case against the depth or diversity of competition.

The *Autosport* editorial and letters page was the place to go for the controversy and handwringing. There were two talking points in particular. Firstly, following the success of returnees Byrne, Weaver and Coyne the previous year, the BRSCC had somewhat tightened the entry criteria, turning away those looking to 'drop down' for the weekend. Whilst this opened up the playing field and would ensure the Formula 3 prize drive didn't go to someone who'd already competed in the category, the move was largely met with dismay. The consensus was that an established name had plenty to lose by pitting themself against the next class of newcomer, so for those drivers the career opportunity and risk were evenly balanced.

The second point of contention was Formula Ford's rapidly evolving technology. Within the tightly defined technical parameters, there were opportunities for innovation. The majority of cars were now packaged in sleek aerodynamic bodywork and suspension had moved inboard, leading to the eventual creation of the original Formula E for outboard suspension Formula Fords. Drivers could now adjust roll bars and brake bias in the cockpit, allowing them to subtly alter the handling mid-race in response to preference or track conditions. Within a couple of years, this would be the norm for the category, but at the time was a big step forward and huge departure from the fill-it-with-fuel-and-off-we-go attitude of earlier years.

The concern was that the increasingly complicated cars would elevate costs, particularly for drivers who wanted to run at the front. The other worry was the trickle-down effect on clubmen who could neither be competitive on the national scene, nor afford to update their machinery in line with the pace of technical innovation. This prediction would be borne out by some of the spiralling budgets over the coming years and the continuing drop in Festival entries from regional Formula Fordsters.

With a backward glance, *Autosport* ran pieces with a near-identical sentiment around the 1972 Festival: cars too tricksy and expensive, well-funded F1 aspirants crowding out those running on tighter budgets. From 1972, instead of declining, the category had enjoyed a bumper decade with strong grids increasingly aligned with professional organisation and preparation – emphatically stating British Formula Ford's place as the proving ground for ambitious drivers.

Fast-forward a decade, and the commentary of the era is remarkably prescient. 1992 would be the final year of the Kent engine, with the Zetec needed to modernise the category, boost interest and compete with the upstart Vauxhall categories. During that period, whilst the racing at the front would remain strong and closer than ever, the number of national championships would be whittled down from five to one. Rising costs in parallel would price many drivers out, and by 1990 just a handful of cars could be mustered for the British Championship.

There is a certainly an argument that the period from 1980 to 1982 represents the apex of the glory days of Formula Ford.

The spotlight would be brighter in the following years and the category would continue to pump out stars of the future with regularity. However, with rising budgets and rapid technological advances, it would be increasingly tough for the lesser-funded or circuit specialists to compete on equal terms. Within a decade, the split between 'ladder' and 'club' single-seaters would be complete. From 1993 onward, only a handful of hardy club drivers would enter the main Festival itself before being shunted into the margins altogether in 1997.

Those concerns, whilst strongly expressed, were for the future. The paddock turned itself to the business of what promised to be another bumper meeting. Replicating the 1981 format (eight seven-lap heats, ten-lap quarter-finals, 12-lap semi-finals, and 15 laps for the final) with 12 cars progressing from each race, the competition would be fierce.

In a repeat of the previous year, the first heat went to David Wheeler who converted pole position. Although the final order reflected the top five from qualifying, the reality of the race was rather closer than the results sheet suggested, with Ross Cheever fending off Maurizio Sandro Sala and Martin Donnelly and the fifth-placed Andy Middlehurst several seconds distant. The second heat further ramped up the excitement with a fierce battle between Andy Wallace and 1981 sensation Anthony Reid – the former having to use every trick in the book and inch of the circuit to keep Reid at bay. Another future BTCC frontrunner, Karl Jones, finished third.

The entry for heat three looked particularly intriguing with Gugelmin pitted against Euroseries and German Formula Ford champion Volker Weidler. After applying pressure early on, Weidler's engine cried enough, allowing Gugelmin to take a comfortable victory. This was the fastest of the heats so far and the first run under six minutes. Trevor Stiles and Dave Button enjoyed a close tussle for second, with Stiles claiming the place by 0.1s. The race was marred by a sizeable incident between Adam Wallis and Paul Mathers, which saw the latter launched towards a marshal's post, fortunately landing short and escaping without injury.

With the gauntlet laid down by Gugelmin, it was Bailey's turn next. He duly took victory and outpaced the Brazilian to record the fastest of the heats. Initially pressurised by Joey Greenan, Bailey soon broke clear, with Greenan gradually demoted through the order. Second went to Bjorn Langrekken from David Hunt (brother of James) and future Lotus F1 pilot and Le Mans winner Johnny Dumfries, Greenan eventually coming home fifth.

In a year of entertaining heats, the fifth continued the trend. John Pratt (best known to non-fans for his appearance in Channel 4's *Faking It*) took his first-ever victory, leading the way from John Booth. There was a similarly engaging battle for third, with the polesitter – promising German Uwe Schafer – fighting Len Bull for the duration. Bull, in an ageing 1979 Van Diemen, kept Schafer behind for the first half of the race and was briefly demoted before decisively slipping through on the final lap.

Heat six provided a rare runaway win, with Keith Fine over three seconds clear from Donington Park champion Mark Peters. Third went to John Village who prevailed after a frenetic battle with Antonio Albacete and Thomas Jans. *Autosport* reserved withering comment for the performance of Joachim (Jo) Winkelhock. Then best known as the younger brother of rising star Manfred, Jo would take his revenge on the British circuits by winning the 1995 BTCC for BMW.

The penultimate heat pitted local knowledge and innovation against the might of a works Van Diemen. The latter, in the hands of Gianfranco Cane, took the spoils, with local star John Oxborrow finishing runner-up ahead of Mike Thompson in the Quest. The heats were rounded out by victory for Rick Morris, once more running in the works Royale. Kept honest by circuit specialist Andy Ackerley in the Ray, Morris was able to build up a 1.5s buffer by the flag. The podium was rounded out by Castle Combe regular Bob Higgins, who had to work hard to keep Martin Holman behind him throughout the seven laps.

Fortunately, the weather stayed dry for Sunday, with the draw keeping the three main protagonists – Gugelmin, Bailey and Morris – apart for the quarter-finals. Gugelmin was first into action, with a superb performance and victory. The Brazilian made it look easy as he eased seven seconds clear of the fight for second. The battle for the remaining podium positions was a good one though, with Wheeler and Cheever picking up where they left off in the first heat. Wheeler took the honours, just 0.1s clear of Cheever. The top five was rounded out by Donnelly and Sala.

Bailey sought to follow suit in the second quarter-final. His initial challenge came from Wallace, who was fractionally ahead on the initial approach to Paddock, but Bailey was able to turn in just in front to lead for the duration. The results sheet made it look closer than it was, with Bailey building his ultimate 1.3s advantage throughout, easing clear of Wallace on every lap. Wallace's challenge was made tougher by the super battle progressing in his mirrors with Langrekken and Reid fighting tooth and nail. Langrekken eventually prevailed to complete the podium. Meanwhile Dumfries retired after hitting an abandoned car (this being an era where wreckage was left where the accident finished), one of several to crash out.

The third quarter-final was truly frantic with chaotic incidents throughout the field. Pratt, building on his heat success, took victory, leading home Booth and a tactically astute Uwe Schafer who picked his way up through the order. It was behind that chaos reigned – a rolling series of incidents at Paddock on lap four left Peter Rogers' Merlyn (the driver fortunately uninjured) abandoned on the kerb at the exit of the turn. Today the safety car would be scrambled in an instant, and even in 1982 there was a question of stopping the race to clear the wreckage. As it was, the stricken vehicle was left in situ. As the laps tipped by, there were liberties taken before, on lap eight, Mark Ratcliffe smashed into the Merlyn at high speed, destroying both cars but fortunately escaping injury.

The entertainment factor remained high for the closing quarter-final, although the chaos was dialled down. The crowd was treated to a superb display as the fast-starting Ackerley, having taken the initial advantage, attempted to keep Morris and Fine at bay. Morris, in trademark style, launched into the lead with a bold outside line move at Paddock on the second lap. Fine claimed second after a similarly brave pass to demote Ackerley to third.

For the semi-finals, the draw put Gugelmin and Pratt at the head of the first, whilst Morris and Bailey would go head to head in the second. As the anticipation built, the afternoon closed in, with chilly, drizzly mist forming over the circuit.

The first semi-final was a non-event. As he'd done earlier in the day, Gugelmin again made it look easy, taking a commanding victory some six seconds clear of Pratt. The latter had needed to work his way past Wheeler, who was then shuffled off the podium by Schafer. The fight for fifth provided the best value of the race, with Booth and Cheever being near inseparable throughout.

If Gugelmin had laid down the gauntlet, Bailey more than accepted the challenge. In an *Autosport*-endorsed 'stunning' performance, Bailey completed the 15 laps some seven seconds faster than the Brazilian, setting up a tantalising final. Bailey didn't have it all his own way, with Morris an ever-present shadow, but as in his quarter-final the Lola pilot was masterly in eking out fractional advantages lap after lap. At the flag, the pair were 1.9s apart but a good six seconds up on the rest of the pack. Third went to Fine, who successfully fended off Reid, whilst Wallace and Ackerley finished in a near dead heat for fifth and sixth.

Unlike previous years, it had been the quarter-finals that proved attritional, with few high-profile casualties in the semi-finals. The final was perfectly poised. Gugelmin had been blindingly fast throughout the weekend, but as with Moreno in 1980, not really challenged in any of his qualifying races. Bailey, meanwhile, had won each race but had worked hard in all of them. His pace was improving with each outing and he'd arguably had the tougher side of the draw.

The final would go down as one of the classics. It had everything: largely clean racing, the protagonists fighting at the front and a dramatic incident to decide proceedings. It was Bailey who led from the start, with Gugelmin swarming on his tail, looking every which way to find an opening. On the third lap, the Brazilian pushed too hard at Druids, allowing Morris up to second, and giving Bailey the glimmer of an opportunity to pull clear. He duly grasped the moment as Gugelmin fought to find a way back past Morris, eventually slipping through at Clearways. By this point, Bailey had a decent but not unassailable advantage.

Although Bailey's pace never eased, Gugelmin – arguably the fastest driver of the weekend – was able to inch ever closer until, with just three laps remaining, the pair were together. By now, Morris had fallen out of contention but held a solid third place. Gugelmin could pick his moment.

Arguably he went a lap too soon. Having just closed on to Bailey's tail, Gugelmin challenged into Clearways with just over two laps remaining. Once more caught to perfection by Kreisky's Videovision, Bailey left a gap to the inside and Gugelmin went for it, hurtling sideways into the corner far quicker than his rival. Bailey gave Gugelmin plenty of space, but the Van Diemen pilot used it all, his rear left wheel locking with Bailey's front right as the pair turned into Clark Curve. The inevitable collision launched Gugelmin into a roll that finished upside-down, balanced by the tyre wall at the edge of the circuit. It was a spectacular incident, but other than biting through his tongue, Gugelmin emerged unscathed. Bailey's driving was commendable – as many have done before and since, it would have been easy and tempting for him to close the door and risk eliminating the pair of them.

Those behind wondered if the incident would serve to remove both from the race – the Lola being notoriously fragile in a category where bumping was far from unknown. But somehow Bailey's car was undamaged from the contact (it was the angle rather than velocity of the collision that launched Gugelmin) and it completed the final laps to take victory and the Formula 3 prize drive. Morris was runner-up once more, with Pratt getting his just reward for a fine weekend's work with third. The top six was completed by Fine, Schafer and Reid, all of whom had shown strongly throughout the competition.

The podium photographs show Morris looking far from euphoric, which 40 years on remains the case: 'That was the one that got away. I was behind the Bailey and Gugelmin crash, but had made a mistake a couple of laps earlier, so couldn't immediately nip through. The Lola was so fragile, though, and Gugelmin drove right over the front wheel – I've no idea how it didn't fall off. How did that Lola stay in one piece?'

Both Bailey and Gugelmin eventually made it to Formula 1. Bailey, the first of the 'rat pack' to find success (the others being Damon Hill, Johnny Herbert, Martin Donnelly, Mark Blundell and Perry McCarthy), discovered his career wasn't a straightforward path to the top. Graduating to Formula 1 with Tyrrell in 1988 and then having a part-season with Lotus in 1991, Bailey never quite established himself at the top level. As he readily admits, fun and an incompatible lifestyle of smoking and drinking got in the way, but combined with world sportscar and BTCC stints, he enjoyed a successful career. Post-retirement he enjoyed a level of anonymous fame by performing as The Stig on *Top Gear*.

Gugelmin also never quite hit the heights. After winning the 1985 British F3 championship, he moved to Formula 1 in 1988 with the Leyton House/March team. Blessed with a sleek Adrian Newey-designed chassis, his best season was his first, although his only podium came in Brazil at the start of the 1989 season. After five years in Formula 1, Gugelmin moved to the IndyCar series in the USA, where over eight full seasons he was a popular frontrunner, taking his sole victory in Vancouver in 1997. In truth, neither Bailey nor Gugelmin quite enjoyed the successes of other Festival challengers, but for one October weekend they both provided displays of superb driving and great racing.

For much of the 1983 season, several of *Autosport*'s warnings the previous autumn came to pass and Formula Ford experienced a marked drop in fortunes – the combination of increased costs and expiring sponsorship agreements made prior to the recession serving to dwindle grid numbers. Motorsport generally feels the impact of a recession some 12 to 24 months later, and this proved to be case in 1983 when British motorsport at all levels experienced much reduced grids.

This trend continued into the Festival with a marked reduction in the number of entries – 128 drivers finally taking to the track, compared with 179 a year previously. Not that the variety was hit too badly, with 20 different chassis and 29 variations of tuned engines available throughout the field.

In the battle of the manufacturers, for the first time in the decade the Van Diemen wasn't the car to beat. The distinctive rear bodywork on the RF83 was a clear departure from the neat packaging of previous editions. The main challenge came from Reynard and Lola. The former was a driver's dream, working best when sideways and inspiring confidence from its pilots. By contrast, the sophisticated Lola was tricksy, but, as shown by Bailey the previous year, very effective in the right hands.

It had also been quite an open season on the driver front. The British charge was led by Andrew Gilbert-Scott, John Pratt, Andy Wallace and Mark Peters – the former taking the British title. Other likely challengers included Maurizio Sandro Sala, Ross Cheever and the increasingly impressive newcomer Gerrit van Kouwen. Making an appearance on a Marlboro scholarship would be Spaniard Carlos Sainz.

With 50 fewer cars participating in the heats, progression to the quarter-finals would, barring disaster, be more straightforward than in previous years. In 1982, roughly ten drivers went home after each heat; in 1983, it would only be four from each opener.

The format benefitted from two changes. Qualifying now took place on Friday, making the meeting a true three-day event. With the timetable somewhat freed up, the races had been made a bit longer, with heats of ten laps, quarter-finals of 12, 15 for the semi-finals and a 20-lap final.

Cheever was on pole for the first heat and duly took victory, despite Andy Middlehurst taking an initial lead. Once through, Cheever was untroubled thereafter. The second encounter was a bit more entertaining, with Peter Rogers taking victory despite the close attentions of Antonio Albacete – both drivers comfortably clear of the field and disinclined to risk all at this stage.

The message about preservation didn't make its way to heat three's contenders. None of the favourites were present, but lots of solid frontrunners were – three of whom had an early trip home. John Village was the first out, booted into the catch fencing at Druids. At the front, Star of Tomorrow champion John Penfold and John 'Butcher' Booth disputed the lead. Heading into Clearways for the final time, Booth made a lunge with the inevitable consequences for Penfold who was despatched into the scenery. Although he made it to the flag, Booth was excluded by the stewards for aggressive driving, any hopes of a successful appeal being scuppered by Booth's car being found 4kg underweight during post-race checks. Paul Mather was the foremost of the survivors being awarded victory.

Heat four was a steadier affair, with Peters easing to the win from Brands specialist Andy Ackerley, future Stig Perry McCarthy and Sainz. The following race also threw up a clear winner in Mark Newby, who benefitted from mechanical and driver failures from his closest rivals. Van Kouwen and Wallace were the stars of heat six, the pair enjoying a precariously close duel. Wallace led most of the way, before van Kouwen finally found a way past on the penultimate lap. Wallace fought back into Druids for the final time but brushed the Lola pilot into a spin. A relieved van Kouwen recovered in time to still claim second.

It was a similarly tight battle in heat seven, with Sala and Pratt romping clear of the field and enjoying their own private battle. Pratt tried every trick in the book and a bit more to find a way past, but some robust defence and blocking from Sala was enough to give him victory by a fraction of a second. This left the most dominant performance to last, with Gilbert-Scott claiming the final heat by some seven seconds.

For all those advancing to Sunday, the quarter-finals would see a step-up in intensity. After only a handful departed on Saturday, half the remaining field would head home after the day's opening quartet of races. Adding to the fun was the presence of Videovision cameras filming the action, with comprehensive highlights of the day being released shortly after on home video, for the first time providing the opportunity for armchair enjoyment of the thrills and spills of the Festival.

Perhaps inevitably with reputations on the line, several prospective frontrunners failed to progress. Cheever wasn't one of them. He took the first encounter with relative comfort after the initial scrapping for position, with only Middlehurst able to maintain a decent challenge.

The start of the second race was the first of the day's big talking points. Starting from pole, Peters was joined on the front row by Rogers and Ackerley. It was the latter who made the better start, squeezing his front-row companions as they headed away. Peters was left with nowhere to go and interlocked wheels with the entirely innocent Rogers. Peters was lifted into an aerial pirouette before crashing down and damaging his suspension. The chaos at the front triggered a train reaction further back, bringing out the red flag. Rogers was out on the spot, whilst the best efforts of Peters' mechanics appeared to have him ready for a pit-lane start before his driveshaft gave out.

This left Ackerley all alone on the front row for the restart, but despite the advantage Albacete put him under huge pressure throughout. Ackerley's defence used every trick in the book – some crossing the line of what could be considered fair – and Albacete, after one near miss too many, decided to settle for second.

The third quarter-final was a lively head to head between Pratt and Sala. In a precursor of races to come, Pratt had the pace but Sala had the wiles. Pratt's every challenge was rebuffed, the Brazilian holding on to win by a couple of tenths of a second. No such excitement for the lead was to be found in the fourth quarter-final as Gilbert-Scott once more departed from the pack, finishing four seconds up the road from Wallace with third-placed van Kouwen another few seconds back.

The first semi-final was, as hoped, keenly contested between Sala, Pratt and Cheever. Of the trios Pratt was the quicker, but it was Sala who took the advantage at the lights. As in the pair's earlier races, Pratt was on his case, looking every which way for an opening, but this time Cheever was hovering with intent. Up front as Sala was producing a masterful display of defensive driving, Cheever managed to find a way around Pratt at Druids. There was to be no way past Sala, who completed the 15 laps fractions of a second clear of Cheever and Pratt.

Gilbert-Scott had it slightly easier in the second semi-final, although for the first time in the weekend he was kept busy. Initially the challenge came from Brands specialist Ackerley, who forced an error early on but was unable to capitalise for a lasting lead. As the race progressed, Ackerley dropped back into the clutches of Wallace and van Kouwen, the pair reigniting their battle from the heats. At the flag, Wallace was just ahead to take second from van Kouwen. Gilbert-Scott took victory by four seconds, his race time quicker than the earlier race, giving him pole position for the final.

The grid for the final was headed by an all-Reynard front row of Gilbert-Scott, Sala and Wallace. Cheever and van Kouwen were next along, whilst on speed alone Pratt was unlucky to be on the third row. Gilbert-Scott judged the start to perfection, leading the way into Paddock as Sala got the better of Wallace into the right-hander. Immediately, Gilbert-Scott set about trying to break away from the field, his pace proving a clear step-up on his rivals, possibly aided by tyres he'd managed to keep warm during the break between races.

Gilbert-Scott was soon well away, with attention turning to the fight for second between Cheever and Sala. On lap seven, the American snuck through at Clearways, but Sala was instantly on his case. Heading into Paddock for the ninth time, Cheever left half a gap and Sala pounced. Cheever looked to shut the door, forcing Sala kerbwards and giving the Reynard pilot no choice but to stand his ground. Their wheels intertwined and Cheever was launched into a spectacular barrel roll down the hill and into the tyre wall (once more perfectly captured by the Videovision camera). Fortunately, both drivers escaped uninjured, Cheever attributing the collision to a 50/50 racing incident.

This promoted Wallace to second, with a hard-charging Pratt looming in his tail. In the early stages, Pratt had been down in tenth but had scythed through the pack. The pair were some five seconds back from Gilbert-Scott, enabling Wallace to invest all his energies in maintaining second. This he duly did, crossing the line just 0.04s clear of Pratt in third. Up front, there was no doubt as to the winner – Gilbert-Scott had been the class of the field for the weekend, and much of the season, coming home a worthy Festival winner.

Both Gilbert-Scott and Wallace went on to enjoy successful careers, but neither quite made it to Formula 1. After his opportunities in Europe started to dry up, from the late 1980s Gilbert-Scott predominantly raced in Japan where he became well known in the well-supported and funded national scene. He was also close to the Jordan team, managing their one-time driver Takuma Sato and occasionally driving the cars for promotional purposes.

Wallace went further, taking the 1986 British Formula 3 title before winning the 24 Hours of Le Mans in 1988 at his first attempt as part of the Jaguar team. This established Wallace as one of the top sportscar drivers of his generation, racing for both McLaren and Bentley and winning his class at Le Mans on a further three occasions.

Of the class of 1983 it was a quarter-final retiree who subsequently became a legend. After deciding to focus all his energies on rallying, Carlos Sainz became the face of the sport for much of the 1990s, winning two world titles and 26 WRC rounds between 1990 and 2004. To many, he is arguably best known for the championship he didn't win. Leading the 1998 title race, and just a few hundred metres from the season-closing Rally GB finish line, his Toyota ground to a halt, handing the title to Tommi Makkinen. The clip of Sainz's distraught co-driver Luis Moya flinging his helmet through the Toyota's rear windscreen made newsreels worldwide. Sainz's son, Carlos Jr, followed in the family tradition but stuck to circuit racing. After serving his apprenticeship in British Formula 3, Sainz Jr graduated to Formula 1 and, at the time of writing, partners Charles Leclerc at Ferrari.

Despite the euphoria of a Festival weekend, the strength of national-level support for Formula Ford continued to wane throughout 1984. Several long-running championships folded at the end of the season, consolidating to a single national championship – the RAC, BRSCC and BARC series all combined for 1985, alongside the junior series and the enduringly popular circuit series.

For the frontrunners of 1984, there were a total of 37 meetings available in which to challenge for the various championships – within 20 years most campaigns were limited to just ten or so competitive weekends, highlighting the consolidation of racing activity.

Despite the fragmented and relentless calendar, the Festival continued to grow in stature. After the home video release of highlights from the 1983 meeting, the 1984 final was shown in full the Saturday following the event as part of the BBC's hugely popular *Grandstand* programme, complete with commentary from Murray Walker. This brought the event to a mainstream audience, although with full grandstands the Festival remained a must-do for die-hard motorsport enthusiasts.

After the comparatively disappointing 1983, interest bounced back in 1984 with over 160 cars entered, including a far stronger continental presence, placing far more jeopardy on the heats than 12 months previously. As ever, the cream of the British scene was joined by European challengers, and regional circuit specialists. Sixteen manufacturers were represented, continuing to show the diversity of the category (albeit a drop of a third compared to two years earlier) along with the usual plethora of engine-tuners.

The pre-event favourites were naturally drawn from those who'd seen success during the 1984 campaign, with John Pratt and Gerrit van Kouwen probably the most fancied. However, there was massive strength in depth, with Dave Coyne (again), Mark Peters, Damon Hill (son of two-time Formula 1 champion Graham Hill) all in the mix. Equally, Brands specialists Tim Jones and Karl Jones (unrelated) were quietly confident of their chances. As son of the circuit commentator Brian Jones, Tim could at least rely on some support from the commentary box. Of the lesser known (at least to the British fans) foreign contingent, Uwe Schafer had gone well on previous visits, but it was Bertrand Gachot whose pace was turning heads in practice. Gachot came into the weekend with fewer than ten races under his belt, having spent much of the season in hospital following a crash. Many paddock insiders would be following his progress.

The competition among the manufacturers remained close. The latest Lola was a sleek and technologically astute package, whilst the Reynard retained its driver-favourite status, continuing to be fast when sideways. Van Diemen were in the mix too, but the 1984 edition, despite its striking looks, followed its 1983 forebear in being a beat off the ultimate pace – although that would change with the introduction of the RF85, unveiled during the Festival weekend. Whilst the tightly constrained regulations kept things close, the cars had evolved by a degree of magnitude from those at the turn of the decade and the cars of even two years earlier could no longer be considered competitive.

The format rolled forward in its now familiar way, with no changes from the previous year. The first heat was a typically fraught Festival encounter. Qualifying pacesetter Harald Huysman was pipped to pole position by Anthony Murray's Crosslé, which led for the first lap. Heading into lap two, Huysman slipped past and was thereafter able to pull away, taking the flag four seconds clear of Murray. Behind was somewhat more chaotic, with future BTCC champion Winkelhock just one of the many casualties whose weekend finished early on Saturday afternoon.

The second encounter was a little more sedate, with Alvaro Buzaid taking the honours after a race-long battle with Gary Ward, third-place man Glenn Board finishing fractions of a second behind the leading pair. Heat three provided a dominant winner in the form of Schafer, but there was some superb battling behind. Second went to John 'Brolly' Booth (so named to differentiate him from John 'Butcher' Booth – the nicknames referring to their professions), with Hill in third – the latter having spent the entire race in the midst of a seething pack. The casualty of note was Mark Blundell, who crunched into the tyres whilst trying to improve his grid position for the following round.

In the following heat, Dave Coyne was comfortably the class of the field, the category veteran kept honest but never under real pressure by Ross Hockenhull and Alan McGarrity, who completed the podium. A far more entertaining fight for the lead could be found in heat five, where novice champion Jonathan Bancroft almost held off the more experienced Mark Peters. However, Peters' experience in clearing backmarkers allowed him to snatch the advantage late on. Pre-event tip John Pratt lived up to the hype in heat six, taking the flag by eight seconds from the closely matched Drew Barwick and Chris Hall. Pratt, widely regarded by his peers as one of the fastest drivers of the era, was felt to be near unassailable when he could break free of the pack – as he duly demonstrated.

The penultimate heat saw another favourite, van Kouwen, make his bow. The aimiable Dutchman had relocated to the UK to pursue his racing dream, feeling that British scene was the strongest in Europe and success in the UK was essential to furthering his career. With the works Lola and a formidably successful season behind him, van Kouwen put in a scintillating performance for comfortably the fastest heat of the day. A distant second went to Johnny Herbert, who was challenged late on by Ruari O'Coileain, whilst another BTCC champion, 1996 winner Frank Biela, took fourth.

Saturday's final race introduced a degree of bias over the tannoy as Brian Jones' son, Tim, lined up on the front row alongside Gachot and Peter Rogers, all equipped with the latest Reynard. Jones, who had funded his start in motorsport through a year in the Royal Navy, had worked his way up through the Champion of Brands ranks and was now a bona-fide frontrunner.

Such was his focus on the Festival and belief that this could be his year, Jones had asked his then girlfriend to move out for the week before and during the meeting. With laser-like focus he took to the grid, only to look to his left. Jones recalls thinking, 'Oh for f**k's sake, there she is screaming my name and jumping up and down. So much for all the preparation.'

It was a superb race that showed Formula Ford at its finest, the leading trio clear at the front in a close dice. Gachot was arguably the fastest, but a combination of a broken anti-roll bar and limited circuit smarts saw him come home third. Rogers pressured Jones all the way but couldn't find a way through, enabling Jones to take victory by just two-tenths of a second. Understandably elated tones could be heard from the commentary box.

Reflecting on the race, Jones feels that it was his finest at the Festival: 'It was like Tai Chi, everything I was doing felt slow and deliberate. The battle was completely clean, no touching, no desperation.' The accompanying photograph in that week's *Autosport* shows the leading trio completely sideways through Paddock, almost balletic in their choreography.

Fortunately for those in the grandstands, Sunday dawned warmer and brighter than the preceding day. As Jones recalls, 'I always arrived early to hear the place wake up. The sound of generators takes me right back there. There was this atmosphere and sense that something amazing was about to happen. I adored it.'

The first quarter-final brought the first and third heats together with the top 13 once more progressing. After some early battling, Schafer pulled clear of Huysman to take a relatively comfortable victory, some three seconds clear. More value could be found in the scrap for third where 'Brolly' Booth just had the better of Hill.

With the huge crowd nicely warmed up, the second race was a thriller. Coyne and Buzaid had a nail-biting scrap with the places swapping regularly. Every time Coyne moved through, Buzaid seemed to have a response. Despite the Brazilian building a small buffer, Coyne had a superb run through Clearways for the final time, drawing alongside Buzaid – to some observers getting his nose in front – but it was the Brazilian who got the verdict. The official gap was 0.07s.

Van Kouwen was the clear favourite for the third quarter-final but he was jumped from the line by Peters with Herbert in close attention. By now a category veteran, Peters knew how vital the first lap would be, building a small lead. It was to no avail as, by the end of the second tour, van Kouwen was through. Thereafter, the Lola pilot consistently set lap times none of his rivals could live with, completing the 12 laps in a tenth of a second over ten minutes – comfortably the fastest race of the round. Peters ran out a clear second from Herbert.

Friends and rivals Pratt and Jones were the class of the field in the closing quarter-final, breaking clear of the pack when Rogers and Gachot tangled, both fortunately continuing. Jones initially had the advantage before Pratt sneaked past. The combination of Jones's circuit knowledge and (according to Jones) Pratt's tendency to over-consult his mirrors kept it desperately close, until a snapped throttle linkage coming out of Druids put Jones out of the race. Jones recalls, 'I pulled up on the Bottom Straight and my bottom lip was going. I know it was the same for Dad in the commentary box. I had the confidence in the car that year to give it a good go, I really think I could have won it.'

With Jones out of the running, Pratt came home a mammoth ten seconds clear of Drew Barwick in second and the impressive Ulsterman Eddie Irvine in third.

The first semi-final pitted van Kouwen and Schafer against each other. With the Dutchman needing to check the tendency of the Lola to roll forward on the grid, Schafer jumped into the lead. As the leading pair tried to break away, there was some ferocious dicing behind – the semi-finals requiring both progression and a good finishing position for chances in the final. Peters, Huysman, Hill and Herbert were all in the mix, although Peters' chances diminished after contact at Clearways. Heading into lap two, van Kouwen took the lead into Paddock and thereafter flew clear. His pace was quickly into the sub-49-second bracket, earning him a substantial cash bonus, and allowing him to open up a tidy lead over Schafer. The leading duo stayed that way to the flag, with Huysman in third, after mechanical issues forced Herbert into retirement.

The second semi-final saw some even more frantic battling. Pratt had pole position, but with Buzaid and Coyne also on the front two rows it promised to be close. Buzaid made the best start, leading from Pratt, whilst Coyne with a freshly fettled car (his bent engine valves had been changed in the gap between races) was also in the mix. Pratt, frustrated by his early demotion, pushed too hard, too soon and collided with Buzaid at Clearways, spinning into dead last. This released Coyne and Buzaid to resume their quarter-final battle, with Gachot and Barwick behind and then a fierce nine-car train. Over the 15 laps, Coyne got the better of Buzaid by just two-hundredths of a second, the pair remaining inseparable, whilst a trouble-free run for Gachot landed him an impressive third. Pratt staged a remarkable recovery drive, carving through the field and on to the cusp of qualification for the final, until a collision in traffic put him into the barriers and out of the race.

As ever, the build-up to the final got the grandstand chatter going. On the one hand, van Kouwen had been devastatingly quick all weekend, and his only rivals on pace – Pratt and Jones – were out. On the other, Buzaid and Coyne had shown great racecraft all weekend and would be hard to overhaul if they made the better starts.

With the BBC cameras rolling, van Kouwen took his place in pole position. The Lola driver had scrubbed in five sets of tyres during testing, using (in his view) a better set with each subsequent session throughout qualifying and the races. Therefore, with his best set of tyres and pace that had been unmatched during the weekend, he had every right to feel confident. Alongside him on the front row was Coyne. Supremely fast in his heat and in the thick of intense battles with Buzaid throughout Sunday, he would be hard to pass if he could lead into Paddock. However, Coyne took to the grid with a new engine, the Van Diemen crew changing the power unit in just 35 minutes. Completing the front row was Schafer who had been consistent and mature throughout but hadn't yet shown winning pace.

Ultimately, this proved to be a Festival where the final fell short, at least in the entertainment stakes. Van Kouwen obliterated the field. Making a superb start, he was quickly able to shake Schafer from his tow, and thereafter spent the bulk of the 20 laps with a comfortable gap over the rest. Schafer likewise took advantage of his good start and early running with van Kouwen to clear the pack, enjoying a comfortable run to second.

More entertainment, although not much of it, could be found for third. Huysman and Coyne took themselves out of the running with an early collision – Coyne finishing 11th and Huysman in the barriers – whilst Buzaid blew his engine trying to chase down Schafer. This elevated Gachot to take a superb third – and with the Frenchman stating his intention of racing in British Formula Ford the following year, it signalled a clear favourite for 1985.

It was an imperious weekend for van Kouwen and one which marked him out as a star of the future. However, it wasn't quite to be. A strong debut year in Formula 3 in 1985, during which he scored three victories, was followed by a disappointing 1986. Thereafter his single-seater career remained stuck at that level and attempts to move into touring cars never yielded the success his talent deserved. A massive fan of Formula Ford and the Festival in particular, Gerrit van Kouwen was an ever-present until he was unable to make the 2020 Covid-disrupted event.

Stars are made here

ALL SPORTS and all teams can point to a golden generation, that period where, for a handful of years, there was an unending train of thrilling talents breaking through. The Formula Ford Festivals of the late 1980s are the quintessential example in motorsport. For five years, the Festival was truly motorsport's junior world championship, attracting the very best talent from around the globe. The racing was ferocious and nail-bitingly close. All bar one of Formula 1's champions from 1994 to 2004 raced at the Festival in these years, but a glance at the entry list for any of the heats is a who's who of international motorsport for the next 20 years.

These were very special years that, at least to a wider public, wrote the legend of the Formula Ford Festival. The Festival truly became a multinational affair, with drivers travelling from around the world to test themselves at Brands Hatch. The margins of success and failure were painfully close – the margin from first to nowhere being as little as an exhaust that was four millimetres out of line in qualifying. This action was played out in front of the BBC's cameras (the Festival sometimes getting up to an hour's exposure on *Grandstand*) and packed stands with a slot at Paddock Hill Bend requiring advance booking.

It did come at a cost. Entries now came almost exclusively from the cream of the British and other European national championships, together with the Champion of Brands frontrunners. The type of driver who had previously instigated and propelled the Festival now stayed away, knowing they stood little chance of progressing beyond their heats. Even within such white heat of competition, some years stand clear among others; both 1985 and 1988 can stake strong claims to being the greatest Festival of all.

1985 was a weekend of light and shade that showcased the best and worst of the category: an astonishing rags-to-riches tale, incredible racing as a remarkable generation of drivers coalesced in Formula Ford, and tragedy with the death of a marshal following a fatal incident.

For the Formula Ford scene, 1985 had a vastly different look. Nationally, multiple series had been condensed to a single championship – 37 events, down to 14. Breakthrough star of the 1984 Festival Bertrand Gachot had taken the title, winning four races along the way. Gachot was equipped with Van Diemen's RF85, *the* car to have. Slimline and far less bulky than its predecessors whilst being about as high tech as Formula Ford got, the RF85 won every single race of the national championship.

Van Diemen were aided somewhat by the 1985 Reynard being tough to master – works driver Tim Jones reflected that the feel of the car changed from day to day, making it very difficult to build confidence. Jones switched mid-season to Van Diemen and would count amongst the favourites in the Festival, as would Mark Blundell and Damon Hill, both returning in 1985, and Jonathan Bancroft, who had shown well as a novice the preceding season. Also hotly tipped for the weekend was Johnny Herbert in the Quest. Both car and driver had shown great potential, but neither had yet had the breakthrough result they desired. However, leading the pundits' picks in the programme was the Brazilian Paolo Carcasci.

As with Formula Ford, Brands Hatch itself was at an inflection point. The following year, Grovewood Securities would sell the venue to John Foulston and Brands would host its final (to date) Grand Prix. For now, the circuit was basking in the glow of the last-minute hosting of the European Grand Prix where a gigantic crowd cheered Nigel Mansell to his debut Formula 1 victory. Under the stewardship of John Webb and Grovewood, despite being very much a commercial proposition, Brands Hatch was run by motor racing people for motor racing people – something that would change dramatically over the following decade.

The entry once more hovered around 160 cars, with 18 to 20 starting each of the eight heats. The remainder of the event would then follow the tried and tested format building up to the 20-lap grand final.

The underpinning story of the weekend started to unfold on Friday. Herbert, drawn in the first heat, pitched his Quest into the Paddock catch fencing at the start of his first qualifying lap – thus condemning him to start from the back of the grid with a ten-second penalty. This set the scene for one of the great Festival stories. Herbert's initial task over the ten laps was to get into the top 13, enabling him to progress to the quarter-finals. Any placings beyond that point would help to make his Sunday morning a little easier. The race itself wasn't a classic. The field quickly spread out, with Alan Seedhouse taking a comfortable victory. For Herbert, the absence of a swarming pack slowing itself down made his life harder, but nonetheless he scythed through the field to finish an impressive sixth.

The second heat might not have had the storyline, but it did have pedigree, with Hill and Rick Shortle as the coming men up against category legend Rick Morris and the experienced Mark Peters. The leading quartet remained close throughout but Hill was largely unchallenged up front due to the intensity of the Shortle, Peters and Morris fight behind – the latter trio finishing in that order covered by just over three-hundredths of a second.

More quality was to be found in heat three, with Carcasci and Bancroft going head to head. The Brazilian had taken pole by the slenderest of margins, but Bancroft made the better start as Carcasci was briefly down to third. It didn't take long for Carcasci to claim second and he was rapidly on to Bancroft's tail. However, Bancroft hit his stride and seemed more confident as the race progressed, taking the win.

The ever-rapid Peter Rogers took victory in heat four, he and runner-up Roland Ratzenberger benefitting from two strokes of good fortune to run clear at the front. Firstly, polesitter Phil Andrews jumped the start and spent the bulk of the race trying to overcome the ten-second penalty he'd received – he was eventually classified seventh. Secondly, third-place finisher 'Brolly' Booth blocked and weaved excessively to keep a pack behind him, allowing a huge gap to open up to the leaders – *Autosport* was disdainful of his antics.

Tragedy struck in the fifth heat. The lead up to and start of the race was a scrappy affair, with several drivers starting from the back of the field due to mechanical infringements spotted in qualifying, and others being penalised for jumping the start.

As Steve Robertson and Ruari O'Coileain led the way up front, there was a fierce squabble for the qualification places.

By lap seven one of the drivers starting from the back of the grid – Paul Bishop – had joined the main pack. Although secure of his progression, he attempted a bold move on Kristyan Ingram into Paddock. The pair collided and Bishop's Crosslé was launched into a series of rolls, the car barely touching the ground and appearing as if it might fly directly into the crowd. The potentially larger disaster was avoided, but the car did clear the barrier, striking two marshals as it landed. The drivers both escaped serious injury, but tragically one of the marshals – an unnamed 26-year-old – was killed as a result of the incident. A collection the following day raised over £2,000 for the family and the competitors from the weekend donated their winnings.

Autosport's leader the following Thursday drew attention to the safety issue. At the time a low Armco barrier protected by tyres, a rising bank and wire fence were all that separated the spectators from the circuit and they were potentially in the path of flying debris. The point made by *Autosport* was that if such an incident could happen in the relatively low speed Formula Fords, the consequences of something similar in Formula 1 didn't bear thinking about. Today's venue, whilst working with the same space constraints, is now largely lined by high fencing around the circuit to prevent vehicles entering crowd areas during similar incidents.

Not that it really mattered, but the race result was declared after seven laps with Robertson taking victory. After an understandably lengthy delay, racing did resume with the remainder of the heats to complete.

Another scrappy start punctuated heat six, with Blundell being the main beneficiary of others' hesitation, but thereafter producing an emphatic performance to win by seven seconds. The action was to be found in the midfield, the podium completed by Alan McGarrity and Vivion Daly.

The start and opening corners would prove decisive too in the penultimate heat, where Gachot took no prisoners in swooping into the lead through Paddock. He, Eddie Irvine and Adrian Wilmott were the class of the field, building a good margin over the rest, where somewhat unusually all 16 starters safely made it to the finish. As he did 12 months previously, Jones took victory in the final heat and, once more, he had to work for it. A leading trio of Jones, Jason Elliot and Frank Biela were inseparable, covered by under a quarter of a second at the chequered flag.

Compared to prior editions there was a definite increase in intensity throughout the heats, with ferocious to over-the-line dicing for places in many races, coupled with scrappy starts and other infringements, highlighting just how many competitors were pushing the limit.

Sunday dawned a little warmer and without fog. The first quarter-final would see Carcasci and Bancroft starting up front, whilst Herbert would be starting from the fifth row and needing further progress to be in the mix for the semi-finals. The flatter outside grid position once again proved its worth as Carcasci swept into the lead at Paddock. For the win, that was the decisive moment as the Brazilian set a comfortable pace up front. In second, meanwhile, Bancroft was under token but rarely serious pressure from Seedhouse, the pair completing the podium. Instead, all eyes were on Herbert. By the end of the opening exchanges, he was seventh, and by lap six he was up to fourth. Although able to join the train for second, Herbert opted to keep his powder dry, settling for progression.

Rogers, Hill and Shortle were the expected frontrunners for the second quarter-final and duly delivered with a clean and entertaining battle at the front. Shortle was always there or thereabouts but remained third for the duration as the leading duo went at it.

Tenacious defence kept Hill in front despite Rogers buzzing all over his gearbox. Heading into lap six, Rogers made an ambitious bid for the lead into Paddock and for a moment it looked as if it would end in a monster incident, but Rogers' skill prevailed (aided by Hill giving him the space he needed) and he was through to victory.

It was another three-car train that dominated the penultimate quarter-final. Gachot took victory but was made to work hard for it by O'Coileain. An unexpected move into Paddock was the decisive factor after the pair had swapped places throughout much of the early running. Third place went to Robertson, all three drivers placing preservation over victory.

Blundell completed the roll call of quarter-final winners, his consistently impressive lap times ensured victory five seconds clear of runner-up Jones. The battle was better for second as Jones once more needed to rely on circuit knowledge to keep Elliott and the rest of the pack behind him.

There was no runaway favourite heading into the semi-finals. Several drivers had all shown they had the pace – Carcasci, Hill, Blundell, Rogers, Gachot and Jones to name six. Then there was Herbert, still making amends for his qualifying misadventures, but clearly going well in the Quest. Very few of the races had breakaway winners, confirming the high and closely matched level of competition.

It was Carcasci, Gachot and Bancroft who took the front placings, lining up three-wide for the opening semi-final, with Herbert starting back on the third row. At the lights, Bancroft once more took advantage of the outside starting position, chopping across into the lead, squeezing Gachot. In turn, Gachot was trying to dispute the issue whilst also giving Carcasci little room for manoeuvre, the Brazilian having made a slightly sideways start.

The Festival then experienced another of its most iconic moments. Neither Gachot nor Carcasci wanted to back off, but there was only space for one car. With Carcasci now pushed on to the grass and their wheels locked, Gachot was tipped into a barrel roll in front of the whole field. The Marlboro-backed Van Diemen disintegrated and Gachot's helmet almost scraped along the tarmac. His luckiest escape came at the very end of the incident as the rear wheel of O'Coileain's car missed his head by millimetres. It was a truly spectacular accident, which featured prominently in motorsport crash compilations throughout the 1980s and remains an online favourite.

Inevitably the race was stopped, with the consequence being that two solid favourites, Gachot and Carcasci, were out of the event – both uninjured but with badly damaged cars. For Bancroft, and Herbert in particular, their task had just become a lot easier. It wasn't quite the race it could have been but was still a good one. Bancroft was able to ease into the lead, taking O'Coileain with him. Herbert, meanwhile, stayed out of trouble at the start before he set about picking off his rivals. By mid-race he was up to third and on O'Coileain's tail, the pressure paying off on the 11th lap, when the Van Diemen pilot made a mistake at Surtees and slid on to the grass. Herbert was immediately through and set about Bancroft, finishing second to him by just 0.02s. With oil dropped during the race this would likely be the faster of the semi-finals, giving Bancroft pole and Herbert the coveted third place (the outside of the front row) for the final. O'Coileain rounded out the rostrum with a close third.

If the first semi-final produced an infamous moment, the second was an iconic race described in *Autosport* as having 'produced some absolutely breathtaking racing, which is so absolutely typical of the Festival'. It was the leading quartet of Blundell, Hill, Rogers and Jones who produced the entertainment. Blundell was yet another to endure a difficult start from pole position as Jones moved across into the lead, taking Rogers with him for company. With the yo-yo effect coming into play amongst the leaders, Jones was under the most unbelievable pressure from Rogers on some corners, but half a lap later he had a glimmer of an opportunity to romp clear.

Reflecting 35 years later, Jones remains rueful: 'I should have won it that year, with better race and self-management. In that semi-final I just wish someone had taped up my mirrors, so I'd get my head down.' It all came to a head at Druids on lap nine. Jones was slow out of Paddock, giving Rogers half an opportunity into the hairpin. Arriving three-wide – Rogers to the inside, Jones in the middle and Blundell committed to the outside line – they all braked desperately late. Rogers had no option but to slither wide, pushing Jones and Blundell even further off-line. This allowed an elated Hill to dart to the inside to assume the lead.

Jones recalls, 'I wish I'd just braked a bit earlier, that would have let Pete through but I'd still have been second. Pete and

I would often push each other on to the grass and be laughing about it. It didn't strike me as anything particularly dirty, we were just racing hard.' As it was Rogers immediately set off after Hill, attempting a repeat of his quarter-final move at Paddock. This time around he overcommitted and ran wide, allowing Hill to jump back into the lead. Hill duly took the flag and front-row slot for the final, from Rogers and Jones.

It had been a truly fantastic race, albeit one that still gives Jones painful memories: 'Until earlier this year I'd never watched the race back. It was only after Dad's [Brian Jones'] passing that I decided to watch it – mainly to hear him in full flight on the commentary. It was a fantastic race.'

This then set the scene for the final. Would it be a fairy-tale victory for Herbert, or would either Bancroft or Hill get their rewards from trouble-free weekends? As *Autosport* noted, unlike the first semi-final, 'the occupants of the front two rows had a combined IQ of something more than double figures this time,' which ensured that everyone made it cleanly through the opening exchanges.

It was Herbert who got the jump leading up the hill to Druids for the first time, with Bancroft and Hill then O'Coileain and Rogers all chasing. At the front, Herbert found himself under constant but not insurmountable pressure from Bancroft. At times Herbert relaxed too much, easing up sufficiently to bring Bancroft back into the fight before easing away. The leading duo were well clear of the rest. Whilst Hill was kept busy by O'Coileain, Rogers and Blundell, O'Coileain was the first to falter, spinning into retirement early on, whilst Blundell frustrated behind Rogers tapped him into a spin coming out of Druids.

For Herbert and the Quest team, taking victory was a result beyond their wildest expectations following Friday's disaster. Herbert was just over half a second clear of Bancroft when he was greeted by the chequered flag. Meanwhile for third, Hill and Blundell were credited with an identical race time, Hill getting the decision by a nose.

For the tiny Quest team, this was quite a result – the marque had shown well at Festivals throughout the decade, but to see off the hordes of hitherto dominant Van Diemens was a formidable achievement.

This was the last hurrah of the 'rat pack' at this level as Hill, Blundell, Herbert, and Perry McCarthy (who had a shocking weekend) would all move on to Formula 1. The 'rat pack' might have hogged the retrospective headlines, but there were plenty of others with the talent, Gachot and Carcasci to name but two.

Tim Jones reflects, 'Some of these guys were so good. Damon [Hill] – none of us knew how good he was until he got to Formula 1. I remember talking to Johnny [Herbert] and saying I can't believe Damon won the World title, Johnny was right to say that people improve and people change – Damon was one of those. Of the others, Gachot – Christ he was quick, and Carcasci should have made it to Formula 1. Ultimately to get to Formula 1 you need a bowl of 20 of so characteristics – being a sublime driver or having the budget is just part of it. I had some of them, so did plenty of others, but when you move up to Formula 3 things change – it gets really serious, the cars are fast, difficult and you need to be aggressive. Some of us responded to the step-up, others didn't. Part of me regrets not doing what Rick [Morris] did and staying at the Formula Ford,

Formula Ford 2000 level, that way I would have kept enjoying myself and been at the front.'

If the 1985 Festival was Herbert's fairy tale, the same circuit almost brought it to a shuddering end. A horrific 1988 Formula 3000 incident on the Grand Prix loop left Herbert with massive leg injuries. Amazingly, he recovered to start (and finish in fourth) his first Grand Prix the following March, his F1 career producing three victories over his 12 years in the top flight. However, the legacy and pain of those 1988 injuries mean that, to many, Herbert's potential was never fully realised.

Hill, meanwhile, was a late bloomer, taking a winding road through Formula 3 and Formula 3000 before making his Grand Prix debut for Brabham in 1992. Propelled into a plum Williams seat the following year, Hill's 1994 and 1995 title fights with Michael Schumacher captivated the nation and he was a hugely popular 1996 World Champion.

Michael Schumacher may well never have got his Formula 1 break had it not been for Gachot, 'a lovely guy, but I do remember him attacking me at Silverstone with a spanner,' laughs Jones. After breaking into Formula 1 in 1989, he secured a seat with the new Jordan team for 1991, scoring a number of promising results through the first part of the season. Immediately ahead of the Belgian Grand Prix, Gachot faced trial for actual bodily harm following an altercation with a London taxi driver the preceding December where Gachot used CS gas as part of the incident. Anticipating a suspended sentence, he was in fact landed with 18 months in Brixton prison. This opened up the seat to Schumacher for his sensational debut weekend. Upon his release, Gachot had lost the Jordan drive. Although he remained in Formula 1 for another couple of seasons, Gachot's career is another example of talent unfulfilled, his part-year with Jordan being his only time in a competitive car.

The mid-1980s found Brian Jones at the peak of his powers, an integral part of the Festival weekend. Jones' booming voice, unhurried delivery and crystal-clear diction cut through the noise of the cars over the public address. Being able to describe a race accurately is only part of the commentator's job. With his affability and friendship with almost the entire paddock, Jones was able to effortlessly weave insider knowledge into his commentary with the effect of making everyone watching feel they had the inside track too. Despite his friendships, Jones never ducked asking difficult questions in post-race interviews, and was trusted by competitors not to have an ulterior motive to his enquiries. The Saturday evening Festival Forum was a social highpoint of the weekend, with relationships rekindled, beer flowing and increasingly 'relaxed' interviews seeing Jones in his element.

The 1986 Festival once more boasted a bumper entry, the change being that grids that would have once been occupied by local and regional competitors were now filled by continental challengers. The meeting was now truly an international event, and one that was increasingly professional.

In Britain, Jason Elliot had taken the national title, although he did most of his winning in the first part of the season. Philippe Favre had been the driver to beat during the early autumn, with Phil Andrews, Roland Ratzenberger and Steve Robertson all taking victories too. Meanwhile the junior title had gone to Paul Warwick, younger brother of Formula Ford alumnus and Formula 1 driver Derek.

As in previous years, Van Diemens had won every round of the national championship and all bar one round of the junior series. After the Quest fairy tale of 1985, no one was expecting it all to go the way of the Norfolk marque again. Category veteran Peter Rogers was out in the Laser, whilst the Crosslé favoured by many Irish drivers always seemed to go well at Brands Hatch, as did the Reynards.

The format remained identical, but there was a big change in how the cars lined up – shifting from the 3-2-3-2 grid formation to today's more familiar 2-2-2-2. After the start-line chaos of the previous year, this was hardly a surprising decision, but it did have a tactical bearing on the weekend with less opportunity to make ground at the start from a lower grid position.

The big story of the Friday's practice was the near exclusion of several drivers during post-session checks. The drivers, all competitors from European championships, were found to have ineligible fire extinguishers – empty, partially empty or disconnected – the weight saving (worth a couple of hundredths per lap) being prioritised over the risk of incineration. After much discussion, in the words of *Autosport* the matter 'was brushed under the carpet', but it left a sour taste. The magazine also noted that trick fire extinguishers injecting nitrous oxide into the engine had been observed in Europe during the season.

Damp conditions greeted the drivers as they formed up for the first heat. The smart money was that this would favour circuit specialist and pole-position holder Chris Hall. After Hall muffed his start, Tomas Mezera was one of several to briefly lead before Hall was able to assert control over the race. The Jamun pilot put his local knowledge to good use to win from Gary Ayles and an impressive Niko Palhares, who would climb from 13th to finish third.

Jeremy Packer claimed the second heat, his Van Diemen enjoying the conditions far more than the Rays that surrounded him on the grid. There was some brilliant action behind as both Chris Cresswell and Ruairi O'Coileain moved through the pack to complete the podium.

Two of the pre-event favourites were drawn together in heat three, but whilst Favre started from pole, Andrews was at the back with a ten-second penalty after trashing his car in practice. Favre didn't have it all his own way, but by mid-race he'd found his stride to win by eight seconds from Anthony Russo. Andrews, meanwhile, would move on to the quarter-finals, but never looked comfortable on his way to eighth.

Robertson was the clear favourite for heat four. He did claim the victory but only after race-long pressure from Andy Stapley and Rolf Steinberger. Stapley had the best shot at a move for the win but was pushed on to the grass ('reprehensibly' in *Autosport*'s opinion) by Robertson. Future Festival favourite Neil Cunningham took third after Steinberger suffered late mechanical issues.

There were high expectations for Elliott in the fifth heat and the national champion duly led away from pole position. Then disaster for Van Diemen and Elliott – his throttle cable snapped, putting the pre-event favourite out of the meeting after barely a mile of racing. Barring that mechanical failure, it's hard to argue that Elliott wouldn't have been well in the mix for the final. With other attrition, all 12 survivors would go through to the quarter-finals. John Davis took victory after a close battle.

Next up was the fight of the day between Warwick, Antonio Simoes and Marc Hessell. Although the positions didn't change frequently, the trio were so closely matched that it was clear any error would shake up the order. Warwick defended well to win, whilst Hessell took second after a last lap-bid for victory by Simoes was unsuccessful.

Heat seven continued the multinational trend, with Dutchman Gerald van Uitert and Finn JJ Lehto (known contemporaneously as Jyrki Jarvilehto) pitting their wits against category stalwarts Rick Shortle and John 'Butcher' Booth. Over ten laps, circuit knowledge couldn't trump van Uitert and Lehto's pace as they finished first and second, a wide Shortle in third.

The final heat brought Ratzenberger into the fray, his practice pace marking him out as one of the fancied men. He duly delivered, with a five-second margin over Rogers in second and French challenger Jacques Goudchaux in third.

With Saturday's work completed, two of the main challengers, Ratzenberger and Favre, returned to the same guesthouse in Trottiscliffe – Favre staying there on his rival's recommendation due to the proximity of the circuit. The ability to leave on-track rivalry at the circuit gates was something that characterised many of the 1986 frontrunners, something of a departure from some previous and future editions.

Run the same weekend as the dramatic Formula 1 title decider in Adelaide, there will have been a few bleary eyes on Sunday morning among those that were up in the early hours to share in Nigel Mansell's ultimate disappointment. Fortunately, the day was warmer, with dry weather forecast to improve the track conditions and hopefully lead to some good racing.

Favre was the first of the favourites to show their hand, dominating the opening quarter-final. The Swiss pilot made short work of heat one winner Hall, whose Jamun wasn't quite as effective in the dry. Nonetheless, Hall enjoyed a smooth run to second, aided by Ayles and Mezera tangling and consequently opening up a gap to those behind. The fight for third was the best of the race, Alan McGarrity deservedly taking the place after an audacious move on Russo at Paddock.

Packer and Robertson shared the front row for the second quarter-final. The latter made the better start to pip Packer, but thereafter couldn't break away. Instead of working together to open a gap to the rest of the field, the pair kept fighting aggressively, allowing a train to form for the lead. Whilst Robertson was able to retain the lead and take victory, contact at Druids between Packer and Rowan Dewhurst left Packer well down the order, finishing eighth – effectively out of contention for the weekend. Dewhurst wasn't so delayed taking second from Cunningham.

Next van Uitert and Lehto continued their battle from the earlier heat. Whilst Lehto's sideways driving style was certainly entertaining, it was also fast enough to stay within a tenth of a second of van Uitert. Despite the proximity, there was no way through for Lehto. Another Finn, Matti Sarilo, took third, whilst Booth and heat five winner Davis tangled, ending their day early.

As with Favre, Ratzenberger took the opportunity to stamp his authority on his quarter-final. Matching Favre's best lap time to a hundredth of a second, the popular Austrian was once more kept in sight but rarely challenged by Rogers. What could have been a superb battle was spoiled early on as Simoes misjudged a move on Warwick into Druids with the inevitable consequences – yet more frontrunners out before the semi-finals. This left Hessel to take a rather lonely third.

The revised starting formation meant there was no repeat of the previous year's semi-final carnage, but the outside of the front row remained the preferable slot for several drivers. Pole position is situated on a slight incline, meaning that to make a good start the polesitter must perfectly balance the engine revs and clutch biting point (1980s Formula Fords not having any of the electronic trickery of current cars) whilst anticipating the lights. The outside line is slightly flatter, making it easier for a smooth getaway without either bogging down or over-revving the engine.

With Favre and van Uitert sharing the front row, it was the Dutchman starting from the outside who took the immediate lead, sweeping across into Paddock. Favre, as he'd done all weekend, wasted no time in fighting back, feinting to the outside, then darting to the inside as they headed into Paddock for the second time. Slow through the turn, Van Uitert also allowed Lehto to slip past into second. Initially Lehto took the challenge to Favre, but after an overambitious lunge into Paddock, Favre was able to consolidate his lead. Lehto and van Uitert then enjoyed or endured, depending on your viewpoint, a close scrap for second, with Lehto rebuffing all challenges to finish two-tenths of a second clear.

The second semi-final provided some even more ferocious dicing, but not for the lead. Perfectly converting pole position, Ratzenberger led away and was quickly able to establish a gap out front as the pack behind started battling. Once the Austrian was in clear air, he could mind his own business, claiming pole position for the final with a race time almost two seconds quicker than Favre's.

The battle for second was spectacular. Robertson had proved near impossible to pass all weekend, and it was the case again throughout the 15 laps. Rogers and Dewhurst were the challengers and at times it was precariously close – the tell-tale smoke from rubbing tyre drifting along the Brabham Straight. Somehow the anticipated accident was avoided, with the trio crossing the line in the order Robertson, Rogers and Dewhurst, separated by 0.13s after almost 20 miles of racing.

The final with a Ratzenberger and Favre front row was a tantalising prospect. Throughout the weekend neither had been bested, but on pace there was just the suggestion that Ratzenberger had the edge. It would prove to be a final that showcased the Festival in all its flavours, some brilliantly close racing alongside more than a small helping of incident.

Ratzenberger once more took advantage of pole position to lead away from Favre. As in his semi-final, Favre made some early attempts to move into the lead, but once these were rebuffed he decided to work with the leader to try and build some daylight over the rest of the field. Their gambit was aided when Lehto and Dewhurst came together at Clearways, removing them from fourth and fifth.

As the leaders moved clear, attention turned to the robust battle for third between Robertson and Rogers. Their tussle in the semi-final had got uncomfortably close, and this was the case once more. Robertson did everything to keep Rogers at bay, receiving the driver warning flag as, even by the standards of Formula Ford, he was felt to be crossing the line. Rogers, though, was not short on commitment and gave as good as he got. Eventually Rogers manoeuvred the Laser alongside Robertson into Paddock and a too-late attempt to shut the door resulted in a collision which fired Robertson off into the barriers. This left Rogers in a secure third, which he would hold for the remainder of the race.

No such histrionics were needed by the leaders who waged a different sort of battle. Favre's focus was on trying to force an error from Ratzenberger rather than attempting a lunge that could put both in Dartford General Hospital. The Austrian was too assured to put a wheel wrong, but Favre was able to stay on his gearbox throughout. The waiting game gave Favre one last shot for the win as the pair exited Clearways for the final time. Favre popped out of the slipstream at just the right moment, but he couldn't quite get in front. After 20 laps just a nose cone separated them, Ratzenberger winning by five-hundredths of a second. Enjoying the race and savouring their success, the pair partied long into the night.

It was a great Festival but one with a bittersweet legacy. All three drivers on the podium died young. After a journeyman career, including stints in touring cars and Japanese Formula 3000, Ratzenberger would finally get his Formula 1 break in 1994 with the Simtek team. Tragically, he was killed at Imola trying to qualify for the San Marino Grand Prix. The following day Ayrton Senna stowed an Austrian flag in his Williams to pay tribute to Ratzenberger at the end of the race, but it was not to be as another black day befell the sport and Senna also crashed and lost his life.

Beloved by all those who came across him, Ratzenberger remains fondly remembered in motorsport paddocks across the globe.

Second-placed Philippe Favre never quite made it to Formula 1, but he was a race winner in Formula 3000 and successful in sportscars before perishing in a skiing accident in 2013. In third, having been one of the fastest and most liked drivers in Formula Ford, Peter Rogers was a dreadful loss when he was killed at Donington Park the following year in a round of the British Championship.

With hindsight, the photographs of the drivers on the podium are uneasy to see. The euphoria from Ratzenberger and Rogers is palpable. They'd just achieved a top-three finish in the world's most prestigious junior motorsport meeting – everything was at their feet, but sadly none of the three enjoyed the successes their talent deserved.

The same could not be said for the some of the frontrunners in 1987, who went on to achieve great things in motorsport. The clear favourite ahead of the weekend was Ulsterman Eddie Irvine, who had claimed victory in both the RAC and Esso Formula Ford championships. Racing in a Van Diemen run by Duckhams (whose iconic navy blue and yellow livery would become synonymous with the Festival), Irvine was looking to become the first driver since Andrew Gilbert-Scott in 1983 to win a national Formula Ford championship and the Festival in the same season.

Irvine's main challengers would be three fellow British Championship frontrunners, the Swiss Alain Menu and the Portuguese pairing of Pedro Chaves and Antonio Simoes. But then there were the unknown quantities; the rapid Irish drivers headed by Vivion Daly would always feature: promising Swede Kenny Brack, a Japanese cohort including Taki Inoue, Scottish newcomer Allan McNish and Finnish teenager Mika Hakkinen.

It is worth briefly touching on the age of the drivers. Hakkinen was the find of the year and the event programme makes a point of noting his age (18 years old) and marking his standout youthfulness. Although there were a few other drivers in their teens (including McNish), most of the favourites were in their early 20s. By comparison, contemporary drivers at the equivalent level are generally five years younger, with most debuting aged 15 and progressing through the ranks at speed, with the most promising knocking on the door of Formula 1 whilst still in their teens.

For the favourites, the tactics for the weekend were relatively simple: qualify well, stay out of trouble and towards the front in the heat and quarter-final. Thereafter it was a case of finishing as high up the order as possible in the semi-final, providing a decent starting position for the final. In total, 137 cars were entered for the weekend, 17 or so per heat, meaning that for the favourites staying out of trouble on Saturday should be enough to progress. However, the heat split drew some comment, with the initial quartet of races featuring the bulk of the expected winners.

For the British drivers, there was also the Peter Rogers Memorial Trophy at stake for the outstanding British driver of the weekend. Rogers had been killed at Donington Park two and a half months prior to the Festival following a collision with Menu. The loss of the 25-year-old was keenly felt, but the trophy in his honour was a fitting tribute.

The opening heat was particularly strong, featuring Menu, a returning Steve Robertson, the fancied Ringo Hine, promising German Meik Wagner and emerging talent McNish. Menu and Robertson, both equipped with the latest Reynard, found the car wasn't suited to the damp conditions in qualifying, leaving them with work to do. Once they were under way it was Hine who was foremost after the early exchanges, with Menu quickly moving into second and chasing the leader. For much of the race, it was a five-car group that headed the field, but with third-placed Wagner keeping his powder dry, Menu was free to challenge for the lead late on. The Swiss tried hard over the closing laps, but Hine took the win by just six-hundredths of a second, with Wagner in third.

Controversy overshadowed the second heat. Marlboro-backed Mexican Adrian Fernandez had qualified on pole alongside Tim Sugden. With the BBC filming the meeting for broadcast the following weekend, there was a clear edict for tobacco branding not to be on the cars (logos, in this instance the red Marlboro flashes as seen on McLaren Formula 1 cars, were acceptable, but brand names were not). After qualifying in an all-white car, Fernandez took to the grid in full Marlboro livery – including the sponsor name. Informed the paint job was unacceptable, the team attempted to tape over the lettering on the grid, but couldn't quite complete the job in time.

As the race got under way, Fernandez took the lead and looked comfortable before being black-flagged on the third lap. The senior BBC producer had spotted the infringement and threatened to pull the plug on the corporation's coverage of the meeting if Fernandez continued. Word came down from on-high and Fernandez's weekend was over – pleas to start from the back of a later heat in a compliant car went nowhere. The team asserted it was an honest mix-up, having prepared the car on the understanding that only Sunday's racing would be shown. In the event they were correct, highlights of the heats never made it on air, and the general consensus was that Fernandez had unnecessarily lost out.

The front row seemed to be cursed as Sugden also only completed a couple of laps before being punted into the scenery at Clearways. This left the way clear for Neil Cunningham to take the win from Piet Bouwmeister and

Emily Newman – the first female driver to finish in the top three at a Festival race.

In 1986, Jason Elliott's much vaunted works Duckhams Van Diemen drive came to naught as he retired on the opening lap of his heat. A year later and Irvine had not dissimilar thoughts: 'I can only lose the Festival – everyone else can win it.' He need not have worried. After Andy Stapley got the better start, Irvine immediately took the lead through Paddock and drove into the distance. Taking the flag ten seconds ahead of his rivals, it was the perfect start to his weekend.

Antonio Simoes was the favourite for heat four and he duly delivered but was aided by the adventures of Derek Higgins. Simoes initially led, but Higgins, having fended off the attentions of Mika Hakkinen, briefly took the lead. A few moments later, an error at Clearways saw him back down to fourth and gave Simoes the opportunity to build an unassailable advantage. Higgins recovered up to second, with Hakkinen coming home third.

Heat five provided more good racing, although sadly not for Brack, whose car failed on the warm-up lap. The revelation of the race was the 'little-known' Mika (known in 1987 as Mikka) Salo, who took the win after a race-long scrap with Julian Westwood. The pair were together throughout, the outcome decided when Westwood left a bit too much space at Clearways on the last lap, allowing Salo through.

All the action was behind the leaders in heat six, where returning category veteran Dave Coyne dominated, taking a comfortable victory from Karl Frahm and Miles Johnson. Coyne's cause was aided by some of the fancied runners in the heat – most notably Michael Bartels – being late withdrawals.

The heavy hand of officialdom loomed over the penultimate heat as first and third on-the-road finishers – Jose Cordova and Ellen Lohr – both received ten-second penalties for practice starts on the formation lap. Nico Palhares, who finished second on the road (but with the pace to win), inherited victory. Tomas Mezera was the final heat winner, the Czech-born Australian, benefitting from an attritional battle for second that was eventually headed by Richard Dean. The heats had been lively, but almost all the favourites made untroubled progress to the quarter-finals, paving the way for a close day of racing on Sunday.

Whilst Saturday's rain had cleared overnight, the fog had set in, so that once proceedings got under way on Sunday morning Druids and Clearways were obscured from the view of the faithful at Paddock.

The seeding drew the two outright favourites, Menu and Irvine, together in the first quarter-final, leaving the pair with a tactical quandary – whilst they wanted to test each other, neither would be keen to do so at the risk of an incident or showing off all their tricks. Irvine got the better start as Hine moved around Menu at Druids, before the Swiss repassed a couple of laps later. Proceedings were then halted due to an accident at Clearways, precipitating a fairly lengthy delay. Once more Irvine got the better start, as Menu (demoted to third on the count back) had to repass Hine before setting about Irvine. That allowed Irvine to build a comfortable advantage at the front of the field, with Menu similarly secure in second, Hine taking third a second further back. Arguably, the most impressive performance came from McNish who spun down from fourth to 20th before recovering to eighth.

The second quarter-final was frenetic throughout the field, topped by an interesting dice for the lead – at least to start with. Cunningham jumped Simoes into Paddock, thwarting the Portuguese's hopes of driving away. On pure pace, though, Simoes was likely to have too much for Cunningham and soon the pressure began to tell – the Australian running wide a bit too often. Simoes eventually found a way past at Druid and charged into the distance. Cunningham was further demoted late on by a flying Higgins busy with atoning for a poor start. Hakkinen was another to slide down the order in the latter stages, finishing fifth.

Salo, Palhares Chaves and Westwood were the star turns in the third encounter, the Finn starting from pole in just his eighth Formula Ford race. Not unsurprisingly, he spun up his tyres at the lights, allowing Palhares to best him into Paddock. Westwood, though, soon made his way to the front as the intensity of the competition started to lead to attrition throughout the field. The position couldn't hold at the front either, with each place worth a row on the grid for the semi-final.

Into Paddock for the final time and Palhares finally found a way past Westwood, with Chaves also chancing his arm at Druids. Westwood fought back and went for a gap to the inside of Palhares along the Brabham Straight. Palhares squeezed Westwood, putting him into the pit wall. Carnage ensued with cars, including Salo who got caught in the accident, pinballing across the circuit. After some initial confusion, the race was stopped and the result taken back to the placings at the end of lap ten – thus giving Westwood the win, from Palhares and Chaves – the question now being whether the cars could be repaired in time for the semi-final.

The last of the quarter-finals was more straightforward, with Mezera and Coyne the clear favourites. The pair emphatically proved to be the class of the field, finishing over 15 seconds clear of the rest, as Coyne, engine misfiring, used his wiles to fend of Mezera for the duration.

Westwood started the first semi-final on pole from Irvine, with Menu being the other likely contender for the honours. Making the perfect start, Irvine then set about ensuring the spectacle was for runner-up – a job made easier as Westwood defended from Menu, the pair slowing each other. It wasn't too long before Menu was through into second, but over the remaining 14 laps he was unable to anything about Irvine – five seconds being the margin of victory, *Autosport* reflecting, 'In Festival terms that might as well have been one minute.' Third went to Jose Cordova who had been stealthily climbing through the field throughout the meeting, from Westwood and the steadily impressive McNish.

Another stoppage blighted the second semi-final as Hakkinen and Cunningham among several others tangled exiting Druids on the first lap. It was a lengthy delay as Cunningham needed to be cut from his Swift, fortunately without serious injury.

This incident eliminated some of the quicker drivers (including a future double world champion) but there was still plenty of talent lining up for the restart, particularly Coyne, Mezera and Simoes. The trio then produced the best race of the day, a 15-lap, three-car train that at the end was covered by four-tenths of a second. Simoes prevailed, his tactical astuteness paying off, after first preventing Mezera (powered by the famed Patch) from really going at Coyne, and then picking his moments to climb into the lead. Coyne took second, with Mezera in third.

After all the drama of the weekend so far, a thrilling final would surely mark out 1987 as one of the great years. Unfortunately for the spectators, it didn't play out like that – in fact, after a day marked by stoppages and sizeable accidents, the decisive race proved to be remarkably incident-free, with just two retirements and somewhat processional racing. Irvine took an immediate lead and proceeded to hold the advantage for the full 20 laps. Menu and Coyne briefly enjoyed a good scrap for second, the Swiss determined to get by and set about Irvine, whilst Coyne also fancied his chances. By the time Menu made the decisive move, Irvine was some three seconds clear with enough in reserve to hold the gap despite Menu's best efforts. In third, Coyne just dropped back from Menu but had a sufficient buffer from Simoes, before proper daylight to McNish.

Irvine had been imperious all weekend, giving a delighted Ralph Firman Van Diemen their first works victory since 1981. Second-placed Menu commented to *Autosport*, 'I want to cry now. Without Coyne it could have been possible. Maybe.' The story of the weekend suggests that Menu was taking an optimistic view. Coyne, meanwhile, would not be deterred, his partnership with Swift being set to continue for years to come as he chased that elusive Festival victory.

Subsequent years would show that the 1987 Festival produced a stellar crop of graduates, arguably the most storied of the decade. Twelve years later, Hakkinen and Irvine fought for the Formula 1 title. McNish and Inoue both raced in Formula 1, whilst Chaves attempted to but could never get the hopeless Coloni near the grid. McNish subsequently focused on sportscar racing, enjoying multiple successes in the 24 Hours of Le Mans.

After single-seater opportunities dried up, Menu switched to saloons, claiming the 1997 and 2000 British Touring Car titles at the height of the series' popularity. Meanwhile with doors closing in Europe, Brack set his sights on the USA, winning the Indianapolis 500 in 1999 before his career was effectively ended following an horrific accident in 2003.

It is now set in motorsport folklore that 1988 is one of the best Festivals, if not *the* best. Beyond doubt it was the most exciting and dramatic final since 1982, with quality racing, high drama and controversy all going hand in hand. The whole weekend had a rough and tumble feel to it, with multiple sizeable accidents, many races punctuated by abandoned cars left on or immediately adjacent to the circuit and a couple of highly fortunate near-misses. After a couple of close escapes, circuit and event safety would be reviewed ahead of the following year.

The grandstands were absolutely packed for the weekend, this representing a high-water mark for the event as a spectator draw as the Festival reaped the benefits of being firmly set as one of the highlights of the British motorsport calendar. The circuit had experienced a turbulent 20 months since John Foulston acquired the track, along with Snetterton and Oulton Park for £5.25m in May 1986 from Eagle Star Holdings (the latter having subsumed Grovewood Securities), offsetting concerns that the site might become a supermarket or housing. A side effect of the deal was that Brands Hatch ended up losing the British Grand Prix from 1986, Silverstone securing an exclusive five-year deal. This forced the track to focus on other events and non-motorsport ventures to retain a decent level of profitability.

A further shock came when Foulston was killed in late September 1987 testing his McLaren Can-Am car at Silverstone.

This once more caused behind-the-scenes disruption, with Foulston's widow Mary inheriting the venue. For the remainder of the 1980s, John Webb still controlled much of the strategic direction and day-to-day operation of the venue, although this would change going into the 1990s, with the atmosphere and clubhouse feel evaporating.

A closely contested and well-supported British Championship had gone to Derek Higgins, one of several winners propelled by the Van Diemen RF88. The Norfolk marque enjoyed another marquee year, claiming all but two rounds of the national series, leaving Richard Dean in the Swift and the Jose Cordova-piloted Reynard to pick up the crumbs. Of the other Van Diemen frontrunners, both Vincenzo Sospiri and Pedro Chaves had been consistently at the front of the field, scoring several wins. The RF88 is the quintessential late-80s Formula Ford, a beautifully narrow and compact package, with sleek styling that made the car look as good as it was fast.

Alongside the UK championship regulars, Champion of Brands frontrunners such as Chris Hall and Andrew Guye-Johnson would be in the mix, as would those familiar to Irish series watchers, with Jonathan McGall, Vivion Daly and Bernard Dolan most likely to be prominent. The foreign charge included the promising Germans Michael Schumacher and Michael Krumm, whilst Mexico's Adrian Fernandez was back hoping for better luck and the same could be said for Finland's Mika Salo.

With a larger entry than recent seasons, the heats wouldn't be quite the perfunctory stay-out-of-trouble exercise of 1987.

McGall was the favourite for the first heat, and he duly converted pole position to victory. As was often the case, those at the front chose to save their pyrotechnics for later in the weekend, but McGall was run close by Andy Charsley and Krumm. Of those expected to be in the mix, the most disappointed was double junior champion Kurt Luby who was classified seventh after acquiring a ten-second penalty for a jump start.

Perennial frontrunner Rick Morris once more showed off his wiles in the second heat, his Reynard constantly in all the right places to keep the similar car of Sweden's Peter Aslund behind. Kelvin Burt finished an impressive third after a quiet but effective climb through the order. An impressive sixth went to Spain's Jordi Gene who broke the lap record, climbing the order after starting with a ten-second penalty due to an exhaust infringement in qualifying.

The 1988 Festival remains one of Morris's favourites: 'The late 1980s Reynard was a fabulous car, I did a lot of the testing on it. The main Reynard driver for the weekend was Jose Cordova, but they needed someone to look after him which was me. Formula Ford was still all about the drivers, but the technology was more of a factor by now. The chassis dynamic changed quite dramatically in the late 1980s into the early 1990s. Everyone understood the suspension better, which meant we could do more with ride height, which in turn changed the pitch and handling of the car. The ultimate example of this was the 1991 Van Diemen; Marc Goossens was able to drive it with such a stiff setup.'

Higgins had the invidious honour of being the pre-event favourite, the Ulsterman keen to get the speculation over with and the racing under way. The works Mondiale of Dolan would be his main challenger in heat three. It was Dolan who made the better start, holding the lead until the third lap, when Higgins was able to get through. Once up front, Higgins was unable to make his escape, late traffic giving another opening to Dolan as they raced to the line. In a near replay of the 1986 final, Higgins held on by just six-hundredths of a second – far too close for comfort for the favourite at this point in the weekend.

The works Swift of Richard Dean had pole position for heat four, but wheelspin on the line allowed Nick Hart to jump him into Paddock. A collision at Paddock between Bobby Verdon-Roe and Gavin Wills, who had shared the second row, gave the leaders a bit of space to sort themselves out. Dean claimed the advantage on lap two, with Hart chasing him all the way for the remaining laps, the pair joined by Alan Kelly and Andy Stapley – the quartet finishing in that order covered by just under one and a half seconds. Not progressing was the rapid Christophe Bouchut; demoted to the rear with a ten-second penalty (more qualifying technical woes), he started with everyone else and ignored three black flags, earning him a one-way trip to the clerk of the course's office and disqualification from the event.

Pedro Faria was on pole for the next ten-lapper alongside the works Van Diemen of Nico Palhares. Of the pair, it was Palhares from the outside of the front row who made the better start, chopping across Faria into Paddock. In what would prove to be the best race of the event so far, Palhares led all the way, heading an extremely tight five-car pack. Jan Nilsson took second after an audacious move at Paddock where he jumped both Faria and Mark Bailey. Faria came out worst from the scrap, finishing fifth, with Bailey completing the podium.

Another tight train for the lead was the story of heat six, with Chaves, Chris Creswell and Salo separated by four-tenths after a frantic eight minutes of racing. As had been the case in earlier heats, once the initial leader – in this case Creswell

– had been demoted early on, the order remained static if incredibly close.

Neil Cunningham had pole for the penultimate heat ahead of Daly, Schumacher and Guye-Johnson, taking the early lead chased by Daly. First-lap drama came at Graham Hill Bend as Schumacher and Guye-Johnson tangled, the Brands regular continuing, the German forced into retirement with a wheel askew. With his mirrors suddenly emptied, Daly seizedthe opportunity to challenge Cunningham taking a decisive lead at Clearways on the second lap. Arguably with the faster car underneath him, Cunningham couldn't find a way back through, allowing Daly to take the honours, with third going to Minoru Tanaka.

The concluding heat once more brought the seeding system into question with Cordova and Sospiri sharing the front row. After an early three-car incident meant there were fewer cars than qualifying spots left in the race, Cordova and Sospiri disputed the lead more than may have been expected or needed. Cordova prevailed, but not before Sospiri had taken his turn at the front, surprising Cordova at Paddock.

Many but not all of the likely contenders had safely made it through to Sunday. Bouchut and Schumacher would be two big losses, the Europeans having shown enough pace to have challenged the British regulars. The heats had also shown there was no clear favourite; the likes of Higgins and Chaves who had been tipped pre-event had not emulated Irvine or Ratzenberger from previous years by looking comfortable in their heats.

Given the closeness of the field and prospects of tight racing, it was a relief for participants and spectators alike when Sunday's weather was sunny but cold. The first quarter-final saw the top finishers from heats one and three combined, giving a front row of Higgins and McGall. Fractionally creeping in anticipation of the lights, McGall took the lead from Higgins into Paddock as the second Mondiale of Dolan slotted into third. Unfortunately for McGall, his movement on the grid had been spotted by the officials, who duly awarded him a ten-second penalty. In the excitement he didn't notice the penalty board, but Higgins did, turning his attention to fending off Dolan.

Behind the leading group, the Sunday carnage got under way in earnest, the most spectacular incident involving Ellen Lohr. The German's car launched some seven feet above the circuit after contact before somehow landing on its wheels and retiring into the gravel. Luby was another to go no further as he crashed out whilst pushing too hard for a higher semi-final grid slot. McGall took the flag thinking he'd won, but once the penalty worked through he was classified in sixth, giving Higgins the win from Dolan and Charsley. McGall would be one to watch in his semi-final, albeit with plenty to do from the sixth row.

The cream of heats two and four set the grid for the second quarter-final, the experienced Morris starting from pole alongside Dean. Unlike so many others, Morris made the best of the inside starting position, although Dean stayed with him on the outside track all the way through Paddock. Trying to force the issue at Druids, Dean locked his brakes, slid wide and reclaimed his place in the train down in 11th. Hart was initially in second before another bold move from Aslund into Paddock elevated the Swede. Meanwhile Dean had a premature end to his weekend, tangling with Derek M Daly (a fixture competitor at the Festival) at Druids, a move born of frustration as he struggled to make progress.

Most eyes were fixed to the front where it was another excellent race, Morris digging into his wells of experience to keep Aslund behind. Joining the leaders were Hart, Gene and Burt, the quintet covered by just over a second. Gene was the big mover, snatching third from Hart late on, whilst posting another fastest lap. Meanwhile Morris and Aslund's one-two signalled that in the face of Van Diemen dominance, Reynard was a force to reckon with.

Given the damage to cars and scenery, it was some time before the third quarter-final got under way, once more with a Reynard to the fore – this time Daly's, with Palhares alongside. It was the Brazilian who got the better start to sneak into the lead at Paddock, with Cunningham slotting into third. Initially getting a jump on the pack, the ferocity of the leading pair's fight allowed the others to close up, resulting in a six-car chain at the front.

By this point, the circuit was somewhat hazard strewn. In the pre-safety car days, crashed vehicles remained where they'd been abandoned – even if, as in the case of Hall's Jamun, this was adjacent to the racing line at Paddock. This meant almost the entire circuit was covered by yellow flags, preventing overtaking and obliging the drivers to slow (with varying degrees of compliance), and this kept the order more or less static until the final lap, when Palhares (in Daly's version of events 'he just seemed to go in real slow') was clipped by Daly at Clearways, spinning in a cloud of tyre smoke. Daly duly took the win, with Cunningham and Tanaka rounding out the top three. Palhares recovered to finish tenth, but his hopes of Festival victory were effectively over.

The closing quarter-final promised to be the best of all with Chaves, Cordova and Sospiri, all solid favourites, taking the top three spots on the grid. Despite not getting the best of starts, aggressive manoeuvring into Paddock kept the Portuguese clear of Cordova, with Sospiri slotting in to third.

The talking point of the race came on the third lap when, pulling out of the tow on the Brabham Straight, Cordova tagged Chaves' gearbox, pitching the Van Diemen into a sizeable accident. An uninjured and furious Chaves stalked down the pit lane to await Cordova's return to the post-race parc fermé, where he grabbed Cordova by the helmet to make his point. For now, Cordova's focus was on keeping Sospiri at bay, which he managed to do – just – as Sospiri tried every which way to get through. The consolation for the Italian was second and a new lap record, as Creswell took third despite an exhaust oil leak for much of the race.

The first semi-final was felt to be the weaker, although with a Higgins/Daly front row and Dolan, Cunningham and McGall scattered through the field, there was plenty of strength in depth. Another controversial clash for the lead was the race's main talking point. Having taken the lead Higgins didn't have the edge on pace over Daly, particularly at the key passing point along the Brabham Straight and into Paddock.

It was a matter of time before Daly would attempt to move to the front. After some parrying, the battle came to a head at the start of lap three, when Higgins squeezed Daly to the outside, leaving no leeway. The ensuing contact saw Daly pitched into the barriers and retirement, an unnecessary incident coming so early in the race. The press consensus was that Higgins had been overaggressive in defence and not allowed Daly enough space.

For all the trackside handwringing, the incident meant Higgins had a reasonably comfortable run to the flag, with his chaser Dolan around 1.5s adrift. The main entertainment came behind as McGall's impressive drive briefly saw him climb as high as third before a wayward moment relegated him back to eighth. Keeping a level head was Cunningham, whose consistency was rewarded by third and a podium-challenging grid position for the final.

Before the start of the second semi-final, there was drama when a bizarre paddock incident befell Morris. Driving through to the assembly area for the race, his nose cone was clipped by a passing motorbike. This necessitated a last-minute change of the damaged bodywork before he could take his position on the outside of the front row alongside Cordova. They would be chased by a strong second row of Sospiri and Aslund. Morris recalled, 'I just pulled out of the awning and a kid came past and ripped the nose off. Fortunately it wasn't too bad, we fitted a new one and I went out and broke the lap record.'

Cordova led away from Morris and Sospiri, the trio immediately showing their speed and building a gap on the rest of the pack. For Cordova, the first part of the race was relatively straightforward as Morris again went into defensive mode from Sospiri. For several laps, it looked as if there would be no way through for the Italian until he successfully executed a brave move at Paddock. Morris immediately fought back, but, after weathering the initial storm, Sospiri was able to gradually ease towards Cordova but could never quite engage him in battle. The pace of the race was sensational. Morris set the fastest lap of the weekend and Cordova was rewarded with pole for the final. Gene took fourth after once more showing stunning form and raising the question of how his weekend would have unfolded but for a few millimetres of misalignment in qualifying.

This set the scene for what promised to be a thrilling final. Unlike Irvine the previous year, there was no obvious favourite. Cordova hadn't been bettered but he'd been run extremely close on every outing. Higgins also had won all his races but had never looked truly convincing. The likes of McGall and Gene had arguably shown superior pace in penalty-blighted weekends. The faithful were wondering if this could be Morris's year, and Sospiri clearly couldn't be discounted.

As the cars rolled on to the grid at 3.25 for the 20-lap final (about 16 and half minutes of racing), no one could have predicted the 90 minutes of drama that would unfold. It had been a beautiful late-autumn day but now the sun was beginning to dip, causing those at the front of the grid some difficulty when looking at the lights.

As the red lights came on, Cordova, confused by the solar reflections on the gantry, thought the lights had turned green and departed for Paddock, with Higgins setting off alongside him. Sospiri crept a tiny bit before thinking better of it. Soon realising their mistake, Cordova and Higgins completed the lap at low speed before weaving back to their grid positions.

On their return, it all kicked off. After hearing the drivers' explanation, clerk of the course John Nicol announced the race would start afresh with no penalties. Unsurprisingly, this decision did not go down well with the other drivers, all of whom were hardly disappointed at the prospect of the front row being sent to the back of the field.

Setting aside the usual gamesmanship, many had seen their weekends ruined by what appeared to be far smaller infringements, in Gene's case his exhaust being 4mm out of position in qualifying, to no performance benefit. There and then, with Sospiri's team manager John Village the instigator, £200 was stumped up in order to convene an immediate stewards' enquiry. As Brian Jones attempted to keep the crowd entertained, and with the drivers waiting on the grid, the matter was debated for some 40 minutes. Eventually, the decision came down that Nicol's original ruling would stand, the reasoning being that as the race had never actually started the drivers hadn't jumped the start. A harassed Nicol conveyed the news to an ad-hoc drivers meeting on the grid, with BBC cameras recording the moment for posterity. To avoid a repeat performance, it was also decided that the race would be started with a wave of the Union flag.

The race finally got under way at 4.07 and would prove to be one of the greatest Festival finals, if not one of finest-ever Formula Ford races. Many of those at the front decided to err on the side of caution when anticipating the flag, Sospiri being the tardiest, accidentally leaving his car in neutral and dropping down to eighth. Cordova led away with Higgins into second ahead of Dolan and Morris.

The form of the weekend suggested Cordova would be near impossible to shift, but, having saved a fresh set of tyres for the final, the Brazilian found his Reynard to be out of balance. It would take him a few laps of anti-roll bar adjustments (achieved by twisting a lever in the cockpit) before he got the handling closer to how he wanted it.

This served to keep the field tightly bunched, everyone simultaneously attacking and defending. The uneasy status quo held until the fifth lap when the order started to shuffle – Dolan passing Morris, before a lap later Sospiri also found a way past Rick. Then a pivotal moment. Higgins' pressure paid off, forcing Cordova to leave a gap into Clearways. Higgins was through, and with his momentum sapped Cordova was soon demoted to fifth as Dolan, Sospiri and Morris all shot past.

Dolan now had his sights set on Higgins whilst also needing to fend off Sospiri. Weaving along the Brabham Straight was effective for the latter, much to the Italian's frustration. It got worse for Sospiri as Morris pounced, darting into third. At Clearways for the 13th time, Morris saw daylight to Dolan's inside and went for the move, but the gap closed and the pair collided, spinning into the gravel.

Sospiri was now released to challenge Higgins with Cordova in third, the trio having six laps to play with. The next pair of McGall and Gene were there too – realistically any one of the quintet could prevail. McGall was the first to gain ground, passing Cordova, as Sospiri got ever closer to Higgins. Sospiri pulled the pin into Clearways for the penultimate time, launching to the inside, banging wheels but making his way through.

Ordinarily, this would have had the crowd out of their seats, but instead attention was drawn to Paddock where Palhares, following contact between Aslund and Salo, had been launched into a series of somersaults. It was a monumental accident, with photographs capturing an inverted Palhares some six feet in the air. Palhares was initially slumped in the cockpit, prompting marshals and medics to sprint to the scene to assist the Brazilian.

As efforts were under way to aid Palhares with his car still half on the circuit, the field piled into Paddock for the final time. The leaders scrabbled through safely, but further back Colin Lees and Jan Nilsson tangled, the latter's car spinning into the Palhares accident, striking several rescuers. Dr Mark Downes was the worst affected, sustaining serious facial injuries, whilst several marshals were treated for cuts, bruises and shock.

It could have been so much worse; little more than good fortune prevented a tragic end to the weekend.

The debate would continue as to whether the race should have been stopped. However, the observer-post request for a stoppage (which according to protocol at the time was the means to instigate a red flag) only came midway through the final lap, so events ran through to the chequered flag. The incident capped a weekend where driver and official safety had frequently been called into question. With almost every race featuring wrecked cars marooned on the circuit, it was good fortune that only the Palhares incident resulted in serious injury.

Sospiri took the flag, fractions of a second clear of Cordova, Jose having a fantastic final lap, ousting McGall before a good run through Clearways allowed him to out-drag Higgins to finish runner-up by four-hundredths of a second. A euphoric Sospiri took the honours following a superb weekend of racing that is still regarded as one of the Festival's watershed moments.

'It was a brilliant race,' remembers Morris. 'The team found this set of tyres that they thought were the ones for Cordova, so put them aside for the final. Then they didn't work and we all queued up behind him. Once someone was through [past Cordova], I had to go for it as well. That was one that got away, Sospiri was behind me and Dolan, and then came through to win. Higgins struggled with bent valves in the last few laps, had we not collided I may well have won that one.'

Despite Festival glory, it took until 1997 for Sospiri to have his shot at Formula 1. Unfortunately for the Italian, it was as part of the Mastercard Lola team who entered just one Grand Prix in Australia. The car was hopelessly off the pace and failed to qualify, the team withdrawing altogether before the Brazilian

Grand Prix. Sospiri showed his agility by then heading to the USA and qualifying on the front row for the 1997 Indianapolis 500. A true talent who never got a proper Formula 1 or IndyCar opportunity, Sospiri now runs a highly successful team who most recently won the 2021 International GT Open championship. Even so, Sospiri's Formula 1 dreams went further than either Higgins or Cordova, who never quite reached the top of single-seaters. Higgins enjoyed success in both the USA and Mexico, whilst Cordova continues to race successfully in Brazil.

Of all the talent at the 1988 Festival, it was the driver who only made it through two corners of their heat who had the greatest career of all. Michael Schumacher was already pegged as an emerging talent at the time of the Festival, and within three years of his Brands Hatch disappointment was established as Formula 1's newest star. By the time of his retirement in 2012, Schumacher had won seven world titles and 91 Grand Prix, universally recognised as one of the sport's all-time greats. The driver with whom he tangled, Andrew Guye-Johnson, runs a garage in Kent. Such are the sliding-doors moments of the sport.

The Kent era ends on a high

AFTER THE spectacle and drama of 1988, it was hard to believe the following year could come close to matching it. Instead, 1988 would be prove to be the first edition of a five-year purple patch for the Festival, with extraordinarily close and high-quality racing through to 1992. This was an era where the strength of the Festival would belie the true health of Formula Ford, culminating in the Kent engine being phased out at the end of 1992.

In many regards the junior categories of motorsport – particularly Formula 3 and Formula Ford – were better served by the media in the pre-internet era. *Autosport* and *Motoring News* (aka the comics) were relatively well funded, especially during the late 1980s, enjoying substantial page and word counts. This allowed them to provide detailed coverage of the national scene, including news items, detailed race reports and paddock gossip. Consequently, the frontrunners would be well known (at least by name) to many of those crowding into the circuit on race day.

Following a frustrating season playing second fiddle to Van Diemen, Reynard's Festival form carried into the 1989 campaign. Making the switch from Mondiale, Dolan took the British title with three wins from the 14 rounds. Dolan's team-mate, the Brazilian Gil de Ferran, was also a multiple winner, and arguably the more eye-catching given his relative inexperience. The Swift team also set about taking the challenge to Van Diemen, with the experienced Dave Coyne guiding the works car to a couple of victories.

The Van Diemen effort was headed by Palhares, staying with the works team for another season and notching up four victories along the way. The Brazilian also claimed the Silverstone-centric BRDC title. Another fancied Van Diemen runner would be Michael Vergers, who had shown well the previous year and enjoyed a strong season in the John Village entry – Village having prepared Sospiri's winning effort a year earlier.

The driver making the headlines on the national scene was in the junior championship. Scottish teenager David Coulthard became the most successful driver in the series' history, taking nine wins in his David Leslie-prepared Van Diemen. Although he hadn't been extensively pitted against the category veterans, on pace alone Coulthard was a pre-event contender.

After the previous year had been largely clear, the weekend endured mixed weather with periodic high winds and heavy rain, including for the final.

At the time, the first heat wasn't felt to be one of the strongest, but with the likes of Michael Krumm, Gareth Rees, Giampiero Simoni and Marcel Albers in the field it proved to be high quality. It was attrition rather than action that provided the talking points over the ten laps, with Krumm and French champion William David being two of the more high-profile casualties. Up front, Albers took a reasonably comfortable win from Andy Stapley and Rees.

Local knowledge didn't equate to good luck in heat two, where Champion of Brands Chris Goodwin, having initially run as high as second, rotated down the order and into the scenery, ending his weekend. Instead, it was 1988 revelation Jordi Gene who took the heat from the promising Finn Pekka Herva and Belgian champion Mikke Van Hool.

The third heat turned proceedings up a notch, the seeding system once again ensuring some heats were more equal than others. Vergers and Coulthard were drawn together, with Vivion Daly (brother of 1976 winner Derek) and Alan McGarrity ensuring strength in depth. With the top five in qualifying covered by 0.4s, the race promised much and, unusually for a heat, delivered. As Daly and McGarrity contested third, Coulthard and Vergers went at it for the win. With tactical nous belying his experience, Coulthard kept Vergers at bay until the final lap, when traffic momentarily delayed the Scot, allowing Vergers through to win. For third, Daly edged out McGarrity.

After finishing his 1988 Festival in a heap at Paddock, Palhares took pole for heat four, with Fritz Kreutzpointner, Warren Hughes and Kelvin Burt ensuring another strong heat. It was that quartet who took the top four placings, Palhares having a more comfortable race than the margin of victory suggested. Hughes took an impressive second having made most of the upward progress, with Kreutzpointner in third.

The next heat gave an opportunity for some of the veterans of the category to state their case for the weekend, with Dave Coyne, Rick Morris and Neil Cunningham to the fore. Coyne prevailed in the works Swift, despite prolonged probing from Morris, although both were prepared to avoid drama at this stage. Second on the road, Morris was demoted to third with a ten-second penalty for a jump start to elevate Cunningham; the trio were well clear of the rest.

A burst of rain as the cars were midway through the formation lap for heat six didn't intrude on an entertaining race. After his Jamun finished the 1988 event wrecked in the middle of the road at Paddock, Chris Hall was once more on top form, a pugnacious drive seeing him get the better of polesitter Bobby Verdon-Roe and David Button.

Heat seven was another full of names of the future, including Australian V8 Supercar charger Mark Larkham. Dry weather over the lunch break worked against the fortunes of polesitter Bernard Dolan, the inside pole line still being damp, whilst the outside track was appreciably drier. After fellow front-row man Carlos Eduardo da Rosa jumped the start, it was Larkham who rocketed through to take an unexpected lead. The slippery surface made things tricky with wayward moments at the front and multiple casualties behind. Dolan was unflappable, carving through the early mayhem and winning by a good five seconds – a substantial margin in this era. Second went to Victor Lopez ahead of Louis di Resta, father of future F1 racer and Sky pundit Paul.

The final heat promised to be a good one with de Ferran and 1988 fast-man Jonathan McGall at the front, with Scott Lakin the other driver who impressed during qualifying. Once more rain intruded just as the cars were forming on the grid, this time to the detriment of the racing. McGall took the advantage from Lakin with de Ferran slotting into third. They would stay that way for the ten laps, with clear daylight between them all by the flag. The crowd would have to wait an hour longer than hoped for the action to get properly started on Sunday after two destructive attempts to get the curtain-raising Formula First race under way. The result was called after five laps, when Martin Short hit the starting gantry in a massive incident, prompting both extensive barrier repairs and an apologetic letter from Short to the following week's *Autosport*.

The first quarter-final saw Vergers and Albers sharing the front row from Coulthard and Stapley. Perhaps unsurprisingly, it was Stapley who made the best start, but from pole Vergers did enough to lead into Paddock. Soon Stapley was under pressure for second from Coulthard, but the red flags came out after a collision at Clearways. With five other cars strewn around the circuit, it was safer to pause.

At the restart Vergers once more led away, but this time he had Coulthard on his tail from the outset, with Albers in third, the trio heading a nine-car train. It stayed that way until mid-race when Albers and Stapley tangled at Druids, the pair retiring on the spot. Eventually, it was Vergers who cracked, a small mistake on lap nine giving Coulthard the opening he needed to zip through, the Scot reeling off the remaining laps with aplomb. The earlier retirements elevated Daly to third, fractionally ahead of McGarrity, the pair being credited with identical race times.

The second quarter-final was tipped to be the strongest with Gene and Palhares on the front row. Whilst it was a close race, the leading protagonists knew they had good chances for overall glory later in the day and kept things just the right side of polite. After taking the lead at the start, Gene was demoted by Palhares early on. Thereafter the Duckhams Van Diemen stayed at the front, despite constant probing from Gene. Third changed hands on a couple of occasions, Herva coming out on top, a third-row start for the semi-final keeping the Finn in contention.

The penultimate quarter-final was highly anticipated., Dolan on pole position was felt to be a white-hot favourite, whilst grandstand sentiment would go to Coyne alongside him, and Morris wasn't much further back. Coyne made the better start, squeezing Dolan into Paddock, giving him no option but to concede the corner. As could have been expected, it then got robust, with the pair going wheel to wheel for the opening couple of laps. Racing of that intensity couldn't hold and, heading into Paddock on lap three, the pair were overcommitted. Coyne understeered out from the inside line, pushing Dolan to put two wheels into the gravel.

A fired-up Dolan re-joined in fourth behind Morris and Cunningham, despatching the pair in fairly short order over the next couple of laps. With clear air and a growing tow from Coyne's Swift, Dolan was soon with the leader, setting a new lap record in the process. By lap six he was through, before building up just enough of a buffer not to be seriously threatened, Coyne coming home second, ahead of Morris.

The closing quarter-final didn't have the through-the-field battling enjoyed in the other races but did have a superb race for the lead. From pole position, McGall led all the way to the final turn. His chaser was de Ferran, who made the best of an early mechanical failure from Verdon-Roe to pick his way up the order and latterly reel in the leader at a rate of 0.4s per lap. At Clearways for the final time, de Ferran made his move, a replica of the one that had given Sospiri success a year earlier – this time there wasn't quite enough room, the rubbed wheels rotating McGall. The Mondiale pilot recovered to take third, a delighted Lakin elevated to second, behind de Ferran.

With barely a moment's pause the drivers were already on their way to the assembly area for the first semi-final. This promised to be a cracker, with Dolan and Coulthard on the front row and Vergers, Coyne, Morris and dark horse Herva all at the sharp end. This would also flush out the chassis battle with Reynard, Swift and Van Diemen in full competition.

For the purposes of these 15 laps, the answer was decided in favour of Reynard, with Dolan emphatically the class of the field, posting the fastest lap of the weekend (and netting a £3,300 bonus into the bargain). Behind, Coulthard continued to impress, unshakable in a defensive performance that ensured there was no way through for Coyne. Afterwards, Coyne reckoned he was down on power compared to the Scot. In any event, a third-row spot for the final would leave him with plenty to do. The race's only casualty was Morris, who lost his engine on the second lap, whilst Vergers was never really in the hunt for victory, taking fourth.

The light rainfall that accompanied the last couple of laps of the first semi-final intensified as the cars gridded up for the second, prompting lots of last-minute setup changes. It was Palhares on pole from Lakin, with Gene, McGall and Hughes all expected to challenge. Lakin headed the field into Paddock for the first time, but it was McGall who was really catching the eye, moving through the pack to take the lead at Druids on lap three.

Palhares and Lakin disputed second until mid-distance when Palhares challenged around the outside of Paddock. Despite navigating the corner side by side, they made contact on the exit, Lakin spinning down to 16th and Palhares continuing in fourth with damaged suspension. However, the Duckhams Van Diemen was suited to the conditions, and before long Palhares had cleared both Gene and Hughes. Despite chasing down McGall, he ran out of laps, so it was the Mondiale pilot who took the win and secured a front-row start for the final, Palhares an eventful second with Gene in third.

After excelling in his drier semi-final, Dolan would start from pole; the Reynard was felt to be a more sympathetic car in wet conditions. Alongside, in the Mondiale, McGall had already shown he could make the car fly. With the circuit conditions sufficiently different from the semi-finals, the drivers had two formation laps to familiarise themselves, enabling both Herva and Hall to have spins but recovering to their grid positions.

As the lights changed, Dolan had his first setback of the weekend, bogging down as McGall swept into the lead at Paddock from Palhares and Coyne. The next twist came at Druids when Vergers plunged into the gravel, re-joining in 20th. All this released McGall and Palhares to dispute the lead, the Brazilian making a bid into Paddock on lap three, using the superior traction of the 'wet' outside line. Both spun exiting Paddock, and whilst Palhares resumed at the cost of a handful of places, McGall spun to the inside and on to the grass. His engine still running, McGall attempted to continue, but his wheels spun hopelessly on the wet surface, leaving him with no option but to retire.

Coyne was now elevated to the lead, with Coulthard and Gene taking on the immediate challenge. The spectators didn't know where to look. Vergers and Palhares were getting started on remarkable recovery drives and Daly had a monumental accident at Paddock, his Reynard vaulting the barriers and stopping just short of the viewing area.

As if this wasn't enough, the rain restarted and intensified. Dolan was the most affected by the change in the weather. The Reynard hadn't been set up to respond to this turn in the conditions and he faded eventually to finish sixth – had it been dry, he would arguably have been a runaway winner. Also suffering from the inclement weather was Coyne, the Swift slipping out of its sweet spot as the track dampened. It wasn't Coulthard who demoted Coyne but Palhares, recovering from his earlier spin. The Brazilian carved back up the order, passing Coyne through Clearways, Coulthard sneaking through as well.

At three-quarter distance Palhares appeared reasonably assured of victory, but for one caveat, the storming progress of Vergers. Clearly relishing the damp conditions, by lap 15 he was up to third, but with ground to make on the leading pair. On the penultimate lap he found a way past Coulthard, leaving the slenderest of chances to snatch a last-gasp victory. He came remarkably close and was on course to line up a move into Clearways. However, the car snapped sideways at Surtees, meaning that Palhares was in the clear to claim a remarkable victory, Vergers a sensational second and Coulthard an impressive third.

It was a superb final to close another great Festival, and yet another event that would unearth the stars of the future. In the case of the class of 1989, it was Coulthard who would make it to the very top. After a strong year in Formula 3 in 1991, by 1994 his career was on the cusp of running out of momentum and a Williams testing arrangement was his only link to Formula 1. Then came the events of the black Imola weekend that saw the death of Ayrton Senna, and Coulthard's sudden break into the top flight with Williams as his replacement. This initiated a 14-year Formula 1 career that yielded 13 wins, but never that elusive world title.

Unlike many of the 1980s Festival winners, victory didn't supercharge Palhares' career. In 1990, he was back to defend his title after attempts to crack British Formula 3 went nowhere. By 1995, his career was winding up, second in the 1992 Italian Formula 3 season being his best subsequent result.

The 1980s were the glory decade of the Festival. On track, the racing seemed to get better with each passing year and the runaway wins that characterised many of the heats early in the decade had all but disappeared by 1988.

Off track, it was a decade of transition – the technology had heightened, with competition between the manufacturers intensifying year on year. The Van Diemens of 1980 were unrecognisable from those of 1989. With technological progress came increasing costs – the clubmen and regional stars that filled the grid in 1980 had all but disappeared by later in the decade, replaced by hordes of Formula 1 aspirants from around the globe.

A popular event at the turn of the decade, by the late 1980s the Festival was one of Brands Hatch's biggest meetings of the year, the Paddock grandstand in particular near guaranteed to sell out. The Sunday morning atmosphere and anticipation as the meeting unfolded is the foremost memory of every contributor to this book. Those days were very special, and as Tim Jones said, 'We didn't appreciate just how good it was.' With the benefit of hindsight, did it ever get better for Formula Ford than a crisp afternoon with a lowering sun in 1988?

For all the success of the Festival, entering the 1990s Formula Ford itself was not in good health. The combination of rising costs pricing out many drivers and new, more glamorous categories attracting those that could, left Formula Ford at a crossroads. The category would adapt, and with increased interest and support from Ford adopt new regulations to remain current. Formula Ford would remain (along with the Festival) relevant throughout the 1990s, with the majority of the brightest talents still choosing to spend at least one year taking part.

The 1990 British Championship was a sparsely supported affair with barely ten regulars. Given than just over five years previously there had been four national championships in Britain, it was a dramatic change in fortunes. Michael Vergers took the title with four wins in an eight-race season. The campaign is probably best remembered for a start-line accident at Donington Park that eliminated almost half the field and was immortalised in several crash videos of the time.

This put the Festival organisers in something of a bind. Whilst the single circuit and regional championships were still going strong, recent Festivals had shown these runners (excepting some of the Champion of Brands pack) to be a step back on pace – hardly unsurprising given the budget and equipment disparity. Likewise, there had always been an international flavour to the meeting, but the unpredictability of entry levels and eligibility issues in recent Festivals (the fire extinguisher saga of the late 1980s being the best example) meant that it was hard to bank on a solid number of cars.

The response was to ease some of the more stringent entry criteria, particularly those that had discouraged drivers from 'stepping down' to Formula Ford for the weekend. The more inclusive entry policy, along with just generally appearing more welcoming, reaped rewards, with the Festival enjoying its largest ever field – just under 200 cars turning out to practice on Friday. With a glut of drivers from several European series deciding late on to make the trip across the Channel, the 1990 Festival had quality and quantity. With an average of 25 cars per heat and just 14 progressing to Sunday's quarter-finals, Saturday's eight-race programme would be anything but a formality.

It was also all change at Brands Hatch too. Following John Foulston's death, his daughter Nicola had increasingly stepped into management roles at the circuit, being appointed commercial director in October 1989. It was immediately apparently that she and long-serving chief executive John Webb would be unable to work together. From Foulston's perspective, she felt that the circuit retained too many outdated business practices from the 1960s, whilst Webb had his reservations about the changes Foulston wanted to make to the circuit. The blow by blow of the boardroom discussions are superbly covered in Chas Parker's history of Brands Hatch, but the overall result was that on 28 February 1990, Webb left Brands Hatch with Foulston taking over as chief executive, remaining in post until November 1999. Foulston immediately set about putting the circuit on a more commercial footing, moving on long-serving members of circuit management, with 17 directors departing during the first two years of her tenure. Whilst there were investments in upgrading the circuit – the gravel trap added to Paddock Hill Bend in 1991 being a particularly welcome addition – for many supporters of the circuit there are few fond memories of the Foulston era and an enduring sense that the circuit lost something of its soul during this time. Initiatives such as the grading system that effectively excluded some series from racing at Brands Hatch-owned venues and charging event marshals for their race-day programmes felt tone deaf to the grassroots of the sport – even if they were sound ideas on a spreadsheet.

The Festival weekend drama started on Friday, where qualifying for all except the last two heats was held in unrelentingly wet conditions and a catalogue of incidents and technical infringements mixed the expected order from the outset.

The first heat was one of those so affected, where Gareth Rees, who'd dominated the largely Silverstone-based BARC championship, crashed on his third lap of qualifying, placing him 19th on the grid. Instead, Simon Harrison would start from pole position, ahead of the German challenger Joachim Koscielniak.

Harrison made the better getaway to lead from Koscielniak in the early stages, the pair joined by Brands regular Sean McCarroll. Meanwhile Rees, having initially made good progress, hit trouble when he made contact with Ivan Arias sending him to the rear of the pack. Lap four brought the first stoppage of the weekend when Raphael Real del Sarte rolled at Clearways. The restarted race was to be run over six laps, which would be added to the two full laps already completed to give the aggregate result.

Once the race got under way again Harrison had a more comfortable time of it, taking the win from Mike Edgar and McCarroll – Koscielniak down in 12th following parc fermé confusion during the stoppage. Rees finished eighth on the road in the restart but on combined time was down in 18th and his weekend was over before Saturday lunchtime.

Coyne was fastest in qualifying for heat two but would start from the back with a ten-second penalty due to a yellow-flag infringement. This meant the front row would be shared by Vivion Daly and Marc Goossens. Daly made the better start, but before long Goossens was through and into a safe lead and two-second margin of victory. Instead, attention turned to what proved to be an excellent battle for second – Bobby Verdon-Roe eventually prevailing, two-hundredths of a second clear of Daly.

Heat three, whilst light on potential event winners, proved to be hugely entertaining, with Brands regulars Chris Hall and Andrew O'Hara making much of the running. O'Hara ran out the winner, having taken the lead mid-race. Hall, meanwhile slipped to fourth after having to back out of a three-wide moment into Paddock. The same couldn't be said of heat four. 1989 winner Palhares headed the field in his first outing in the Van Diemen RF90, from 1990 Champion of Brands David Germain and Rick Morris. Other than Morris being demoted to fourth by Franc ten Wolde, very little happened at the front.

It was Reynards to the fore in heat five, with Fionn Murray in the works car leading all the way to take the flag a couple of seconds clear of Swedish and Finnish champion Tommi Saloma. Oscar Middeldorp made it an all-Reynard podium, finishing a second clear of future McLaren Formula 1 driver Pedro de la Rosa. Heat six was another somewhat scrappy affair with a red flag after two laps of the first attempt. When they did get going, polesitter Bradley lost his engine on the line – the pilot was adamant he didn't stall. The ensuing confusion enabled Martiyn Koene from the outside of the front row to take a fairly comfortable win from Franck Thouvenel and Thomas Winkelhock.

Practice for heat seven delivered something of a minor upset when Frenchman Eric Angelvy out-qualified Hughes, one of the pre-event favourites. Angelvy's Van Diemen wanted to creep at the line, so Hughes jumped into an early lead. Meanwhile, Angelvy was in a battle with Russell Ingall (both driver and car making the trip from Australia) and Alastair Johnston. A second-lap error at Druids from Angelvy was enough to give Hughes a decisive lead whilst ratcheting up the fight for second. In the event, Ingall prevailed from Johnson, albeit five seconds adrift of Hughes up front.

The concluding heat had a line up stronger than seen in some quarter or semi-finals of years gone by. It was a multinational affair, with French star Jean-Christophe (Jules) Boullion taking pole and German championship frontrunner Sascha Massen alongside. This put British champion Vergers (in the plum Duckhams Van Diemen seat) down to the second row. Meanwhile, Neil Cunningham and German Formula 3 star Jorg Muller were amongst a multitude of drivers starting with a penalty after practice infringements.

Progression was the primary focus, but every place was worth a row for the quarter-final. Vergers put his experience to good use, passing Massen on the first lap before setting off after Boullion. After setting a strong initial pace, he was reeled in by Vergers on lap four, the Duckhams car swiftly assuming the lead. Boullion astutely slotted in behind, taking advantage of the two, whilst closely examining Vergers' lines. The pair crossed the line covered by just 0.18s, Vergers largely untroubled despite the slender margin. Massen was a further three seconds behind, as both Cunningham and Muller made it safely through.

With such a strong field, no obvious favourite and very few frontrunning casualties in the heats, Sunday promised to be another sensational day of racing. Overnight rain meant the circuit was wet but rapidly drying when the first quarter-final got under way. Harrison was in pole, O'Hara alongside him. Unfortunately, the first attempt only lasted three corners before Stuart Dawson ploughed head on into the barriers at Graham Hill Bend whilst avoiding a spinner. The severe impact trapped the driver in the car for 40 minutes as he was extricated with injured ankles.

After the inauspicious start, when the race got going in earnest it was a good one. Harrison converted from pole but was immediately under pressure from Edgar and Adrian Cotterill. The latter pair had the edge on Harrison, both finding their way through at Paddock on the sixth lap. Two laps later and Edgar took a decisive lead, although Cotterill chased him all the way to the line, Harrison trailing home third. Although the field spread out, the race claimed some casualties, the most notable being music producer Matt Aitken (of Stock Aitken Waterman fame), whose weekend ended in the wall.

The second quarter-final also served as a Christmas party fundraiser for parts manufacturers as the wreckage from the race put the day's programme over an hour behind schedule. For the survivors, it was a tale of two races. At the front Palhares and Goossens were separated by under two-tenths, but once more the gap at the line didn't tell the full story. Although the Belgian had been with Palhares throughout, he never launched a serious bid at overhauling the previous year's winner, watch and learn proving a more prudent course of action. Morris was a solid third, whilst much of the attention was focused on Coyne.

Still recovering from the penalty in his heat, Coyne could go no further than ninth, after being frustrated by robust defensive driving from Jason Pollock – this would put Coyne 18th on the grid for the semi-final.

A close and clean battle up front showcased the better side of Formula Ford in the third quarter-final, as Hughes and Murray diced for the lead. After swapping places throughout, events were decided in Murray's favour when Hughes spun into the tyres at McLaren. Amazingly escaping damage, Hughes restarted in eighth but, like Coyne, faced a mammoth task in his semi-final. This allowed Murray to take a comfortable win from Ingall and Saloma, whilst the older faces in the grandstands were pleased to see 1972 winner Ian Taylor finishing in tenth.

The closing quarter-final was, after a fashion, a repeat of heat eight, with Boullion getting an in-depth view of Vergers' gearbox. Once more the Frenchman trailed Vergers home by fractions of a second, his pace obvious; it was just a case of whether or not he could find a way past. Some six seconds further back, Koene completed the podium.

In the gap before the semi-finals the weather once more turned, with an ever dampening-circuit giving the drivers a tyre and setup dilemma. The front row comprised Murray and Edgar. Initially it was Murray who made the better running as Edgar slipped into the clutches of Ingall, the pair trading places. Arguably the weather then swayed the race in Edgar's favour – he certainly seemed happier in the conditions, taking the lead at Paddock on lap seven and immediately pulling away. The opposite could be said for Ingall, who slid back to fifth. Meanwhile, Murray managed to successfully fend off Cotterill for second. From the eighth row, Hughes was climbing the order but having gone with well-scrubbed (near slick) rear tyres the conditions went against him, sixth being a fine result but leaving him much to do in the final.

It was an all-Duckhams Van Diemen front row for the second semi-final, Vergers heading Palhares. After excelling in damp conditions 12 months previously, the pair were surely favourites to romp clear. Initially, that seemed to be the case as Vergers led away from his team-mate Boullion, with Goossens and Morris lurking as Coyne sought to make ground from the ninth row.

It all changed on the second lap as Vergers went off at Surtees, clouting the tyre wall and re-joining in 21st – the simple arithmetic being seven places required just to progress, then every position thereafter worth a row in the final. It was a huge task. He would eventually climb to 14th, making the final on the last row, after a contact-laden battle with Frank Bradley.

Maybe Vergers and Coyne had a karmic arrangement because by the end of lap two the Swift was up to sixth and two laps later he was in fourth. At the front Palhares and Boullion were the pace-setters, with Morris still close. Incredibly, Coyne would best them all. After despatching Morris, he was with the leading pair on the 13th lap. After passing Boullion at Clearways, Coyne had the momentum for the Brabham Straight, squeezing into the lead at Paddock. It would transpire that Palhares had a broken anti-roll bar, so he was content with second position, despite late pressure from Boullion. For Coyne, it was a remarkable performance, showcasing his tenacious best and further enshrining his legendary status among spectators. Whilst this was just the semi-final, he would not hesitate to fight through the order in the final.

Despite having the slower semi-final, Edgar lined up on pole position (ironic considering he had at one point looked like being the event's first retirement before the red flags came out in the opening heat), with Coyne to the outside of the front row. The Duckhams Van Diemen charge was headed by Palhares in third, with team-mate Vergers starting at the very rear.

Once more the outside line worked a charm as Coyne immediately moved clear of Edgar, with Palhares into third. The 1989 winner, freed from the earlier mechanical issues, was on the pace immediately, passing Edgar on the second lap; the leading group was completed by Murray and Boullion. On lap four, Palhares was at the front, moving past Coyne on the way to Druids after keeping his nerve with the wide line at Paddock. Meanwhile, Vergers was on a missions carving through the pack, and showing what might have been but for that 'off' in the semi-final.

It wasn't to be back-to-back victories for Palhares, an engine coil issue forcing him into the pits on lap eight. Speaking to *Autosport,* he rued, 'It was so easy at the front, I was only really trying at Paddock and Druids.' This elevated Coyne back to the lead, but he was far from comfortable, with Boullion the foremost of the challengers and Murray not far behind.

As would be expected, there were intense battles and subsequent casualties to be found throughout the field. Ingall was jettisoned into the Clearways barrier after contact with Rosa, likewise Morris was pushed into the Druids gravel by Hughes. All the while, Vergers continued to climb the order and by lap 12 was in sixth, having overhauled 22 cars. His first real opposition came in the fight with Cunningham for fourth, finally squeezing through late on after a precarious move at Paddock.

At the front, despite Boullion's best efforts, there was no way past Coyne. As the pair battled, Murray was able to insert himself into the fight, making it a trio by the last lap. Boullion was determined to go for one last shot at glory, taking the wide line at Clearways to try and out-drag Coyne to the finish. The Reynard-sized hole to the inside was too much for Murray to resist. He jumped into the gap, rubbing wheels with Boullion and snatching second in the process. This gave Coyne the gap he needed to take victory by just under three-tenths of a second, Murray fractionally edging out Boullion. Vergers finished a further two seconds back, another remarkable performance from the Dutchman.

For Coyne, this was a dream result. He'd spent most of the 1980s trying to win, often at the front but never having the whole weekend come together. His robust driving style led to Brian Jones tagging him 'the man they love to hate', but Coyne's commitment to the category and the Festival could not be overstated. After several years as a pantomime villain, his was a popular victory, Coyne saying to *Autosport*, 'When I stepped out of the car the feeling was indescribable. It's a fantastic event and I've been trying to win the thing for so long … it's great.' Having been on the scene for the past decade, Coyne wasn't really on the Formula 1 fast track, but he did get a Formula 3000 break in 1991, winning a couple of rounds of the national championship.

Fionn Murray also moved up a class in 1991, progressing to Formula Renault, where a solid but unspectacular season proved the peak of his climb up the ladder. In 1998 he was killed in a light aircraft crash alongside his father-in-law.

After his superb showing at the Festival, Boullion's star burned brightly. In 1994, he won both the Formula 3000 championship and was signed as a Williams test driver. The following year he got his shot in Formula 1, starting 11 races for Sauber but never really matching team-mate Heinz-Harald Frentzen. He didn't get a second chance, his career winding the path of touring cars and sportscars throughout the following two decades.

Outside the paddock bubble, during 1991 Formula Ford faced a new threat to its hegemony. Launched during the winter, the new Formula Vauxhall Junior category, with investment from the manufacturer, was pitched as a professional entry-level formula for top karters looking to graduate. Also powered by a 1600cc engine and running a tubular-frame Van Diemen chassis, Vauxhall Junior cars ran on slick tyres. Immediately securing a BTCC support slot, the inaugural champion was Dario Franchitti, who opted to progress his career to Formula 3 via the Vauxhall not Ford route.

Motorsport broadcaster Simon Hill, who was racing in the Champion of Brands at the time, recalled, 'Nobody really saw anything as a threat to Formula Ford at that time, it was so entrenched in the fabric of motorsport. I don't think anyone realised the impact that going away from the Kent engine [announced in the winter of 1991/92 ahead of the 1993 season] would have. People generally saw the Vauxhall pathway as an alternative not an instead of.'

Over the decade, Formula Ford would see off FVJ and its bigger sibling Formula Vauxhall Lotus, but the impact of the Vauxhall categories gave other manufactures the confidence that they too could create their own racing ladder. Over the next 15 years, these efforts would ultimately topple Formula Ford from its position.

The 1991 Festival would again enjoy a mammoth entry coupled with some superb, if wild, racing. The British Championship had been claimed by Marc Goossens in the works Duckhams Van Diemen. The Belgian won eight of the 18 races but hadn't visited the top step of the rostrum since mid-August. His Van Diemen team-mate, Australian Russell Ingall, had also enjoyed a successful season with four wins throughout the campaign. Looking to break the Van Diemen hegemony would be Reynard's Dino Morelli, who had triumphed in two of the final three races of the season. Meanwhile, Andrew McAuley, who'd won four times in the works Swift during the year, would switch to a Van Diemen for the Festival.

Also in a Van Diemen would be the promising youngster Jamie Spence, whose speed and robust style were already turning heads. Oliver Gavin was another relative newcomer impressing the paddock, landing the works Swift drive for the weekend. Others to reckon with included Bryan Herta in the Team USA scholarship entry, a pair of Finns ,Tomi Veijalainen and Tommi Anttalainen, and a relatively unknown Austrian from a rallycross family, Alex Wurz.

For Herta, who would subsequently become one of the top IndyCar drivers of the 1990s, inspiring Herta-mania, the trip to Brands Hatch was a new experience, 'I had never travelled outside of the United States prior to coming to the UK for the Festival, so I truly had no idea what to expect other than an amazing adventure. Looking back I met so many great people that played roles later in my career or remain friends or acquaintances to this day. Peter Windsor showed me around the Williams GP factory, I met Adrian Reynard and Rick Gorne, Steve Horne, John Bright, Jackie Stewart, Paul Pfanner, David Philips, Alan Docking, the list goes on. On track I am sure I was hoping/expecting to win as all the young lads were, and even though that did not happen, what I actually received was an education in motorsport that helped me for the entirety of the rest of my career.'

The Team USA scholarship had placed Herta with the Lanan racing team, but all had not gone smoothy in the run up to the weekend: 'The original plan was for me to compete in a home-built Lanan chassis. John Bright, Bill Bray and Robin Webb ran the team and built the car I went to the UK to test and I recall the event was suddenly getting very popular again and we realised the Lanan car was going to struggle and we did not have the time (or money) to develop it, so the decision was made by the team to make a deal to lease the Reynard chassis for the event instead.'

Neil Cunningham took pole for the first heat, but a hydraulic issue on the formation lap left him with no option but to jump the start with the consequent ten-second penalty. This gave Morelli a clear run for the ten laps, Marc Delpierre and Derek M Daly the nearest but distant challengers. Cunningham, meanwhile, was able to race around his penalty to eventually be classified in eighth, securing his passage to the next round.

Anttalainen set the pace in practice for heat two but struggled with twitchy handling as the race progressed, dropping down to sixth. It was Gavin who laid down his marker, setting an impressive pace in the Swift to come home four seconds clear of Irish Festival winner Jason Pollack and Vincent Radermecker. Spence defied expectations, taking pole for the third heat ahead of Ingall and Franck Guibbert. Spence was impressive in the early laps, fending off Ingall's attentions until gearbox issues forced him to concede the lead.

Even without a fully functional third gear, he still had enough to retain second from Guibbert.

The next heat was the first truly entertaining race of the weekend, as Australian 'Driver to Europe' winner Troy Dunstan went wheel to wheel with Chris Hall, the Brands Hatch instructor who'd taught him the circuit earlier in the week. The first attempt only got as far as Druids before Mark Younde rolled into the gravel, the race being stopped to release the unharmed driver from under his car. From the restart, Hall and Dunstan treated the ten laps as if it were the final, Hall's local knowledge just giving him the edge.

Local pride continued in heat five, where Andy Stapley prevailed in an entertaining race-long scrap with Steffan Nielsen. An impressive third went to Herta, who poached the place late on from Simon Harrison. Today Herta notes of the tactical advice he received, 'Funny I don't remember anything specific. I knew the racing was fraught at Brands in FF, that there were national champions from countries all over Europe entered. I think I was told to protect the inside line when defending at all costs as it was very hard to pass around the outside there.'

Goossens got his Festival challenge off to a good start in heat six, despite Veijalainen leading for the first lap or so. Once the Belgian was through, he looked comfortable and was never seriously threatened and set the fastest race time of the day. The largest margin of victory came in heat seven where Warren Hughes romped home eight seconds clear of Darren Edmonds, third going to an occasionally wayward Luca Alessandrini. The final heat was scrappily taken by French championship frontrunner Patrick Lemarie, who'd benefitted from early leaders David Wright and Andy Charlsley spinning on oil at Surtees.

The recovering pair dead heated for second, the drivers unable to be separated by the timekeepers.

Fortunately, the fine weather continued into Sunday, with another decent crowd descending to enjoy the action. The first quarter-final immediately hit the spot, a tight and clean battle for the lead coupled with numerous excursions to the tyre wall from those behind. Ingall made the best start to lead away from Morelli and Spence. As the latter two swapped places, eventually in Morelli's favour, Ingall kept the pair at arm's length, easing to victory. Behind, there were casualties aplenty, Cunningham the most high-profile after he got caught in Mark Redgrave's accident.

The second race was equally fascinating with the wily Hall up against Gavin, and Dunstan also in the mix. For the first laps, it was Gavin who had the advantage, until he made a mistake heading into Clearways, dropping down to sixth. This briefly elevated Dunstan and Pollock until the pair clashed and spun a couple of laps later. Dunstan would have a further spin before the flag, still able to progress to the semi-final but with his hopes of an overall podium dashed. With all the action behind, by the chequered flag Hall had a decent gap to Radermecker and Rafael del Sarte, with the recovering Gavin next along.

Hughes was the comfortable winner in the third quarter-final, which only ran to three-quarters distance before being red-flagged. It wasn't the most entertaining race of the round, Hughes taking the lead from Stapley into Paddock before maintaining a hefty gap. Likewise, third-placed Nielsen was no particular threat to Stapley, the main mover being Herta who raced up to fourth. By this point, the American was starting to turn heads, surprising others but the not the driver himself:

'At the time I recall thinking it strange that everyone was so surprised as I had already had a decent amount of success in the US junior categories. In my mind we were there to try to win the race, but I guess not many others had considered us much of a threat.'

As anticipated, Goossens won the closing quarter-final, but was pushed all the way by Veijalainen – although the extent to which the Duckhams-backed driver was keeping his power dry was a matter of conjecture. Third went to Lemarie who spent the race dicing with Irish champion David Wright.

The first semi-final was anticipated as a duel between Ingall and Hughes, the pair sharing the grid for the first time in the weekend. The action got off to a false start with a plethora of accidents over the opening laps – the most spectacular of these saw Swift's Frank Bradley perpendicular at Paddock, unsurprisingly necessitating the red flag. Once the survivors had reconvened, Hughes made the better start to lead from Ingall and Morelli. It was a superb fight as for lap after lap Hughes had everything thrown at him, but he held strong. On the tenth lap another incident, this time at Clearways, blocked the track and brought out the red flags. After an already stoppage-filled day the result was declared at eight laps, with a relieved Hughes the winner.

Goossens had it more his own way in the later race, concluding the main business by leading Hall into Paddock. Once he had established a gap, he was able to control the pace, winning by six seconds but with more in the tank if it had been needed. Hall meanwhile, had a race-long job fending off Veijalainen which he accomplished, albeit by just two-hundredths of a second. In fourth, Gavin had a race of adventures, his latent pace offsetting one or two missteps.

Anticipating the final, there was still no definitive favourite. Goossens' race times hadn't been the fastest, but he'd also not yet been seriously pressured. The same couldn't be said of Hughes, Ingall and the rest. By dint of his semi-final pace, Hughes had pole position, but the upward incline meant this wasn't necessarily where he wanted to be.

The curse of pole struck again as, from the outside of the front row, Goossens jumped into the early lead, with Hughes, Ingall, Morelli and the rest immediately behind. The first time it all got a bit too close was on lap four when Morelli found a way around Hughes at Druids. It stayed uncomfortably tight for several laps, with the leading quartet alternating between bunching up and fighting their own private battles. Just behind Veijalainen was the best of the rest, as Gavin slipped down the order after clouting Spence.

The decisive moment wasn't for the lead but for second, when Morelli tapped Ingall into a spin at Clearways. Inevitably, accountability for the blame differed – Ingall thought 'it was a bit desperate', Morelli said 'he kept lifting at the exit of Clearways and this time I hit him' – but the net result was that Ingall spun out of contention. The Australian will certainly have felt karma was served when Morelli's clutch failed with just a couple of laps to run. All this elevated Hughes to second, but with Goossens setting a new lap record on the penultimate lap, there was little he could do, finishing just over one and a half seconds back. The beneficiary of the casualties was a delighted Veijalainen who took third a couple of seconds clear of Spence.

Goossens fully deserved his Festival success, a standout performer throughout the weekend who pushed exactly when he needed to. The Belgian twice finished third in the Formula 3000

A 1972 dice at Brands Hatch illustrates why the category became so beloved of spectators and competitors

Here interviewing Niki Lauda at the 1982 British Grand Prix, for over three decades Brian Jones was the voice of Brands Hatch

Aside from tightening Graham Hill Bend the Brands Hatch layout has barely changed since 1976

A packed Paddock grandstand surveys the action and carnage of the 1996 'Kent' Festival

Modern Formula Ford 1600 racing remains as close as ever

Just 18 months after winning the Formula Ford Festival Jenson Button was in Formula 1 with Williams

Despite being hotly tipped, Nigel Mansell didn't make it through his heat in 1977

Late season form in 1992 saw Jan Magnussen (8) head to the Festival as one of the favourites

Formula 1 success seemed near inevitable for Johnny Herbert after his 1985 triumph

Despite only a handful of races in Formula 1, Tommy Byrne's Festival performances remain the stuff of legend

The RF88 remains one of the most potent and best-looking Formula Fords

The Ecoboost cars were neither lovely, nor loved signalling the end of the category

championship, but was never quite propelled into Formula 1. After an enduring and successful career in Belgium he now runs his own team in the European NASCAR series.

1992 was the last great Festival. If later events could point to standout races, this was the final time that eight full heats of cars were drawn from across the Formula Ford universe. The entry once more topped 170 cars and for the last time until 1996 enjoyed comprehensive coverage from the BBC, the *Grandstand* highlights covering all of Sunday's action.

The reason for the change in future years was that this would be the final Festival run to Formula Ford 1600 regulations. In return for a greater level of interest from Ford, the elderly Kent engine would be retired from the main class at the end of 1992 to be replaced by the heavier, more powerful 1800cc Zetec engine, a powerplant which could be found in contemporary road-going Ford models. The treaded tyres would remain for now, famed for creating excellent racing, and the 1993 cars would not be hugely different from their forebears – although this would change in the coming years. Likewise, Ford were poised to take a more proactive step forward in promoting the category and maintaining a strong field. With both Vauxhall and Renault (the British Formula Renault championship launched for the 1990 season) investing in Formula 1 ladder single-seaters, Formula Ford needed to move with the times.

The 1992 season had been a good one with a number of races held in support of the increasingly popular BTCC, which was just entering its golden period. The on-track action throughout the year had been fierce, the title being claimed by Jamie Spence, whose run of early-season victories had given him a points buffer. Spence, however, would not be racing in the Festival –

following a season of incidents, his licence was suspended after what was felt to be a deliberate collision with Andrew McAuley in the season finale at Silverstone. Devastatingly fast and utterly fearless, Spence would be a big loss to the entry list – although his place in the Swift works team would be taken by Oliver Gavin, the sensational debutant of a year earlier.

McAuley would be one of the other UK title contenders in the mix over the weekend, as would series runner-up Neil Cunningham, Vincent Radermacker and the end-of-season form driver Jan Magnussen. Magnussen had won four of the final five rounds of the season and the Dane was seen as one to watch, switching for the weekend from his bright yellow Van Diemen to the iconic Duckhams colours.

Away from the British Championship frontrunners, there were lots of possibles but few clear-cut favourites. Future F1 competitors Alex Wurz and Marc Gene featured, as did Philippe Siffert (son of Jo Siffert who had been killed at the circuit exactly 21 years previously) and Jaki Scheckter, nephew of 1979 Formula 1 champion Jody. Unusually for a racing driver, Jaki was legally deaf.

For the final time, the Festival would run to the format it had followed for over 15 years with eight Saturday heats feeding Sunday's whittling down through the quarter and semi-finals.

With such a strong entry, progression from the heats wasn't a formality and a lowly finishing position would have repercussions for Sunday. Justin Keen was the star of the opening heat, the works Swift pilot seeing off the Reynard of Finnish champion Kalle Jokinen. Future Minardi Formula 1 racer Gene was initially third before he spun his chances away, eventually creeping into the quarter-finals with a 14th-place finish.

The second race was even more hard fought, headed by a battle between Jonathan McGall in the Mondiale and Andy Stapley in the Ray.

The two Festival stalwarts found the balance between close racing and staying out of trouble. Stapley came out on top making the decisive move mid-race. Scheckter, meanwhile, finished 11th as he overcame a ten-second penalty as post-qualifying checks found his car to be underweight.

Penalties also threw a bit of a cloud over the third heat. From pole position Gavin, in another works Swift, dominated. However, he was deemed to have jumped the start and was awarded a ten-second penalty. On adjusted time, this gave Jamun-perennial Chris Hall victory. Such was Gavin's pace that he still did enough to be classified second.

McCauley in the works Van Diemen was a close winner in heat four, dicing all the way with Andy Charsley in the Ray in what would prove to be the day's fastest heat. Charsley, having claimed the Champion of Brands series, used his circuit knowledge to full effect, but a small error at Druids three laps from home was enough to give McCauley the edge.

In the following heat, experience was once more to the fore as perpetual frontrunner Cunningham took the honours. Cunningham was almost a little too laid back, admitting post-race to easing off a bit too soon. This gave Claudio Piazza-Musso a glimmer of hope, but despite a late bid at Paddock the South African had to settle for second.

More Australian success was to be found in heat six where Russell Ingall took a comfortable victory from Brands regular John Hayden, the latter punching above his weight in a comparatively aged Van Diemen. Further back, Wurz finished tenth, overcoming a ten-second penalty after being caught in a practice incident.

The penultimate heat provided many of the day's talking points. Favourite Jan Magnussen would be starting with a ten-second penalty – the post-qualifying weighbridge claiming another victim. He would seek to be the third driver in seven years (following Herbert and Coyne) to take the Festival despite a penalty in his heat. It was also the day's only red flag, when John Oxborrow came off worst in a multi-car incident at Clearways. Oxborrow broke his neck in the incident, spending several weeks in traction before making a full recovery; his unique Ox chassis was badly damaged.

Once restarted, it was one of the races of the day. Brian Saunders and Mark Marchant engaged in a classic Festival battle. Marchant was quicker than Saunders but couldn't find a way past. On lap eight, they tangled exiting Paddock, Marchant's Jamun being launched over Saunders' cockpit, the latter being fortunate to avoid injury as both crashed into retirement. Saunders' weekend was compounded on Sunday when his girlfriend sustained nasty facial bruising after walking into a transporter tailgate. All this gave Thomas Johansson an unlikely victory, whilst Magnussen took a formidable second, setting a new lap record as he went.

The closing heat was deceptive. Despite being one of the closest races of the day, there was no overtaking amongst the top three. Ken Bowes won from pole, with Kurt Mollekens and a circumspect Angel Burgueno completing the podium.

After a largely dry Saturday, it rained hard on Sunday morning, leaving the track completely sodden for the first quarter-final, although the rain itself had eased off. The cream of heats one and three formed the grid, with Gavin, starting third, the expected star turn. It proved to be the case, the Swift pilot making a lightning start to jump the front row of Hall and Keen. In this heat only Hall could live with Gavin's pace, but even so he remained a couple of seconds back. The entertainment was for the rest of the top ten, where Frederic Lenoir prevailed in an entertaining fight, chased to the line by his ever-improving compatriot Alexandre Janoray.

The first stoppage of the day came at the start of the second quarter-final (the best of heats two and four), where the treacherous conditions contributed to a multi-car pile-up on the run to Graham Hill Bend. Rui Aguas came off worst, fortunate to be diagnosed with little more than heavy bruising after he was cut out of his Van Diemen.

The restarted race was a scrappy affair where a combination of driver and mechanical failures prevented the emergence of a leadership fight. McGall was the beneficiary of others' misfortune, romping home some 17 seconds clear of the rest. The Andys in the Rays – Charsley and Stapley – had mixed fortunes. Stapley stayed clear of trouble but was never near McGall's pace, taking second under pressure from Cunningham. Charsley had the speed, but a mistake at Paddock saw him required to put on a recovery drive from 12th up to fifth. The other pre-race favourite, McCauley, also had a torrid time, initially comfortable in second before issues with a sticking throttle limited him to tenth.

By the time the cars formed up for the penultimate quarter-final, a drying line was beginning to emerge on parts of the track. This gave way to a great fight between Magnussen and Cunningham. The Dane was faster on the dry sections, but Cunningham seemed more comfortable over the damper parts. It was a fascinating see-saw battle, late traffic almost swung in Magnussen's favour but Cunningham had enough and was a deserved victor, albeit by just over a tenth of second. Third went to an impressive Johnny Kane who made impressive progress through the leading group to take the final podium position.

An entanglement at Druids brought out early red flags in the closing quarter-final. The now rapidly drying track enabled some more frenetic racing, with plenty of comings together – Hayden being among the victims. The battle for the lead was initially between Ingall and Bowes before the latter was demoted by Franck Guibbert on lap four. Bowes, feeling he had the pace to win, was a frustrated third behind Ingall and Guibbert – the order remaining static from mid-distance.

The on-off rain continued to make the circuit treacherous for the semi-finals. The first of these brought Cunningham, Gavin and Magnussen together, the trio of pre-event favourites taking the top grid positions. Whilst progression was vital, every place was worth a row for the final. The other driver in the mix was circuit specialist Hall, who could spring a surprise in the variable conditions.

The conditions as the race got under way were wet, but gradually improved as the laps unfolded. This put setup at a premium, with the teams having to use their judgement as to grip levels for the latter laps. It was Hall who got the best start of all, leaping up from fourth to lead into Paddock for the first time. Gavin was immediately on to his gearbox and darted into the lead on the run towards to Surtees. A train of cars for the lead formed with Hall and Magnussen sandwiched by the Swifts of Gavin and Cunningham. It soon became clear that the Swifts were perfectly dialled into the conditions, which enabled Cunningham to apply pressure for third – squeezing past Magnussen at the end of the second lap.

Up front, Gavin was enjoying an easy run to victory, eventually taking the honours by over four seconds. The fight for second was the focal point for much of the race. Once clear of Magnussen, Cunningham was soon with Hall. The Jamun driver struggled for pace due to his full wet setup and by mid-race the Australian was through to second, which he would hold to the end. Magnussen eventually completed the podium after spending several laps struggling to find a way past Hall. He managed it on lap 13, a dart to the outside at Paddock combined with assertive defence at Druids doing the job. However, the pre-event favourite would be starting the final from the third row, with much to do.

The second semi-final proved to be the story of the front-row men McGall and Ingall. This was not the first tango for either driver, and they knew exactly what was required of them – a top-two finish and stay out of trouble. The track was a fair bit drier, so barring multiple stoppages the winner would most likely have pole position for the final.

From the outside of the front row, it was McGall who made the better start to head Ingall into Paddock. From the opening parries, it was clear that Ingall was the quicker of the pair, but McGall knew all the tricks to keep him behind. The pair thus spent much of the race circulating as one, Ingall constantly debating whether to settle for second. It appeared he had decided to do just this when, with a couple of laps left to run, McGall ran slightly wide at Druids. The gap was too tempting for Ingall who tried to dive through. Compared to the rest of the circuit, the track up at Druids was more slippery and both protagonists struggled for grip. McGall's traction kicked in first and as he accelerated he brushed wheels with Ingall causing him to spin.

This gave McGall victory by a deceptively comfortable margin of eight seconds, underlining his and Ingall's dominance. Guibbert and McAuley inherited second and third with Ingall recovering to finish fourth – another with plenty to do in the final.

The clouds continued to hover overhead as the cars assembled for the final. McGall had pole with Gavin alongside him, with a Guibbert-Cunningham row two. Many eyes were looking to Magnussen on the third row and Ingall a further rung back. The rain had abated sufficiently for a dry racing line to have formed, but it was still treacherous for any driver that put a wheel out of step. From the outside of the front row, Gavin made the better start, but was immediately under pressure from McGall, who sought to make the most of his pole. The Mondiale pilot managed to reclaim the advantage at Clearways to lead at the end of the first lap. Meanwhile Magnussen made a stunning start to the race, with the Van Diemen now clearly to his liking. By the start of the second lap the Dane was up to third and rapidly closing in on the leading duo.

Gavin and Magnussen had been the class of the Festival and McGall's spirited defence wasn't quite enough – he was demoted to third on successive laps at Clearways. This duly released the leaders to engage in the battle that had been anticipated throughout the weekend. Magnussen made his first bid for the lead at Paddock on lap five, the pair brushed wheels and Gavin held position.

A lap later and Magnussen tried again. In one of the greatest moves in Festival history, coming from a long way back, the Van

Diemen hurtled into Paddock. Committed to the outside line, Magnussen somehow found the traction to shoot into the lead. It was a phenomenal manoeuvre, but it wasn't the decisive one. Gavin was able to stay right on Magnussen's gearbox and, two laps later, tried his luck around the outside at Druids. There simply wasn't enough grip. With both drivers overcommitted, the leading duo ran wide. Magnussen re-joined without too much drama, but Gavin's race was run – back on track in seventh, he retired a few laps later as there was too much dirt interfering with the pedals.

Cunningham was delighted, if bemused, to inherit the lead, noting to *Autosport*, 'You don't try to pass someone round the outside when it's as slippery and cold as it was there.' It proved to be a short run at the front as Magnussen pulled off his Paddock trick again at mid-race to definitively claim the advantage. The remainder of the race was straightforward for Magnussen as he reeled off the laps without trouble

After such a strong showing, there was to be no justice for the Swifts. Following Gavin's retirement, Cunningham looked set for a solid second until his gear linkage broke just a couple of laps from home. The unfortunate Australian was pitched into retirement, having deserved far more from his weekend. Behind, there had been a highly entertaining battle between Ingall and Stapley, which was eventually decided in Ingall's favour late on. Both had been on the pace throughout the weekend and were deserving of the final pair of podium placings.

Magnussen's performance was stunning. Echoing Herbert's performance of seven years earlier, his heat penalty to outright victory turned heads throughout motorsport. His trajectory continued with the 1994 British Formula 3 title, which landed him a move to Formula 1 – initially as a McLaren test driver (making his debut at Ti Aida in 1995 when Mika Hakkinen had appendicitis), before landing the Stewart drive in 1997. A year and a half of indifferent performances, coupled with a non-F1 driver lifestyle, saw him replaced midway through the 1998 season. A move to sportscars was a career salvation, an over 15-year relationship with Corvette netting him four class wins at Le Mans.

Gavin, the other star performer of the weekend, had an uncanny career parallel to Magnussen, taking the British Formula 3 crown a year after the Dane in 1995. After his Formula 1 opportunities were limited to driving the safety car for a few seasons, Gavin also found a long-term home at Corvette, sharing three of his five Le Mans class victories with Magnussen.

For over 20 years, the Formula Ford Festival had offered one-off competition for competitors from around the globe. The 1980s had seen the meeting transition on to a more professional footing, but even in 1992, the Champion of Brands regulars could mix it at the front. Now the event was stepping into a bold new world. For the next four years, the Kents would continue to have a Festival of their own, but the overwhelming majority of drivers with an eye on Formula 1 would transition to the Zetec class. The Festival would never be the same again.

Enter the Zetecs

1993 WAS a brave new world for Formula Ford, moving on after 25 years from the loyal Kent engine to the Zetec class. Zetec-era Formula Ford enjoyed immediate prominence, racing as part of the extremely popular TOCA package that supported BTCC events. It was a boom period for the BTCC and it meant Formula Ford action would play out in front of crowds of tens of thousands rather than headlining a small Mallory Park club meeting.

Despite the new engine, the manufacturer battle remained much as it had been the previous year, with Van Diemen and Swift the two pre-eminent contenders. Both cars still looked much the same as their Kent predecessors, although the significantly heavier power plant created new engineering challenges. With the tail of the car being much weightier, the handling needed to be adapted to give drivers confidence that the car wouldn't swing round on them mid-corner. Whilst this could be engineered out to an extent, the following year would see the cars taking on a vastly different appearance, being explicitly designed to accommodate the 1800cc engine.

The championship was dominated by Russell Ingall, who took 13 victories en route to the title. Ingall, running with the works Van Diemen team, was joined on the championship podium by team-mate Kurt Mollekens, the pair sandwiching Swift's Guy Smith. Alongside the UK frontrunners, there was no shortage of strength in the entry – Ralph Firman Jr (son of Van Diemen principal Ralph Firman) would make a one-off appearance, having competed in Formula Vauxhall Junior throughout the year. Foreign challengers in the form of Tom Coronel, Gonzalo Rodriguez, Soheil Ayari and Marc Gene once more illustrated the pulling power of the Festival.

Ayari's entry was particularly interesting as a portent of Festivals to come. He, alongside Bertrand Godin, would be at the wheel of the new French Mygale chassis. Featuring a nose-mounted radiator, the car certainly looked unique and showed impressively on the British manufacturer's home turf. If the latter-Kent era had largely (but far from exclusively) been Van Diemen v Reynard and Van Diemen v Swift, how many in the Paddock in October would have wagered the dominant technical battle for the Zetec era would be Van Diemen v Mygale.

Although a successful introductory season, the Zetec class had not been over-populated, with numerous Kent-engined cars padding out the entry at each round. The promotional push from Ford had proved a success in the new regulations being adopted throughout Europe. A field of 48 cars was assembled across three heats, which would directly decide the grid for the final, the error-strewn programme not making clear quite how this would be calculated. The level of support would set the tone for the Zetec era – whilst never great in numbers, for the following decade many Formula 1 prospects would still spend at least some time in Formula Ford. By contrast, the Kent Festival, run alongside the weekend, still drew six heats of cars, and would fill four heats through to it being discontinued at the end of 1996.

It was a bizarrely disjointed weekend, with qualifying on Friday followed by a fallow day on the Saturday, given over to heats from the Kents, and all the race action on Sunday. For the spectators, the rest of the meeting thoroughly compensated – this was a true feast of Formula Ford action, with over 200 Kents and Zetecs across an array of championships. The only non-Formula Ford race was still single-seaters in the form of the Winter Formula First Challenge race.

Certainly, the Festival remained a big draw for spectators, with the grandstands and banking packed for Sunday's action, along with extensive media coverage. Unfortunately, for the first time since 1984, the BBC cameras stayed away. Although the meeting was filmed (many of the crashes ended up featuring on the notorious Havoc crash videos), the loss of BBC exposure meant the Festival would struggle to retain its wider public profile hereafter. Giving this a certain irony was the fact that 1987 Festival winner Eddie Irvine dominated newspaper back pages in the week after the meeting, having been thumped by Ayrton Senna following the Japanese Grand Prix. The debutant Irvine had the temerity to unlap himself from the Brazilian great, to Senna's profound irritation. It was a juicy story with *Autosport* gleefully printing a full transcript of the altercation, which had been caught on tape.

Sunday morning was dry if cold, resulting in good conditions for the trio of heats. The first of these featured an entertaining four-way tussle for the lead between Rui Aguas, Justin Keen, Jonny Kane and Andy Charsley. Aguas was initially to the fore, but at one-third distance his Van Diemen started jumping out of third gear (which he rectified by keeping a grip on the gear lever when in third), enabling Kane to move through into the lead, followed shortly afterwards by Keen. Aguas soon learned to drive around the issue, repassing Keen, but running out of time to do anything about Kane who was just a quarter of a second clear at the end.

Event favourite Ingall had pole for heat two ahead of Gene, before squandering the advantage by bogging down at the start to give Gene the lead. Fortunately for Ingall, the red flags were immediately out as his fellow Australian and Festival veteran Neil Cunningham spun in front of the pack at Paddock before being T-boned at high speed by Jose Barbosa – both drivers were fortunate to escape without serious injury.

Second time around there was no repeat from Ingall and he shot into an immediate lead, quickly building a two-second buffer over Gene. Thereafter the Spaniard was able to match Ingall's pace and the gap remained stable. Third went to the experienced Bernard Dolan who'd needed to clear Vincent Vosse in the early stages. Ingall did exactly what he needed to do and set what he thought would be the fastest heat time to give him pole position for the final.

The concluding heat was the best of the trio, with Firman, Frederico Viegas and Kurt Mollekens all looking like potential winners. Polesitter Firman prevailed, but not before being headed by Viegas on a couple of occasions. A last-ditch effort to reclaim the lead from Firman resulted in Viegas dropping to third as Mollekens followed through the gap created by his works Van Diemen team-mate. During the closing stages, the trio ran very closely as Mollekens looked every which way for a gap, but to no avail. Firman thus took the flag, with just thirteen-hundredths covering the top three.

Once the heat times had been compared, it was an all-Duckhams Van Diemen front row for the final – Ingall on pole with Firman alongside. Kane and Gene would share row two before another brace of Duckham's liveried cars in the hands of Mollekens and Aguas.

The only weakness shown by Ingall thus far had been his poor start to the subsequently halted second heat, with the consequence that many rivals were pinning their hopes on another duff getaway. It wasn't to be. Ingall made a perfect start to take a lead that he would hold, unchallenged, throughout.

Behind, the dicing got under way immediately. Kane made a superb getaway to take second into Paddock from Firman and Mollekens, with Gene in fifth. As in their heat, Mollekens was soon on Firman's gearbox, deciding to make a proper bid at the start of lap three. The pair ran side by side through Druids, emerging with Mollekens slightly ahead. Running downhill to Graham Hill Bend, Mollekens adjusted his line slightly to right, making contact with Firman and spearing both cars at speed into the tyre wall. The drivers somehow emerged uninjured, but the cars were heavily damaged, it being immediately apparent that both were out on the spot (I can claim a little piece of Festival history here, as post-race paddock scavenging for souvenirs netted me the remains of Molleken's nose cone, along with Cunningham's from the heat two incident).

Whilst a disaster for Van Diemen, the incident was good news for Gene and Kane, who were largely released to settle the lower podium placings between themselves, Gene sealing second with a move at Druids. Aguas, meanwhile, was struggling, dropping back from the leaders before being demoted for fourth by a flying Guy Smith and eventually slipping to eighth after a trip through the gravel at Druids. Viegas, meanwhile, finished fifth, his hopes of going further stymied by tyre issues and losing touch with Smith as he tried to clear Aguas.

It was an impressive and almost straightforward win for Ingall, although far from his first attempt at the Festival. Speaking after the event, he reflected, 'Now I know how it feels to win the Festival, I think it's even better than I thought it was going to be.' Gene was an impressive second, although once more the early gap proved insurmountable. Kane was a fine third, the highest-placed Swift representative on a weekend where the Van Diemens seemed to have the edge.

Ingall's career subsequently took him back to Australia, where, nicknamed 'the enforcer' due to his robust driving style, he claimed the 2005 V8 Supercar title in a year where the top three in the championship – Ingall, Craig Lowndes and Marcos Ambrose – were all Festival alumni.

The consensus on the first Zetec Festival was mixed if cautiously positive, and certainly there had been (just) enough action to point to the Festival remaining relevant in the future. However, as the crowds left Brands Hatch, they may also have reflected that the Kent Festival, which had really filled the timetable for the weekend, had been better attended and produced better racing.

The second year of the Zetec class saw the category enjoy the step-up in professionalism and exposure that had been hoped for. Gone were the days of the clubman and aspiring Formula 1 star racing together. In its 1994 guise, Formula Ford was high tech and professional. The British series spent the year running as part of the BTCC TOCA package, with the main event arguably at the peak of its popularity. It was a single-seater-heavy paddock with Formula Renault, Formula Vauxhall Lotus and Formula Vauxhall Junior all competing for broadly the same pool of drivers as Formula Ford.

The title went to the promising Danish racer Jason Watt, who only took three victories from the 16 races, the Vector pilot reaping the benefit of consistency. Jonny Kane in the works Swift had swept to ten victories over the course of the season and he would clearly be a big Festival rival to Watt. The Belgian Geoffrey Horion had also been in the mix, scoring two wins for Van Diemen, the Norfolk marque otherwise enduring a difficult season.

For the second year of the Zetec class, the cars looked markedly different to the 1993 contenders, which were essentially uprated Kents. Sidepods had been introduced at the end of 1993 with two specific safety aims in mind – side impact protection in the sort of T-bone incident that befell Cunningham in 1993 and Aguas in 1992, and to make it harder for wheels to interlock when the cars were going side by side. Recognising the characteristics of the Zetec engine, the Vector in particular had been designed from the ground up as a Zetec car, giving a very different driving experience to the Kent cars.

Although now adopted throughout Europe, the Zetec class was still confined to the national championships, meaning that the talent at the front of the Festival was strong but not supported by eight heats worth of cars. More worryingly for the sustainability of the class was the fact that, instead of Zetecs percolating to club level, the previous years' cars were being converted to Kent specification. Simon Hill had some interesting reflections on the adoption of the Zetec: 'Logically you would have thought it would work as you could pick up a complete car relatively cheaply. Immediately, though, we were converting them back to Kents. They did feel odd to drive, but maybe that's because everyone was so used to the Kents. Whatever the reason, there just wasn't the appetite for them among club racers.'

The format for the weekend would comprise a brace of semi-finals, a last-chance race and final. Given the increased grip levels, greater acceleration and stiffer nature of the Zetecs, it was easier than in the Kent era to maintain a race-long lead by holding a defensive line. A good grid position from qualifying would be essential for any driver with aspirations for outright victory.

Running with the number one on his car would be Hill: 'I believe I was the first person to run with that number, at least that's what Brian Jones told me. It was a disaster though, I had a very late deal with Ted Hawkins to run a year-old Swift. The engine was down on power, and I attempted to replace it in the paddock prior to the race. Unfortunately the car then stopped on the out lap for the heat, so I must have done something wrong. That was my Festival.'

After the usual week of pre-event testing had been completed, attention first turned to the draw, which appeared to be heavily lopsided towards the first semi-final, with arguably five to six outright contenders clustered together. Pole position was claimed by Guy Smith, just ahead of Firman (returning to the Festival once more after his adventures the previous year), the pair somewhat surprisingly demoting Horion and Kane to the second row.

Crisp, clear weather greeted the drivers on Sunday morning, ideal conditions for close racing. The opener didn't lack for intrigue and intensity. The best start went to Kane, who jumped the front row to lead until an error at Clearways on the second lap. This promoted Firman Jr for his turn at the front until he slid off at McLaren. Thus polesitter Smith took his turn at the front, and he stayed there for the remainder, taking his Vector to victory. He didn't have it easy, though, as Kane harried him throughout until the Ulsterman overcooked a move into Paddock late on and ran wide. This promoted Horion to take second, with Kane rounding out the podium.

Qualifying for the second semi-final had produced a surprise result, with Bas Leinders taking pole position from Watt. The second row was shared between Jari de Veirman and French champion Soheil Ayari, the pair both hustling some pace from their Van Diemens. Knowing that a narrow lead would be defendable, the start was all important. Watt did exactly what he needed, jumping Leinders as the lights changed to lead through Paddock. Fortunately for the Dane, the race wasn't red-flagged when Naoki Kurose skittled the midfield at Druids first time round. Out front he focused on reeling off the 15 laps in a faster time than team-mate Smith to give him pole position for the final.

Leinders, meanwhile, was struggling with a fuel injector issue that worsened as the race unfolded, eventually dropping him down to tenth. He was also the victim of a brave move from Ayari for second, the French pilot leaving it incredibly late before lunging at Paddock. The final position on the rostrum went to Bertrand Godin, who was the beneficiary of over-ambition from Vincent Vosse when the latter tried to challenge Ayari for second.

With the top 11 from each semi-final automatically progressing to the final, the remaining six grid slots would come from the five-lap last-chance race. During the pause between races, both Godin and Leinders were excluded due to fuel irregularities, so now eight slots in the final were up for grabs. Despite this, the last-chance race wasn't the spare parts department benefit many were expecting, with Cyrille Sauvage leading throughout and only Peter Dumbreck making significant progress.

So as the sun dipped the 28 contenders lined up for the 20-lap final. From pole position, Watt was the favourite, but the semi-finals had shown there were plenty of potential challengers.

Unusually, it was a clean start with the front rows largely moving away in grid formation, with Watt leading the field through the opening exchanges. It was soon apparent that he didn't have the pace to pull clear and would have his defensive work cut out. His first challenge came from Vector team-mate Smith, who launched a boldly (over)ambitious move into Paddock, which Watt parried by easing him wide. By the time he'd gathered it up, Smith was down to fourth behind Ayari and Horion.

The next incident came at Paddock on lap five as Horion looked to the outside of Ayari. Smith sensed half a gap to the inside, coming from a long way back to attempt the pass. It was too optimistic. Ayari turned in and collided with Smith, the angle of collision spearing the Frenchman into the Paddock tyre wall at near unabated speed. It was a relief to see Ayari walk away. Smith sustained suspension damage from the contact and was also out.

This promoted Horion to second, with Kane in third – the latter having the benefit of some clear road to close up to the leaders. Horion, meanwhile, took his turn to pressurise Watt, and it was uncomfortably tight. Lap after lap, Horion would pull to the outside and draw alongside Watt under braking for Paddock, but Watt's tactic of sticking to the defensive line was paying dividends. That approach, whilst effective, was far from the quickest way to approach the race, which allowed Kane to reel in the leading pair.

For the final five laps, it was three for the lead – Watt, Horion and Kane – the latter having the whip-hand as he had the luxury of letting events play out ahead. Into Paddock for the final time, Horion rolled the dice and made his boldest attempt yet. Watt was unflustered as Horion overcommitted and ran wide, allowing Kane to slip through. Horion tried to fight back, but overdid it at Clearways within sight of the flag and spun down to fifth.

With too little time for Kane to mount a challenge, Watt took the chequered flag and a lights-to-flag victory after a tremendous defensive drive. It was a strong second for Kane, who never quite got the Swift working as he wanted. Meanwhile, third went to Vosse, who was the beneficiary of Horion's late rotation. Whilst there may not have been as many races as previous years, the quality was high and the racing entertaining.

For much of the 1990s, Watt looked a near-certainty for success in Formula 1 and finished runner-up in an extremely competitive 1999 Formula 3000 season. However, an off-season motorcycle incident left Watt paralysed from the chest down, ending his single-seater career. He returned to the circuit in 2001, winning the Danish Touring Car title in 2002 in a modified Peugeot 307. After winning the 1997 British Formula 3 championship, Kane never quite broke into Formula 1 or IndyCar, but a career pivot into sportscars yielded a class win in the 2010 24 Hours of Le Mans.

In 1995, Formula Ford had enjoyed a strong season in support of the BTCC in what was generally a boom period for single-seater racing the UK, with four healthy national ladder series (and that's excluding Formula First) continuing to feed the British Formula 3 championship.

It was also a strong field with Swift works driver Bas Leinders having taken the title, although there was a strong case that the fastest driver of the year had been Van Diemen's Mario Haberfeld. Another Van Diemen peddler felt to be in the mix was Kevin McGarrity, who would be running in Duckhams colours. Also on form was Vector's Justin Keen and the similarly equipped Kristian Kolby and Giorgio Vinella. The programme pundit selection generally all plumped in the direction of Michael Vergers, the experienced Dutchman returning once more to chase victory. Nestled away deep in the entry list running for the Duckhams Van Diemen team was Australian newcomer Mark Webber.

Even in a more professional era, the lure of Brands Hatch in October was still irresistible for drivers. Giorgio Vinella recalled, 'I enjoyed Brands Hatch a lot, it has a soul. The first time I went to the circuit and saw all the famous corners it was fantastic. It is somewhere that even when it's silent, it speaks, you can hear the heroes of the past.'There had also been a big technical change for the season. After sidepods had been added to the cars for the 1994 season, for 1995 (and the first time in the category's history) slick tyres were introduced for the British Championship, elevating both lap times and grip levels. Three years into the Zetec era and the cars were a step removed from their Kent predecessors in terms of both looks and performance. The same regulations didn't apply in European competition and hadn't been adopted in other national championships where cars still ran on the traditional treaded tyre. In order to keep the entry multinational and not overly advantage the British regulars, the Festival would run on treaded tyres.

Heading into the weekend, the drivers who'd raced in both the UK and Europe during the season could well benefit. As Vinella explained, 'Switching between the tyres [slicks and treaded], you had to change the entire setup of the car; the races we did in France meant we knew what we wanted to do for the setup and didn't have to find it in testing.' The weekend format would ensure that every lap would count: a brace of Saturday qualifying sessions forming the grid for two semi-finals on the Sunday morning, followed by a last-chance race and the final. Given the extremely strong field, progression from the semi-final was far from guaranteed even for the favourites.

In total, 52 cars would take to the track for qualifying, with Kristian Kolby being the talk of the first heat. Having just turned 17, the Dane, in a Vector chassis similar to the one in which his compatriot Watt had raced the previous October, had been on the pace throughout testing. This form rolled into the first semi-final where Kolby dominated, fending off McGarrity and Leinders. With a clean race and strong pace, Kolby also set a race time good enough for pole in the final. Another driver marking himself out as one to watch was Miku Santavirta, whose raw pace seemed to be a match for Kolby, although he was frustrated in his efforts to move through traffic. Santavirta, speaking for this book, recalled, 'We had one race all year where we were quick and that was the Festival. The results hadn't been there, but the team was great.'

The second semi-final was a far scrappier affair with two stoppages. Aggregate victory in the three-part race went to French pilot Patrice Gay in the Mygale. Gay hadn't looked particularly emphatic, but the multiple red flags weren't conductive to establishing a good rhythm. The main challenger was Kolby's team-mate in the Olympic Motorsport Vectors, Giorgio Vinella, who was right on Gay's pace for much of the race.

Vinella remembered, 'I didn't have the best qualifying, down in fourth or fifth, but I was good at the start – the stoppages helped me as at each restart I gained some places.' The highlight of his race was a spectacular move on Gay into Paddock Hill Bend that gave him first on the road, second on aggregate times. 'You always plan the move from at least the corner before, and through Clearways I could get on his tail, I could see I was making him nervous. I got a better run out of Clearways and managed to get alongside down the straight. Into Paddock I was on the outside line, and turned in a little sideways with oversteer, but I managed to get through without running over the kerb on the exit and had the speed up the hill.' It was a crash-strewn Festival Sunday, and by the time the final got under way the October sun was low in the sky. From testing, practice and the semi-finals, many pundits were struggling to look past Kolby or Gay on the front row for a winner.

Once more, pole position proved to be more of a hindrance than help. Starts were a chink in Kolby's armour and that, coupled with the low sun, meant that he was slow away and allowed Gay to take the lead. Kolby was also jumped by a fast-starting Vinella and slotted into third ahead of Leinders, who benefitted from McGarrity sliding wide at Paddock.

In the early running, it looked as if Gay had the race sown up. He was flying whilst Vinella battled handling issues, serving to bottle up the field behind him. This all changed on the third lap when Gay arrived at Surtees to find the track covered in dirt following tail-ender Marco Schumann's spin moments earlier. First on the scene, Gay had no time to react and spun into the gravel and out of the running.

This elevated Vinella into the lead, but with over three-quarters of the race to run it seemed unlikely that the Italian would be able to hold on. Kolby was the next to hit trouble, his car jumping out of third gear as he exited Clearways. Moments later, McGarrity was past Leinders at Paddock, moving him to first in the queue to challenge Vinella.

The Vector still not working to Vinella's liking, McGarrity was quickly past, with the Swift team-mates Leinders and Santavirta not far behind. From the start of the race, Santavirta knew he had a chance: 'I immediately realised the speed was there, [it would be] no problem to win this one. We put in a new engine for the race and it worked.'

This set up a thrilling three-way battle for the lead. Of the trio at that moment, McGarrity in the Duckhams Van Diemen was the slowest and Santavirta the fastest. Leinders was caught in the middle, torn between attacking for the lead and defending his position. The dynamic was uneasy, the tension growing as the laps ticked off – Leinders unable to quite find a way past McGarrity.

All the while, Santavirta was growing more frustrated until, finally, Leinders left a chink of light to the inside line as the pair exited Paddock. If the gap was ever really there, it certainly wasn't by the time the pair were halfway up Hailwood Hill, locked wheels resulting in the Swifts' exit. Over 25 years later, Santavirta remains frustrated: 'I realised I was going to win the race, maybe Bas realised he would not win and closed the door. [After the race] there was nothing to talk to him about, it was not worth talking to him about. Everyone realised what had happened.' To compound the awkwardness, the Swift teammates were also housemates in Sheffield.

This left a laughing McGarrity free to reel of the remaining laps from Vinella, the gap between the pair coming down as McGarrity cruised. Third went to Haberfeld who hadn't quite been at the very sharp end throughout the weekend but was able to pip Webber on the line for the podium.

The story didn't quite end there. Post-race scrutineering found an irregularity with Vinella's camshaft and he was excluded. Vinella remains unrepentant: 'I still say I finished second, I had no advantage from the part, and it should have been changed sooner. Every time I speak with Mario [Haberfeld], he says, "When can I have the trophy?" but I'm not giving it to him – I earned it. Mark [Webber] has never pestered me about it.'

The *Autosport* report the week after the event suggested the final was the best race to date of the Zetec era. This was a bold but fair claim. It had been a thrilling race with significant strength in depth at the top of the field. It was Formula Ford racing at its finest, right on the precipice between triumph and disaster. The 1995 final would remain as one of the standout moments for the class, producing thrilling racing that diminished as grip levels increased in future years.

For the main protagonists there was more frustration to come. They all failed to make the final leap to Formula 1, their careers more often than not stalling in the cauldron of late-1990s Formula 3000. The same fate could not be said of the 1996 winner.

Returning for another year in the category but moving across to the works Duckhams Van Diemen team, Kolby took the 1996 title. The Dane won six of the 16 rounds, although the race at Silverstone was declared void after a botched start procedure. Second in the championship went to Webber – the breakout star at the previous year's Festival – who had a solid campaign, netting three victories along the way. Webber was regarded as the team's number two driver (in practice meaning second pick of all the parts and not getting first crack at any new developments), but he was keen to prove the team wrong. Unlike the previous campaign where Swift and Vector had been in the mix, Van Diemen locked out the top four positions in the British Championship – Darren Malkin and Vitor Meira claiming third and fourth respectively – with the French Mygale the only other chassis to claim a win during the season.

Arriving at Brands Hatch, if the weekend went the way of the season, the expectation was that the Festival would be a victory lap for Kolby and Van Diemen. That proved to be just about right.

After two dry years, the weather in 1996 was ferocious and steadily worsening as Sunday progressed; the semi-finals held in greasy conditions, the final in a torrential downpour that at any other meeting might have led to the officials calling an early finish. After a gap of a couple of years, the event would once more be filmed by the BBC's cameras, with 30 minutes of highlights shown the following week.

As expected, Kolby and Webber were at the head of the pack for their semi-finals. Webber duly converted victory, holding off Jacky van der Ende, with the Dutchman getting the most out of his Mygale. A hugely impressive third went to Tommy Field, who fended off French champion David Terrien. Field, in a year-old car, had impressed during the second half of the season as the frontrunner in the 'first division' class of the national championship (for older cars), but was not expected to be in this territory.

The other semi-final went the way of the third works Van Diemen of Vitor Meira, who benefitted from a disastrous race for Kolby. Initially looking set for a comfortable win, Kolby twice slid off at Graham Hill Bend, eventually netting a sixth-row start for the final which all but put him out of contention. Third went to Darren Malkin, whose mid-year run of four wins had shown he could mix it at the front.

Another emerging story from the semi-finals was the pace of Michael Vergers. A Festival star of the late-1980s, Vergers hadn't quite been able to kick on up the single-seater ladder. A ride height infringement had him starting with a ten-second penalty in his semi-final, where he charged through to ninth. The pace was there, but a win from 16th on the grid was a near impossible task.

The final was settled early on. Van der Ende initially led from Webber, the Mygale pilot heading the first couple of laps. It wasn't long before Webber was through and seemed comfortable, although Field in his old car was keeping him honest. Meanwhile, Kolby hit disaster, entirely innocent as he was collected by a spinning Terrien on the exit of Druids.

Webber's progress was interrupted following an incident along approach Paddock as Andy Booth tangled with Swiss champion Iradj Alexander-David. It was the latter who came off worse, thumping nose-first into the tyre wall. With the slightly woozy driver requiring attention, the red flags came out. Aside from those in wrecked cars, the big loser was Vergers, who had been steadily moving through the order and finding the conditions very much to his liking.

The weather remained inclement for the restart. The race, run over the dreaded aggregate, gave Webber an inbuilt advantage over his rivals, particularly the flying Vergers. In the event he need not have worried. After some initial pressure from Field, he was soon able to build up a comfortable gap over the pack. Field and Vergers engaged in battle, but Field knew the aggregate position meant that just keeping close to Vergers would be sufficient. It finished that way, Webber the commanding winner ahead of a stellar Field, and an unfortunate Vergers who might have gone at least one place better but for the red flags.

Webber, after a season where he'd played second fiddle to Kolby, used the Festival victory and BBC *Grandstand* coverage to move onward to Formula 3. Within six years, following a stint as a works Mercedes sportscar driver, the Australian had made it to Formula 1, scoring fairy-tale points on his Melbourne debut. In a career that ran through to the end of 2013, Webber took nine victories for the Red Bull team, whilst becoming a fan favourite and one of the most popular drivers of his generation.

Even after his Festival disaster, Kolby was still seen as a future star, becoming a strong British F3 frontrunner. His career lost momentum during a difficult Formula 3000 season in 2000 where he endured five straight non-qualifications despite running with the crack DAMS team. When his sponsors went under a couple of years later, Kolby's career ground to a halt.

Field also progressed to Formula 3000, albeit under the most bizarre of circumstances. The British Formula 3000 championship had struggled its way through the 1990s, more often than not with fewer than ten cars at each round. For the season opener in 1997, just three drivers arrived at Brands Hatch and Field was among them. In a race punctuated by a spurious safety car, he finished third, earning the rare distinction of a podium and last place, before the season was cancelled. Thereafter, Field has been a regular at Brands Hatch in Super Silhouettes.

1996 would prove to be the Festival's final BBC appearance. The loss of Formula 1 rights at the end of the season and near-exclusive focus on the BTCC ended an on-off 12-year partnership. The 1996 coverage was well produced and full of entertaining action, introducing several names – most notably Webber's – to casual viewers. Hereafter, the Festival would be filmed and televised most years, but coverage would largely be on Sky Sports and Motors TV. Whilst the productions themselves were normally of a high quality, the audience would be appreciably smaller. If the broadcast ambitions were dimmed, the same couldn't be said of Ford's ambitions for 1997, where the Festival would be rebranded the Formula Ford World Finals.

Final years as the World Cup of motorsport

AFTER THE washout of the previous year, 1997 was the first season in which the Festival Sunday would see the frontrunners on slick tyres for the final.

After showing well in 1996, Jacky van der Ende had switched to Van Diemen, landing the plum Duckhams-supported works drive. This proved to be something of a mixed blessing: on the one hand flattered to be courted by the top team from the previous season, on the other Van Diemen had overflowing order books, which meant some rivals got their hands on the '97 car over a month before the Dutchman.

As the season unfolded, it proved to be no hindrance to Van der Ende, who claimed the British title from the pair of Heywood Racing Mygales in the hands of Ricardo Sperafico and Richard Tarling. As is often the case, it was pacy series newcomers who really caught the eye – in this case Dan Wheldon and Aluizio Coelho, both in Andy Welch-prepared Van Diemens. Still running in support of the BTCC, Formula Ford was ever more professional but still fighting for elbow room against Formula Vauxhall Junior and Formula Vauxhall Lotus. Whilst grids were healthy, they weren't huge, particularly as there hadn't been an influx of competitive clubmen to fill out the pack in older cars.

For 1997, the Festival was significantly rebadged in the hope of giving a promotional boost to both category and event. The initial proposals were unveiled at the 1996 Festival, with Formula 1, Formula 3 and World Rally test drives, along with a £20,000 cash award announced as part of the prize pot. The meeting was to be renamed the Formula Ford World Finals, with entries limited to the top six finishers from each of the national Formula Ford series running to Zetec regulations. Intended to boost interest in the Zetec category, which had not been universally adopted, the proposals met with a tentatively promising response – team principals welcomed the investment push but were concerned that the entry criteria could leave many drivers on the sidelines.

The format was also rejigged somewhat, with Saturday given over to pre-qualifying races. Those progressing would then join one of the three heats on Sunday morning. Automatic qualification to the heats was awarded to the frontrunners of the various national Formula Ford championships. With the heats directly forming the grid for the final, the priority for the frontrunners was to progress with as little drama as possible. The winner of the fastest heat would claim pole, but the victor of the slowest heat would start from the second row. For the favourites, the heats proved to be somewhat perfunctory.

Tarling's heat was the quickest, giving him pole for the final. Tarling had never quite seemed on the pace for much of the season but was at one with his Mygale, giving him a comfortable win. Wheldon, meanwhile, occupied the outside of the front row for the final, taking victory in his heat from the works Van Diemen of Vitor Meira. Van der Ende, meanwhile, did what he needed to claim his heat, but the race was held in damp conditions and was thus slower, condemning him to the second row for the final.

With only one race to dial themselves into the weekend, the foreign challengers were at a disadvantage without the opportunity to progress through the field over multiple qualifying races. The week of pre-event testing would help with outright pace, but racecraft tricks would need to be honed in racing conditions. This meant the bulk of the front of the field for the final would be the British Championship regulars.

From pole, Tarling made the best start to take an early lead from Wheldon and Van der Ende. As was so often the case in the Festival final, Van der Ende found the works Van Diemen to be perfectly set up for the conditions. Thus emboldened, he darted to the inside of Wheldon, heading into Paddock on lap two before setting about Tarling. A lap later he tried a repeat, but Tarling was able to repel the challenge.

On lap five, van der Ende tried to the outside at Paddock and this time Tarling had no answer, the lead decisively falling into the hands of the Dutchman. Thereafter, there was no real battle for the lead as Tarling kept the pressure on but was never quite close enough to challenge. Nonetheless it was an impressive end to a disappointing season for Tarling.

With, barring disaster, the first two places settled, the focus turned to lower down the order as the battles became increasingly frantic for the remaining podium places. First to depart was Meira, whose overoptimistic challenge on Wheldon for third ended in the Paddock tyre wall. Wheldon was delayed, promoting Matt Davies and Paul Edwards, before they slowed each other at Graham Hill Bend. Reinstated to third, Wheldon's race ended in the Paddock gravel trap with Davies – the pair colliding after an overambitious move from Davies didn't work out.

Third place seemed increasingly cursed as Edwards now took over in the chase for the final rung on the rostrum. The American almost made it to the flag before being torpedoed by Robert Lechner at the final corner, the Austrian's desperate move removing both from contention. This elevated Sperafico to third. The Brazilian had endured a troubled weekend, lining up 17th on the grid for the final, but ultimately enjoying a fairy-tale result.

Despite the image reboot and enhanced promotion, it wasn't a classic Festival. The condensed format of the main event meant some of the magic of the weekend had been lost. Memories of the Festival depended on the strength of a handful of races – and in 1997, for the first time in the Zetec era, the entertainment levels had dimmed.

The official video also served to sell the event short. Unlike the BBC coverage, which was filmed from high vantage points enabling viewers to get a perspective of the rhythm of the races, the 1997 coverage was filmed from trackside positions with the cars in close-up shots. It was difficult to get a sense of how the races were unfolding and didn't really capture Formula Ford in its best light.

For the winner, success didn't prove to be the career rocket fuel of many of his predecessors. Successive seasons in Formula Opel (the European branding of Formula Vauxhall Lotus), German Formula 3 and Formula Palmer Audi were competitive but didn't yield victories or titles, before van der Ende's single-seater career petered out.

Tarling enjoyed more immediate success, winning the 1999 Formula Palmer Audi championship before hitting the traditional funding barrier and being unable to move up the ladder. However, he has enjoyed something of a second life in Formula Ford and has spent much of the past decade as a perennial frontrunner in a plethora of classic Formula Ford 1600s.

Of the podium finishers, it was Sperafico who came closest to Formula 1, finishing runner-up in the 2003 Formula 3000 championship, having been a frontrunner for a few seasons. He then made the move to the USA, but a season in IndyCar proved frustrating and unsuccessful. For the past 15 years, he has been a perpetual frontrunner in a range of Brazilian sports and touring car series.

After the razzmatazz of 1997, in 1998 the Festival returned to its more traditional format as Ford withdrew backing. Whilst some of the prizes might have disappeared, the prestige remained and interest stayed high. Not least because that season's star, Jenson Button, was already making a name for himself outside the usual motorsport circles. With Button's emergence and nine of that year's Formula 1 grid being Formula Ford graduates, the category remained as relevant as ever.

The British Championship had been won by Button, who had enjoyed a season-long battle with Derek Hayes, with both Dan Wheldon and Nicholas Kiesa snapping at their heels. That Button and Kiesa made it to Formula 1 and Wheldon became a multiple Indianapolis 500 winner gives an indication of the quality at the front of the field.

Button was the narrow favourite for the Festival, but Mygale had yet to get the best of Van Diemen at the event. Alongside Wheldon, Hayes and Kiesa, in the mix were two promising Australians, Marcos Ambrose and David Besnard, again both good picks with Ambrose twice becoming V8 Supercar champion in Australia and a two-time NASCAR winner. In total, the entry exceeded 80 cars, and whilst there were a few club-level drivers filling out the field, it once more felt as if the cream of European single-seater talent would be on the grid. This reflected the wider context of dimming fortunes for both Vauxhall-backed categories and Formula Renault being perceived as an interim category between Formula Ford and Formula 3.

The format, tweaked again from the previous year, saw the reintroduction of heats for all competitors. The field was split across four heats, before progressing to semi-finals and the final with a last-chance race. With no space for quarter-finals, cars would fall by the wayside in every race, leaving no margin for error. For spectators, the event timetable didn't lend itself to a weekend of non-stop Formula Ford action: heats on Saturday, the semi-finals opening proceedings on Sunday morning, the last-chance race mid-afternoon and grand final to close out the day.

Held on a waterlogged track, Saturday's heats swiftly became a matter of survival, with a couple of possible contenders falling by the wayside. The first was Tom Sisley, who dominated much of the first heat until a puddle at Graham Hill Bend a couple of laps from the end pitched him into a spin where he collected an abandoned car, eliminating him. This gave victory to Derek Hayes.

Heat two saw polesitter Craig Murray fail to progress. Having lost the lead early on to Wheldon, he spun in worsening weather at Hailwood Hill, damaging his car and slipping out of the qualifying positions. For Wheldon, it was a comfortable win. With standing water now all around the circuit, the final brace of heats was delayed and reduced in distance. Button won a strong third heat from Ambrose and Kiesa, whilst Rob Collard took a comfortable win in the fourth from Neil Shanahan.

Sunday dawned dry and with anticipation in the air. The strength in depth of the field was formidable, and the slightest error could well mean a poor starting slot for the final or elimination from the meeting. The first encounter saw Haywood Racing Mygale team-mates Button and Hayes locking out the front row ahead of Ambrose in the works Van Diemen. Button made a good start but Hayes less so, allowing Ambrose to challenge for and claim second on the run up to Druids. It was clear that the Van Diemen, as was so often the case in October, was the form car. Ambrose proved the point by making his move on Button into Druids on the second lap. Pushed off-line, Button was also passed by Hayes.

As a queue formed behind Hayes, Ambrose was able to move clear, building up an unassailable advantage. Button started to really apply the pressure as Hayes was pitched off into a nasty accident at Paddock. Initially thought to be an error, the issue was ultimately diagnosed as a broken rose joint, leaving the Ulsterman a passenger as he plunged into the tyres. Given the gap to Ambrose, Button could do little more than settle for second. Behind was Jean Christophe Ravier who finished third following a charge through the pack. For another pre-event favourite, Kiesa, it was a race to forget, fifth place giving him ninth on the grid for the final, his chances of victory slender at best.

The second semi-final saw the works Van Diemens of Collard and Wheldon sharing the front row, Collard with the advantage due to a slightly quicker heat. Collard made the better start, with Shanahan slotting into second – albeit briefly as a broken fuel pump put him out before the first lap was completed. It was a brief respite for Collard, as Wheldon was through at Druids on lap three and led thereafter to the flag. Behind, Collard was pressured for much of the race by French champion Anthony Gheza. Gheza was the innocent victim of a late incident, where he was taken out by Timo Bernhard after the German had been forced on to the grass by Barry Horne.

The protagonists then needed to wait the best part of the day before forming up for the final to decide the winner. With Wheldon and Ambrose locking out the front row, it looked good for a fourth successive Van Diemen Festival victory. Button, however, had other ideas. After passing Wheldon at McLaren on lap three, he then set about Ambrose. Immediately, the pair engaged in battle, with Wheldon poised just behind.

It was an intense fight with the pair swapping places, but Ambrose seeming to slightly have the upper hand as the race progressed. Realising there was no way through if Ambrose stayed on the defensive inside line, Button thought tactically, saying to *Autosport*, 'I knew he would take a defensive line if I was close to him at McLaren, so I dropped a couple of lengths at Graham Hill [Bend]. It worked, and he opened the door at McLaren.'

The manoeuvre allowed Button to get his nose ahead, but as Ambrose inevitably tried to close the door, the pair clashed and the Australian was out. The day wasn't done for Button as Wheldon was all over his tail, but ironically the waved yellow flags for his team-mate's stricken car, which prevented passing, put paid to Wheldon's chances. After his disastrous semi-final, Kiesa put in a powerful drive to finish third.

It was victory then for Button, completing the British Championship and Festival double, and an important win for

Mygale, breaking the run of Van Diemen success and becoming the first non-British manufacturer to win the Festival.

It had been another great Festival. Although it had fewer races than in the past, Sunday's action was spectacular throughout. It was also one of the last 'all-star' Festivals, with many of the main protagonists progressing to the top of the sport.

Speaking to *Autosport* on the podium, Button commented, 'Before the weekend I thought a Festival win would just be a bonus. Now I realise it's much more. It's the biggest moment of my career.' It was, but not for long. An impressive debut season in British Formula 3 led to an invitation by Williams to take part in a shootout for the team's second Formula 1 seat (alongside Ralf Schumacher) for the 2000 season. Button got the drive, kicking off a 16-year Formula 1 career that brought him the 2009 world title.

Like many of his predecessors, Button was propelled to Formula 1 by his Festival success – however, he would be the last Festival winner to make the step to the top of the sport. Formula Ford would remain the pre-eminent junior category for a few more seasons, but Button was the last of the great generation of Festival champions to go all the way.

For Wheldon, there was also glory, but in the USA, where he twice won the Indianapolis 500 and the 2005 IndyCar title. Tragically, Wheldon was killed in an awful accident in Las Vegas in 2011, on the Sunday evening following the 40th running of the Festival. Kiesa just about made it to Formula 1, competing in five races for the struggling Minardi team at the end of 2003, before his career gradually petered out over the coming years.

The 1998 Festival would also be the final event of significance held on the Indy circuit in the layout that had been used since the early 1970s. During the winter, Graham Hill Bend was significantly remodelled, the fast sweep being replaced by a much tighter left-hand bend preceded by a heavy downhill braking zone. Whilst the reprofiled corner created a new overtaking opportunity, it removed some of the rhythm and flow from the lap and received a mixed reception from drivers.

Formula Ford ended the millennium as fiercely competitive as ever, the campaign once more a two-chassis battle between Van Diemen and Mygale. It was the French marque that again prevailed, the Heywood Racing-run cars of Nicolas Kiesa and Craig Murray taking the top two placings in the standings. Third in the points went to Ricardo van der Ende, younger brother of 1997 Festival winner Jacky, who led the Van Diemen charge in the Duckhams-liveried car. Also consistently featuring at the front of the field were the brace of Van Diemen-propelled Australians, James Courtney and 1998 nearly-man Marcos Ambrose, along with Tom Sisley who had been so unfortunate in his heat 12 months previously.

Overshadowing the season was the tragic death of Neil Shanahan on the second May bank holiday at Oulton Park. Involved in a heavy multi-car accident, Shanahan suffered unsurvivable injuries. His death hit the paddock hard. Incidents of this gravity were a rarity in both the category and the wider era of the sport. As with the death of Peter Rogers in 1987, Shanahan's memory lives on at the Festival with the Neil Shanahan Memorial Trophy being presented to the Festival winner. Where possible, Neil's parents Liam and Mary do the honours, stealthily appearing in the commentary box to enjoy the best view in the house for the final.

After being a focal point in the spectator calendar early in the decade, the Festival had slipped down the pecking order and was no longer a top-tier event. Whilst the event still drew a decent (if ever-declining) crowd, the circuit was at its busiest for the World Superbike weekend, with the British Superbikes, BTCC and historic events being the other main draws.

As ever, the Festival build-up consisted of days of testing in advance of the weekend. Alongside the usual suspects from the British title fight were the returning veteran Michael Vergers making his fifth Festival bid in a Tatuus chassis and the relatively unknown Finnish teenager Kimi Raikkonen in a Van Diemen.

A quartet of heats on Saturday would whittle down the field, and from the outset the racing was tense and exciting, with the drivers treating each race as if it were the final. The first of the heats was one of the less entertaining and went to Raikkonen, who led home Sisley. Changeable weather precipitated tyre gambles for heat two, with the front row of Ambrose and Robert Dahlgren opting for wets, whilst many of those behind risked slicks. A brief shower in the early laps enabled Ambrose to break clear, whilst Dahlgren, suffering from mechanical issues, was soon embroiled in a multi-car scrap for second. This came to a head when a flu-stricken Jeffrey Jones challenged into Druids but dropped a wheel on to the wet grass, taking three others with him for company. All this gave Ambrose a fairly comfortable win.

It was a two-way fight for the honours in heat three, with Kiesa defending heavily from Courtney throughout. The Dane in the Mygale had enough in the tank, but, ominously, Courtney's challenge grew stronger with each passing lap. The romantics were denied their day when local hero Mark Marchant, who'd qualified third, wouldn't restart after losing power whilst heading from the paddock to the grid.

It was another duel for the final heat, with van der Ende and Murray engaging in a 'ferocious dogfight' in *Autosport*'s words. Having crashed out of the heats a year earlier, van der Ende wanted the minimum of fuss, but Murray was all over him, losing his nose cone when it all got a bit too close. A late mistake from Murray saw him traversing the gravel at Paddock before he recovered to fourth. This gave Van Diemen their third win of the heats with van der Ende having vanquished Murray's Mygale.

Sunday morning dawned damp and greasy with an all-Scandinavian front row for the first semi-final – Raikkonen heading Kiesa on the grid. The talk overnight had been whether Raikkonen could emerge as a left-field candidate for overall victory, but national champion Kiesa would be a stern test. Kiesa more than rose to the challenge, using circuit knowledge and experience to make the most of his outside grid slot, finding traction in the wet on the wide line at Paddock to move past Raikkonen on the run to Druids. Thereafter, Kiesa was able to control the race, opening up a second or so advantage over Raikkonen without taking any undue risks. It was job done for Kiesa as he took the flag and secured a front-row position for the final.

Behind, the crowd enjoyed a three-way battle for second, with Raikkonen joined by heat rival Sisley and Courtney. Once more hitting his stride as the race unfolded, Courtney made his move on the final lap, cleanly launching to the inside at Paddock to secure second. Raikkonen then came home third ahead of Sisley. Behind, much of the attention was being drawn by Vergers, who eased through from the back of the grid to finish an impressive seventh.

The second semi-final was not dissimilar to the first, albeit with what was felt to be the stronger side of the draw, with Duckhams Van Diemen team-mates van der Ende and Ambrose sharing the front row. Ambrose got the better start and, as Kiesa had done earlier, was able to open a small gap with ease before controlling the race. Crucially, the track was drier than the earlier race, meaning that the winner would be starting the final from pole. With that in mind, Ambrose did exactly what he needed to take a comfortable victory, one that signalled he had more in reserve for the final.

Once more it was the battle for second that provided the entertainment, with van der Ende and Murray picking up where they'd left off in their heat. In itself, this was strong going from Murray, who'd moved from eighth on the grid to take his shot at van der Ende. Much as in the heat, van der Ende proved immovable, with Murray eventually overcooking it in his efforts to move past. A late spin for the Scot ended the battle, but Murray was able to recover to third.

After poor weather for nearly the entire weekend, the track had dried out for the final, meaning the 28-car field were all on slicks. Starting from pole position and given his pace to date, Ambrose was the clear favourite. After almost winning the year before, Ambrose certainly had unfinished business with the Festival.

The Australian converted pole position to lead away from Kiesa with van der Ende and Courtney next along. Raikkonen's hopes were dashed on the second lap when he dived to the inside of Courtney at McLaren, making contact and spinning into retirement. With cars scattering, Murray was the big winner, moving into fifth. Already with a two-second cushion after just three laps, it seemed as if Ambrose was set for an emphatic victory.

Then disaster struck the Australian once more. Midway round the fourth lap, his gear linkage sheared leaving him with no option but to retire into the pits. The rueful Ambrose commented to *Autosport*, 'this is harder to take than last year, because I'd done all the hard work and it was there for the taking.'Kiesa was duly elevated into the lead, but all was not well with the Mygale. Losing third gear during the warm-up lap, the Dane was having to drive around the issue, his subsequent pace meaning escape was impossible. Van der Ende piled on the pressure, forcing Kiesa into an error at Graham Hill Bend, the subsequent recovery allowing the Van Diemen pilot to snatch the lead into Surtees. A leading quartet of van der Ende, Kiesa, Courtney and Murray formed for a few laps before, in the space of two corners, both Courtney and Murray managed to depose Kiesa. The moment of action enabled van der Ende to make a decisive break, aided by Courtney and Murray starting to dispute second.

At three-quarter distance van der Ende had enough of an advantage to see off a late challenge from Courtney, who was finally released as Murray started to suffer from a slow puncture. Thus van der Ende scored Van Diemen's 16th Festival triumph and, alongside brother Jacky two years previously, became the first pair of siblings to win the event. It wasn't quite a classic final, but it had been an enjoyable weekend's racing where some promising new names had taken the fight to the established favourites.

As ever the relative strength of the field only became clear a couple of years after the event as the drivers graduated up the ladder. 1999 certainly had a great strike rate for onward progress, although not for the winner. The Festival was almost van der Ende's single-seater swansong. After a year on the sidelines in 2000, he claimed the title in the sole season of the Formula Chrysler Euroseries (a scarcely supported attempt to bridge the gap between Formula 3 and Formula 3000) before making the transition to touring and sportscars where he has enjoyed considerable success, particularly at GT4 level.

Murray would also struggle to progress his career beyond Formula Ford. A brief run in Formula 3 in 2001 precipitated a return to the Festival a year later. Two of the 28 from the final did make it to Formula 1: Kiesa and Raikkonen. Whilst Kiesa's time in Formula 1 was brief, Raikkonen may well go down as a legend of the sport. Stepping into Formula Renault for the 2000 season (after taking a clear sweep in the 1999 winter series), the Finn won seven of the ten races to utterly dominate the season. Clearly a rare talent, Sauber swooped, signing him to Formula 1 for the 2001 season. Announcing his retirement in the summer of 2021, Raikkonen had racked up 21 wins and 103 podiums across a career topping over 350 starts, his greatest achievement being the 2007 world title.

At the time, however, it was the Australians Courtney and Ambrose who were the ones tipped for greatness. For a brief period at Courtney was regarded by many as a generational talent. He would cement his reputation with a stellar 2000 Formula Ford season, racking up more wins than any other driver in the history of the category. Signed by Jaguar to race in their Formula 3 team and as a Formula 1 test driver, the path to the top seemed assured. Courtney's career momentum was sapped by an enormous Formula 1 testing accident at Monza in 2002. His injuries were more severe and recovery longer than was reported at the time, so Courtney wasn't at peak performance for over a year. By the time he won the 2003 Japanese Formula 3 title, his shot at Formula 1 seemed to have passed; instead he returning to Australia where a 15-plus-year career in the Supercars series yielded one title and multiple race wins.

Without the backing enjoyed by Courtney, Ambrose had a solitary and unsuccessful Formula 3 season in France and the UK before also returning to Australia. He immediately established himself as one of the top Supercars drivers of his generation – he only raced in the category for four seasons, twice taking the title and never finishing below third in the points. Thereafter he moved to the USA to take on the challenge of NASCAR, where he adapted well to the ovals but became a star in the road-course events, winning twice at Watkins Glen.

After the promise of the 1999 season, 2000 was another strong year. Tom Gaymor, who competed in the category a year later said, 'It was box office. People went to the TOCA (BTCC) meetings for the touring cars and Formula Ford. The racing was great'

Courtney in the works Van Diemen took the title following an acrimonious battle with Mark Taylor in the Mackie Motorsport Mygale. Also topping the podium had been another Mygale – Heywood Racing's Anthony Davidson, triumphant 12 months earlier in the Kent class trophy race at the Festival. Finishing the season strongly was Robert Dahlgren in another of the works Van Diemen's, who won two of the final three races. This quartet were certainly the favourites heading into the weekend, but as ever there was scope for surprises to be sprung.

There was a downbeat note coming into the weekend, with the news of John Nicol's passing. For many years Nicol had been the officiating heartbeat of the event and his loss was be keenly felt.

Behind the scenes there had been big changes too. In late November 1999, Foulston sold Brands Hatch Leisure to Octagon, the sporting division of marketing group Interpublic. The circuit had been approached by Interpublic and Foulston, at that point wishing for a change of direction, decided to sell. After a decade in charge, Foulston had kept the track as a motorsport venue and left having earned a significant profit on the family's original investment. Octagon took over the circuit largely on the proposition of bringing the British Grand Prix back to Kent, albeit at what would have been a hugely remodelled Brands Hatch. For a variety of reasons this never happened, and much of Octagon's time as owners was spent looking for an out after it transpired they had significantly overpaid for their assets.

The quartet of heats were run on a wet Saturday afternoon. Taylor was the first into action, winning the opener after withstanding some early pressure from Peter Gray before pulling out an over-six-second buffer. Third place went to future Red Bull and Minardi Formula 1 racer Robert Doornbos. Davidson was similarly emphatic in the second heat, steadily pulling away from the rest from pole, with an equally comfortable second-place finish for German champion Marc Benz. The story of the race was the fight for third, which eventually swung in favour of veteran fast-man Michael Vergers.

The story of heat three was similarly perfunctory, Dahlgren running out a comfortable winner from Adam Carroll. Once more the interest came in the dice for third with Gary Catt making a bold move on Olli Kaurala at Druids to secure the place. There was only really jeopardy for the lead in the final heat, where Alx Danielsson upset the form book by taking a last-gasp pole position in the Vector. This left Courtney with more work than expected, taking until lap four to pass Danielsson. For a time it seemed as if he was set for a comfortable win, but, once he'd raced his way into clear air, Richard Goransson was able to chase down Courtney, ensuring a very close final few laps. Third went to Danica Patrick, the American immediately vindicated in her decision to switch to Heywood Racing for the weekend.

Although Sunday morning dawned without rain, the track was still very damp from Saturday's precipitation, making for treacherous conditions. It was also clear from the early stages of the opening semi-final that neither the Mygale nor Van Diemen teams had got their cars working perfectly for the whole lap. The opening and arguably slightly weaker semi-final saw Taylor and Dahlgren front row, with Gray and Carroll next along. The outcome was decided at the start when Dahlgren made the better start from the outside to head Taylor into Paddock. Whether it was caution or the conditions, Taylor stayed put, leaving Dahlgren to take a clear victory. In what was probably the most settled race of the day, most of the positions remained static. Replaying Saturday's action, the most podium jeopardy came in the early dispute for third, where Gray and Carroll swapped places before the former assumed a clear advantage on the second lap.

Fortunately, the second semi-final was more entertaining, although not for the win. After making the better start, Davidson fended off some initial parries from Courtney before the pair settled down, content to lock out first and third on the grid for the final, with the race being held on a drier and faster track. Third went to the wily Vergers after several laps back and forth with Goransson until the Swede rotated through the gravel at Paddock and dropped to 14th from where he would have to take his chances in the last-chance race. Also in the wars was Benz, whose first-lap spin at Paddock ended his challenge. Whilst Goransson and Benz faltered, both Robin Rudholm and Patrick impressed, the former finishing fourth from ninth on the grid, whilst Patrick maintained the form from her heat to finish fifth.

Steffan de Groot led throughout the five-lap last-chance race whilst Goransson failed to progress – more early incidents preventing him from progressing to the final. Goransson's adventures aside, this was one of those rare Festivals where all the outright favourites enjoyed a trouble-free run through the qualifying races not only to progress to the final, but also to lock out the front of the grid as well.

Davidson had pole from Dahlgren, with Courtney and Taylor just behind. It promised to be a classic final. The conditions had continued to improve throughout the day, with the circuit now fully dry – the paddock view being that this might just favour the Van Diemens.

The leading quartet moved away in grid order and immediately formed a single, inseparable train at the front. The first change in the order came as Dahlgren had a slight lock-up at Paddock into the second lap, allowing Courtney through into second. Whilst Davidson held firm at the front, the chopping and changing continued, although by lap 13 Courtney was shuffled down to fourth, the consequence of his own challenge for the lead and the ripple effect of Dahlgren's next effort. Taylor meanwhile, was quietly in third and waiting for his moment.

Behind, Gray, Patrick and Vergers had also been dicing, Vergers slipping down the order as he couldn't quite overcome an underpowered engine. Lap 14 triggered the next pivotal moment when Ferdinand Kool and Kaurala came together at Paddock in a sizeable incident. Although both drivers were uninjured, the red flags came out to safely remove the damaged cars.

It was decided that the final was to be restarted, as a five-lap sprint, with the quartet of protagonists once more securing the top two rows. As the lights changed, they immediately slotted back into grid order – Davidson from Dahlgren, Taylor and Courtney. The dispute over third became the first flashpoint, not least because Gray, Rudholm and Patrick were all in close attendance.

Courtney, anxious to clear Taylor as soon as possible for a shot at the leading duo, challenged into Paddock on the second lap. The move was only semi-complete as they arrived at Druids, with Courtney running wide. This delayed Rudholm and Patrick but enabled Gray to make it three-wide (with Courtney and Taylor) into Graham Hill Bend. That there would be an accident was visible from the International Space Station as Courtney lunged and speared into Taylor, with Gray also caught in the melee. Amazingly, all managed to continue but were out of the running. Speaking to *Autosport* in the heat of the moment, Courtney commented, 'I was either going to be last or first, it was a bit of a banzai move.' A somewhat more frustrated Taylor responded, 'It was a typical Festival move. His reaction was first or last, but I'd rather have been second than eighth.'The incident promoted Patrick to third and Rudholm fourth, but now with some daylight to the leaders. It was still unsustainably close between Davidson and Dahlgren, the latter constantly tapping the Mygale to try and force an error. Not that this was a particular worry for Davidson – pre-empting this tactic, the Heywood Racing team had reinforced his wishbones for the weekend. When that didn't work, Dahlgren launched a brave all-or-nothing move to the outside of Paddock, which almost paid off before a wet patch forced the Van Diemen to lose traction, ending the Swede's day in the gravel. With just a lap to run, Davidson knew the pressure was off as he took the chequered flag, a hugely deserving winner, heading an unexpected Heywood Racing 1-2 as Patrick took a superb second ahead of Rudholm.

It had been a wonderful final that brought together all the ingredients that drew the fans to Brands Hatch year on year. Any one of Davidson, Dahlgren, Courtney and Taylor could have won it. However, Davidson's astute defence from pole position once more proved that track position can trump all.

The nature of Zetec-era racing did slightly invoke the ire of columnist Marcus Pye, who used his weekly pulpit to reflect that the racing wasn't as good as it had been – the grip from the slick tyres making the cars far less of a handful than they had been and removing some of the excitement. Whilst there was definitely some truth to Pye's assertion – Davidson was not the only Zetec-era winner who achieved that feat by making a good start and sticking to the inside line – it came in the wake of what had been a brilliant Festival. The quality of the racing illustrated that it was possible to find an equilibrium between increasing professionalism and wheel-to-wheel action.

The 2000 season marked Davidson as a talent to watch, his form continuing in Formula 3 the following year when he finished runner-up in the championship to Takuma Sato. A year later, he was in Formula 1, starting two races for Minardi. Circumstances conspired to deprive Davidson of the Formula 1 stint his talent deserved and he only got one full season for Super Aguri in 2007 before more sustained success came in the World Endurance championship.

Patrick, meanwhile, had a seismic effect on American motorsport. Making her IndyCar debut in 2005 and immediately establishing herself as a frontrunner, she became the face of the sport. Scoring her only victory in 2008, a 2012 switch to NASCAR failed to deliver the hoped-for results. Her exposure has not been without criticism, particularly within NASCAR, but there is no doubt that during her career she introduced motorsport to a far broader audience.

After a thrilling 2000 Festival, the 2001 season proved to be hugely entertaining but ultimately Formula Ford's last golden year as a contemporary category. Van Diemen's Richard Goransson had swept the first three rounds of the season, before his form dipped and the title was fought out between Goransson's works team-mate Pat Long and Robert Dahlgren (also in a Van Diemen, but prepared by the Aztec Racing team). The title was decided in acrimonious fashion during the final round at Silverstone where Long and Dahlgren controversially collided. Long felt that Dahlgren had deliberately taken him out. Whilst that was hard to prove, the race footage suggested that Dahlgren had been overoptimistic in his passing attempt.

In all, Van Diemen won 12 of the 13 British Championship rounds, with Mygale scoring a solitary victory in the hands of Heywood Racing's Ronnie Bremer. Bremer's team-mate, Alan van der Merwe, finished third in the championship, consistency netting him six podiums.

2001 was at the height of the Van Diemen and Mygale rivalry. Broadcaster Tom Gaymor had been racing the Junior Formula Ford championship; such was the popularity of the series in 2001 that an overspill championship was needed for newcomers. He recalled, 'You sensed the rivalry from the moment you arrived. It was a bit like supporting Arsenal or Tottenham, you couldn't be on the fence. In Heywood, everything we did was about trying to beat Van Diemen; there were lots of underhand tactics to try and get into each other's head. For example, it was common to remove bolts from the floor, so that it would vibrate to create a different noise on the straights, suggesting a new engine tweak, when really it was just the floor rattling. Alan [van der Merwe] and Pat [Long] were at it all season, they'd do [destroy] nose cones running into each other at test sessions.'

The scene was set for another intriguing Festival, with the expectation once more that the title fight acrimony would spill over. Although the Mygales had struggled during the season, if it was a wet weekend the Heywood Racing cars could be expected to be at the front. In a boost to the Festival's profile, the intention was for Sky Sports to show same-day coverage on the Sunday evening, but on the day this didn't prove possible.

Unfortunately, it wasn't to be a replay of the 2000 thriller and torrential rain throughout Sunday served to temper some of the action. For the favourites, Saturday's task was to get through the heats without drama and into the semi-finals. The first heat saw Dahlgren, Long and Bremer all drawn together. It was the American Long who prevailed, making his move mid-race to decisively sweep past Dahlgren at Paddock. Bremer took third, with the race largely running to the form book.

The expected battle in heat two was between Goransson and polesitter Adam Carroll. Battle was never really joined. Goransson secured an immediate lead and was unheaded thereafter, whilst Carroll seemed content to hold on to second. With the pair well clear of the field, it was Westley Barber who took third after climbing up from fifth. The works Van Diemen squad celebrated three wins from three races with Robin Rudholm taking the flag in heat three following a dominant performance. There was good battling behind as a fine defensive drive from Rob Bell netted him second ahead of Ivor McCulloch. The concluding heat finally delivered something of an upset when Benelux champion Stefan de Groot took a lights-to-flag victory, jumping polesitter Gary Turkington at the lights. A strong drive from van der Merwe elevated him from fifth to second, whilst Turkington completed the podium.

A long-established Saturday night tradition was the Festival Forum at the Kentagon. Liberally lubricated by treats from the bar, Brian Jones would host the evening, interviewing an array of drivers and paddock personalities about their prospects for the following day and the general state of all things Formula Ford.

When Jones took his turn to interview Long and asked what would happen if he were behind Dahlgren the following day, the American made it quite clear that the outcome wouldn't be to Dahlgren's advantage.

The pair lined up together for the first semi-final, which proved to be highly controversial. Two red flags, a subsequent eight-lap dash and an ultimately disqualified winner provided more than enough talking points. At the first attempt, Long led Dahlgren until a pile-up behind the safety car (despatched so Ho Ping Tung could be recovered) on the third lap provoked a stoppage.

One of those involved was Gaymor: 'There was a concertina effect behind the safety car at Graham Hill Bend, we couldn't see anything. It was embarrassing really. The initial contact dislodged a wishbone as I spun off. I went into the barrier at low, low speed, but the damaged suspension pierced the cockpit and hit my foot. The marshal couldn't understand why I was screaming, but I was in agony. My grandad was the England rugby doctor at the time, so we piled into the car and went to the West Middlesex hospital where I was diagnosed with a chipped bone.'

Tung impressively instigated a second red flag too. Spinning once more, this time at Surtees, he was hit by several following cars. The stop-start proceedings were especially frustrating for Long, who had looked comfortable out front but had his advantage wiped out by the red flags. Third time around, it was Dahlgren who got the better start and immediately moved into a decent lead as Long came under pressure from Bremer.

By mid-races Long was snapping at Dahlgren's heels and had brought Bremer with him. It all came down to the final lap, when Long had a decent run at Dahlgren into Paddock. They made contact through the turn,but Dahlgren remained out front. Further contact followed on the way into and out of Druids, the latter incident pushing the Swede out wide. As Dahlgren came back to defend once more, there was further, stiffer contact with Long resulting in of Dahlgren spinning into the barriers and out of the race.

Long took the chequered flag from Bremer and Robin Rudholm, but his joy was short lived as he was excluded from the meeting following the incident with Dahlgren. Given the bad blood between the pair, the Festival was always going to be a flashpoint. Speaking to *Autosport*, Long claimed the move wasn't deliberate but added, 'I think he [Dahlgren] got what he deserved, but we both lost in the end.' Whatever the ins and outs, the leading pair from the British Championship wouldn't be in the final, throwing the overall outcome wide open but depriving the crowd of a repeat of the 2000 grudge match.

It was unreasonable to expect the second semi-final to match the drama of the first, but even so it was a dull race. The weather was slightly improved but the fully damp track didn't really lend itself to great dicing. The outcome was decided on the opening lap as Goransson got a better start than polesitter de Groot. Holding on to the outside line through Paddock, Goransson was decisively ahead into Druids and stayed there for the remainder. Van der Merwe made a superb move through Surtees and McLaren on lap two to secure second position from de Groot. Thereafter, the leading trio were all able to easily hold position, taking the flag in that order with few positional changes in the rest of the top ten.

By the time the final rolled around, the conditions had worsened considerably, with the circuit in a borderline waterlogged condition. Goransson had pole position by dint of his drier and less dramatic semi-final, the Van Diemen heading Bremer's Heywood Racing Mygale. The second Heywood car of van der Merwe would start third, ahead of Rudholm.

As the lights changed, the brace of Mygales made superb starts, Bremer blasting into the lead through the outside line, whilst van der Merwe held his nerve in a brave move to the inside of Goransson. With Carroll taking all Goransson's attention for the rest of the first lap, the Heywood Racing Mygales were able to move clear.

Much as the team might have wanted the cars to hold position, the drivers had discussed what to do in this situation beforehand. 'It was everyone for themselves,' van der Merwe remarked to *Autosport*. Consequently, he was right on Bremer's gearbox as they approached Druids for the second time. There was the tiniest of gaps to the inside at Graham Hill Bend and the South African went for it. Somehow he sneaked through in a move only permitted by Bremer's inherent fairness – the Dane could have easily closed the door at the risk of eliminating both from the race – and thereafter was able to pull away. Having never previously won a Formula Ford race, van der Merwe was in his element, setting fastest lap after fastest lap to build a reasonable buffer over Bremer.

With the top two positions settled, the battle for third commanded attention. Almost immediately Carroll was applying pressure to Goransson, the decisive moment coming on lap five. Carroll launched to the inside at Druids, but, as Goransson moved across, the pair made contact. Despite wishbone damage, Goransson was able to continue, but it was in a frustrated fourth. As he reflected to *Autosport* in the heat of the moment, 'I'm just pissed off … I am sure that if I had got a better start and lead I would have won.' Duly elevated into third, Carroll couldn't quite get on to terms with Bremer, but at the same time had enough to contain the wounded Goransson.

Despite his consistent season, van der Merwe wasn't a white-hot favourite coming into the weekend, but he claimed his first win with some style, taking the Festival final in dominant fashion from Bremer and Carroll.

The South African's subsequent career did take him to Formula 1, but not as a competitor. Having won the 2003 British Formula 3 title, van der Merwe's single-seater career ran out of steam, his last races coming in the A1GP category. Offered the chance to drive the Formula 1 medical car in 2009, he has been in the role ever since, shooting to mainstream prominence for his role in rescuing Romain Grosjean from the Bahrain inferno at the end of 2020.

During the 2001 season it seemed as if Formula Ford could do no wrong. The British Championship was oversubscribed and boasted incredible strength in depth along with superb racing. However, in 2002 interest in the category plummeted, and by the end of 2005 the Zetecs had been retired.

Decline and fall of the Zetecs

AFTER A boom year in 2001, interest in Formula Ford nosedived for the 2002 season, with two powerhouse teams – Duckhams Van Diemen and Panasonic Batteries Racing – accounting for all the victories and the top four placings in the championship. Unusually, the wins were concentrated on just three drivers: Westley Barber, Christian England and Jan Heylen. Compared to the constant fields of 30 cars in 2001, most events in 2002 saw just half that number take to the grid.

It was Barber who took the title after his seven-race winning streak to start the season proved impossible for his rivals to overhaul. Barber, a former La Filiere scholarship winner, had some serious PR heft behind him for the season too, making him the highest-profile Formula Ford driver since Jenson Button some four years previously.

Gaymor finished fifth in the championship, but didn't score a podium all season. Almost 20 years later and with an extensive driver coaching portfolio under his belt, he was clear on the reasons why Formula Ford experienced such a dip in interest: 'What I've now learnt is that junior ladder motorsport is like high street fashion, drivers will go where's cool. Renault, and the

Tatuus [FR2000], was the main reason that 2002 was a bogey year. I remember drivers seeing that car and the Formula Fords just didn't compare.'

Another factor would have been the sensational graduation of Kimi Raikkonen from Formula Renault directly to Formula 1 at the end of the 2000 season, putting stars in the eyes of a generation of hopefuls. Gaymor continued, 'The Zetecs were good cars, they were monstrously quick in a straight line. At places like Thruxton or Snetterton, you'd be catching the Formula 3s on the straights – we were doing something like 152-153[mph]. But then you had to brake really early; they were heavy too, so you had to scrub the speed off for the corners, you couldn't carry it through as otherwise you'd spin. The Avons [the championship tyre] were good tyres once you got the heat into them, but they were a nightmare when cold.

'In Formula Ford, drivers got such an experience that they miss now. The budget for a year was between £100k and £180k and for that you got so much seat time. We were testing so much, easily over 30 days during the season. Some weeks we'd be at Mallory Park on Wednesday and then off to Donington on Thursday. Today's drivers spend all their time in the gym or in a simulator; they don't spend enough time in their performance environment – certainly compared to other sports. In Formula Ford I learnt what it was like to be in a team and how to get the most out of a team – how to engage with mechanics, engineers and the like – and we could do a lot of that in private on test days. Today, drivers have to do all that on a race weekend and you see them making mistake after mistake.' The Festival promised to be an echo of the campaign that had preceded it, with a small field headed by a closely matched leading group. Just over 45 cars made it to Brands Hatch – the season regulars, one-off returnees, drivers stepping up from Junior Formula Ford and the usual continental challengers. Although Barber was the hot favourite, he had only won once in the second half of the season and it was his team-mate Heylen who was the form driver.

Saturday's three heats went largely with the form book, wins shared by Barber, Richard Goransson and Heylen. Goransson had the closest battle for the lead, taking victory in the second heat by just over a tenth of a second from Xavier Massen.

Gaymor meanwhile was having, in his view, a nightmare weekend: 'I'd had a big crash at Donington Park in the final round and although I didn't realise or understand it, I was suffering from the effects of concussion. I was nowhere during the weekend and feeling sick too from the concussion. In the end I had to withdraw.' Gaymor was somewhat self-deprecating as he finished fourth in his heat and seventh in the semi-final – admittedly not quite to the standard he'd want, but far from shabby.

As ever, the semi-finals saw the favourites starting to show their hands. Pitted against each other in the first semi-final, the battle between Barber and Heylen went much as per the form book from the season. Barber took a reasonably comfortable win by just under three seconds, with far closer competition for second where Heylen edged out Craig Murray by a couple of tenths. The second semi-final saw Ben Clucas, leading the Mygale charge for the weekend, take victory from Goransson. In a close race, the top three, completed by Christian England, were separated by under a second.

Barber's semi-final was the faster so he'd start from pole alongside Clucas – the latter looking to make it three Mygale Festival triumphs in succession. Slotting into second, Clucas immediately took the fight to Barber, the Mygale harrying the Van Diemen. On a slippery track and in fading light, the pressure paid off as Barber slid slightly wide at Clearways. Clucas had the speed as they accelerated into Clark Curve, but Barber chopped across the road, squeezing Clucas into the pit lane entry. The inevitable happened: the pair's wheels locked, the consequence being that Barber was fired off to the left, hitting the tyre barrier opposite the pit lane at near unabated speed. Winded, but fortunately without serious injury, while the race was stopped Barber could be helped from the car.

Although able to continue for the restart, Clucas had sustained some contact damage in the incident, which impeded the Mygale's handling. Consequently, he faded to fifth over the course of the 14 laps. Instead, Haylen stepped into the breach, ensuring the Duckhams Van Diemen team scored the win they expected. Goransson took second, whilst Dutch driver Jaap van Lagen completed the podium. Whilst Heylen was a deserving winner, the race-stopping incident between Barber and Clucas had deprived the crowd of a potentially great battle.

Despite the hype surrounding Barber, who was being touted in some quarters as the next Jenson Button, the required sponsorship to go all the way never materialised and his career petered out following a fine second in British Formula Renault in 2004. Heylen, meanwhile, has gone on to considerable sportscar success in the USA and van Lagen is widely regarded as one of Europe's top touring car racers. Once again, despite the relative paucity of grid size, many of the class of 2003 have gone on to enduring motorsport careers.

2003 was the last time until 2013 when Formula Ford was included on the TOCA package, with just over 25 cars to be found at each round. By this time, Simon Hill was working as a television commentator on the TOCA weekends: 'Formula Ford still felt relevant and there were some great drivers doing it, but it was becoming clear that the Renault route was becoming more relevant from a career perspective. Formula Renault just seemed to have stronger presence, and you no longer needed to do a year of [Formula] Ford before doing [Formula] Renault.'

In a season with no single standout driver, the title evolved into a three-way battle between Tom Kimber-Smith, Joey Foster and Finland's Valle Makela. Winning five races, more than anyone else, Kimber-Smith was a deserving champion in a Team JLR Van Diemen, although Makela's robust driving in the Nexa-prepared Van Diemen drew more headlines.

The Festival itself proved to be emblematic of the Zetec era, with the frontrunners all being closely bunched but the racing itself rarely thrilling. Championship runner-up Foster marked himself as the driver to beat, winning both his heat and semi-final.

He was run close by Gaymor: 'I'd worked up to third in the heat, and was going well in the semi. I'd just passed Joey for the lead when my engine seized coming out of Graham Hill Bend, I had to freewheel back to the pits. I was gutted as I would have won that race. The team did an amazing job to change the engine for the final, but it was the spare and I was effectively trundling round [Gaymor finished an impressive 11th]. We then got home to find the house had been burgled and completely ransacked – instead of celebrating a Festival success, we spent the evening with the Met Police.'

Estonian Marko Asmer won the other heat, before the perennially underfunded but rapid Ben Clucas won the semi-final in his Mygale. Clucas, who had been in the mix for victory 12 months earlier, could certainly be expected to take the fight to the hordes of Van Diemens.

Foster's semi-final proved to be the faster, giving him pole position from Clucas. Most expected the start to be all important, and so it proved with Foster slotting into an immediate lead. For the remainder of the 25 laps, Foster never had a substantial margin over the field, but by sticking tightly to the defensive line he was only rarely under significant pressure. Helping Foster's cause was the fact that Clucas gradually faded down the order, with Asmer climbing to finish second ahead of Tom Kimber-Smith.

2003 was a transitional year for Formula Ford. It lost its seat at the top table of junior championships. The Festival itself was notably lower profile, with the spectators barely filling the Paddock grandstand, let alone other spaces. Whilst the field for the British Championship had been healthy and competitive, that would change dramatically over the next two years.

By 2004, Formula Ford in the UK was no longer cool or sexy. The market demanded miniature Formula 1 cars, plush hospitality and slick marketing. The immense driver development benefits that Formula Ford offered were being lost in the noise and glitz of its rivals.

The British single-seater ladder was still topped by the British Formula 3 championship, which remained a direct feeder series to F1. Whilst not that high profile outside the industry, the quality of the teams and competition ensured a high-calibre field attracting top global talent. Many of the drivers in the category were placed in seats by their manufacturer or corporate driver development backers. Formula 3 remained the university of motorsport, building on the racecraft honed in previous years to teach engineering and setup skills, together with the millimetre-perfect precision required for a qualifying lap.

Formula 3 was generally regarded as a year two or three category, attracting graduates from a host of junior single-seater series. As such, it remained a natural bedfellow of, rather than rival to, Formula Ford. Instead, Formula Ford had two main competitors for the top karting graduates and racing newcomers – Formula BMW and Formula Renault. Both were heavily manufacturer-backed categories, running alongside the BTCC in the UK and internationally enjoying far more obvious links to Formula 1.

Launched in the UK ahead of the 2004 season and running for just four seasons, Formula BMW took Formula Ford's place on the TOCA package, supporting the BTCC and immediately enjoying 20-plus car grids. Several eminent drivers came through the series too, particularly in its final season – ex-F1 racers Bruno Senna and Marcus Ericsson and Formula E star Sam Bird being the most prominent – although given the publicity that surrounded its launch, not at a comparable strike rate to the far less fashionable Formula Ford.

Formula Renault was slightly different. Generally viewed as a second-rung category, although it was the entry point for Lewis Hamilton in 2001, in the early 2000s its popularity exploded throughout Europe with multiple well-supported national and regional championships. The success was such that during the decade the Tatuus chassis was the best-selling bespoke race car in the world. With entries well in excess of 25 cars for much of the decade, it was a boom time for the category, which was a natural next step for many Formula Ford graduates as well as top karters.

The Achilles heel for both series was the cost. They were significantly more expensive than Formula Ford – with the right team, it was possible to compete for the year in Formula Ford for the same cost as the bare Tatuus chassis. The financial element alone continued to push many talented drivers towards Formula Ford and it is arguably no coincidence that many of the top drivers from the era, who established their reputations based on talent alone, still came through the Formula Ford route.

Gaymor's reflections are similar: 'Renault and BMW killed Formula Ford; they effectively beat Ford at its own game, but realising they too could have a ladder to Formula 1. However, looking back at that era, Formula Ford had some really good drivers, and so many of them still have careers in the sport today.'

For the spectator, however, Formula Ford remained pre-eminent in terms of entertainment value. The turbulent air generated by the front and rear spoilers on the BMW and Renault cars made it near impossible for drivers to run in close packs. Additionally, the microscopically short braking distances added to the overtaking challenge. Consequently, many races, particularly at Brands Hatch, were crushingly processional, with almost no order changes. In Formula Renault, the qualifying sessions were often more entertaining than the races themselves, and arguably more significant for the outcome of the weekend.

With Formula BMW taking its place on the TOCA package, Formula Ford needed a new home for 2004. It found it running alongside the British Formula 3 and GT championships. From a driver career progression perspective, this was perfect as drivers could build relationships with the F3 teams and knew the environment they hoped to graduate into. However, the F3/GT package was a huge step down in terms of visibility, the tens of thousands of fans that flocked to BTCC meetings were replaced by tens at the F3 meetings – if it was sunny. The less glitzy environment did help push costs down, but whereas the fleet of Formula BMWs ran out of shiny team transporters, many of the Formula Fords were unloaded from a van.

The 2004 championship was still reasonably supported, with heavyweight multi-car entries coming from Team JLR and Nexa Racing, both of whom fielded Van Diemens, and the smaller Jamun squad with its Mygales. The season peaked at 20 cars for the Croft round, with grids at most events hovering between 15 and 18 drivers. The title fight was decided relatively early on, with Nexa's Valle Makela winning eight of the first ten races, followed by a tight battle for second between Dan Clarke and Sebastian Hohenthal – both of whom were consistent rather than spectacular. Instead, it was others in the field who caught the eye with sparkling pace tempered by inconsistency – American's Charlie Kimball and Joe D'Agostino, and Ireland's Charlie Donnelly all marked themselves as ones to watch.

This didn't bode well for a bumper Festival, and so it proved with just 30 cars entered for the event, mainly drawn from the British series plus a couple of Dutch and Scandinavian drivers. Given the grid capacity was 28 cars, only two unlucky competitors would miss out on making the final. On paper, things didn't look too auspicious, but the Festival again proved to be hugely interesting with some good races and moments of drama throughout the two days of competition.

The event also received a promotional push by Brands Hatch's new owners, Motorsport Vision (MSV). Headed by former Festival competitor Jonathan Palmer, the MSV group acquired the circuit (along with Oulton Park, Snetterton and

Cadwell Park) in January 2004. Outgoing owners Interpublic took a significant financial hit and Palmer set about returning the motorsport soul to the circuit whilst retaining profitability. Immediate changes included a smartening up of the venue, with impressive levels of tidiness and cleanliness that continue today. Likewise, there were competitor-centric investments that included extended run-off areas and improved paddock facilities. Palmer's entrepreneurial spirit meant that the 2004 Festival was more heavily promoted than several of its forebears, with a trial innovation of bookmakers setting up shop for the day. The immediate consensus was that all the changes were for the better.

The expected frontrunners were the British title contenders, Makela, Clarke and Donnelly being the main picks. Maybe it was the reduced threat of elimination or the changeable weather mixing things up, but the racing was ferocious throughout.

The format closely followed that of previous years with heats and semi-finals to decide the grid for the final. Given the slender entry, the last-chance race was dispensed with. The brace of heats largely went to form, with Clarke and Hohenthal splitting the wins. The only significant casualty was Donnelly, who crashed early on. If the heats had been intense rather than action-packed, in contrast the semi-finals were two of the wildest races enjoyed by the spectators (and endured in race control) for some time. After initially being stopped due to an incident, Dan Clarke took the shortened first semi-final by half a second from team-mate Joe D'Agostino, having led throughout, as only nine cars made it to the flag.

If that was attritional, the second race was even worse as just eight cars went the distance. There were incidents all over the place. Donnelly (again) and Duncan Tappy tangled early on, then a few laps later Kimball was upside-down in the gravel after a nasty coming together at Paddock. At the front, it was Makela who took victory from Hohenthal by just six-hundredths of a second after a frantic scrap. As the second semi-final went its scheduled distance, it would be Makela who would claim pole position for the final.

In race control, the destiny of pole position was low on the list of concerns for the stewards of the meeting. Only 17 cars had qualified by right for the final, and of those that had crashed, none appeared to have been damaged beyond repair – so how were they to fill the rest of the grid? In the event it was agreed that the drivers would draw lots for the remaining starting positions. Jason Down and Ryan Cannon were the two unfortunates who missed out on a slot as everyone else regrouped for the final.

Setting aside the chaos in the pack, the racing during the weekend had suggested the packed Paddock grandstand would be treated to a close final. So it proved with a see-saw race gradually whittling away the favourites.

At the lights, Makela and Hohenthal picked up exactly where they'd left off, running in precariously close company chased by Clarke and D'Agostino. The race was almost immediately disrupted when Ian Pratt rotated at Graham Hill Bend and was collected by Donnelly, eliminating one of the pre-event favourites. TV footage, still available online, shows a furious Donnelly stalking from his car to give Pratt's helmet a hefty slap, slamming his visor shut. In truth, Donnelly had overdriven all weekend and, whilst largely blameless for his third accident in as many races, starting from the rear of the field had been of his own making.

Once the safety car came in, the fight at the front restarted with unsustainable intensity. Things had to come to a head, and on lap ten they did as Makela was pushed wide at Graham Hill Bend. The kerfuffle enabled Dan Clarke to leap from third to first, with Makela now in chasing mode. Moments later, the safety car was out for a second time as Ian Parson and Suk Sandher collided. Released once more, with just nine laps to run, Makela started to push beyond the limit in his efforts to overhaul Clarke. This saw him drop down to fourth on lap 20 behind Yuya Sakamoto and Hohenthal before, a spin a few moments later demoted Makela to 15th at the flag – once more the British champion had fallen at the final hurdle in the Festival final. Compared with what had gone before the remaining laps were relatively stable as Dan Clarke took victory from Sakamoto and Hohenthal. It was Clarke's final act in Formula Ford before graduating to Formula 3. From there his career took him to IndyCar and, five years later, returned to Brands Hatch to represent Great Britain in the final A1GP event.

The 2004 Festival once more emphatically proved that, even with a depleted field, Formula Ford could still provide some superb action. Clarke's subsequent single-seater career took him to both the A1GP series where he represented Great Britain, and IndyCar, where he raced two seasons, netting a solitary podium.

For 2005, Formula Ford was once more running in support of Formula 3 but endured a further dip in popularity, with only six or so serious frontrunners committed for the campaign. The remainder of the field was padded out by guest drivers and several masking-tape specials – cars of yesteryear run by enthusiastic clubmen enjoying the chance to race at more prestigious meetings.

Behind the scenes, series bosses were taking proactive steps. Zetecs would be replaced at the end of the season by new Duratec regulations – a peppier, more powerful engine would improve performance, whilst the new breed of cars were more enjoyable to drive and contemporary in their appearance than their predecessors.

On track, Jamun team-mates Charlie Donnelly and Duncan Tappy produced an intriguing title fight in their red Mygales. In the early season, Donnelly did all the winning whilst Tappy seemed to contrive ever more unlikely ways not to take the chequered flag. The bad luck had to end, and once Tappy claimed victory mid-season at Castle Combe he was never again beaten to the line. Consistency paid off for Donnelly though, and he was able to massage his early-season points lead through to the title.

Heading into the Festival, the smart money was on Tappy, but with several upset winners over the past few seasons his coronation was far from certain. The event's prestige, combined with Formula Ford's enduring presence in Europe, meant that over 40 drivers made the trip to Kent. With representatives from Japan, Australia, the USA and most European nations, there was still evidence of Formula Ford's cachet. As had been the case since the turn of the decade, the field was almost entirely composed of Van Diemens and Mygales.

Two heats, semi-finals and a last-chance race would decide the grid for the grand final. The heats went to form, with Donnelly and Tappy both leading from lights to flag in their respective encounters, with neither race being particularly close.

The semi-finals, at least partially, told a different story. Whilst Tappy once more enjoyed a comfortable victory, Donnelly was beaten to second by Dennis Retera thanks to a last-lap move. It was another classic Festival thriller. For 17 laps Retera sat on Donnelly's gearbox, the cars running side by side over the line on more than one occasion. The other big twist was that the safety car had come out for two laps in Tappy's race, whilst Retera and Donnelly's battle was uninterrupted. Consequently, by dint of a faster overall race time, Retera would have pole position for the 25-lap final despite having led only one lap all weekend.

Since moving to the one-by-one grid formation, pole position for the final, with the relatively steeper uphill gradient, had proved to be a mixed blessing. So it was for Retera as Tappy took an immediate lead and instantly began to try to stretch the field. The early entertainment was once more provided by Retera and Donnelly, the two of them squabbling for second until Donnelly decisively found a way through on lap six. Released into clear air, Donnelly could do nothing about Tappy, the latter remorselessly consistent with his first 17 laps all within 0.2s of each other.

The drama came late on when Christian Ebbesvik and Linton Stutely came together, prompting a safety car. Tappy, who by this point was almost eight seconds clear of Donnelly, saw his advantage whittled down to nothing. By the time the track was clear, it was just a single-lap dash to the line. Tappy held his nerve to take victory, leading home Donnelly and Retera, the trio having been the class of the field throughout the weekend.

Whilst Tappy didn't quite make it to Formula 1, he progressed to the tier below (and secured the 2007 Formula Renault title for good measure), racing in Formula Renault 3.5 before establishing a successful career in sportscar racing. At the time of writing, he remains a frontrunner in the European Le Mans Series.

The Festivals of the slick-shod Zetec era are rarely seen as classics, but in truth many of them were entertaining, with 1995 and 2000 being the standout years. The style of racing was distinctive and suited level-headed defensive driving, the grip of the slick tyres allowing drivers to tightly hug the inside line as trains of cars formed, running nose to tail. The racing was close, hugely competitive and the class still propelled more than its fair share of drivers up the ladder to Formula 1, particularly prior to 2001.

What the Zetecs lacked was the romance. The cars weren't as pretty as their predecessors and they certainly weren't as fun to drive. The heavier engine upset the balance as the weight transferred mid-corner, making the cars a real handful. This was manageable for the aspirant professional out there to beat their rivals, but no fun for the club-level drivers who had supported the Kent class for almost 60 years. The trend of converting Zetec cars back to Kents had already started in 1994, and today there are only a handful of Zetec-specification cars racing in the UK.

The 'other' Festivals

ONE OF the greatest pleasures of the Formula Ford Festival was that it allowed the humble clubman to directly take on the latest hot tip for stardom. However, even in a category with as close regulations as Formula Ford, older cars become uncompetitive and, when a new headline class is introduced, obsolescent.

This conundrum is something the category has grappled with for the best part of 40 years and has played out both successfully and unsuccessfully at the Festival.

The biggest headache of all came in 1993 with the move from the Kent to the Zetec engine. To many, Kent (Formula Ford 1600) is the true Formula Ford. The category has always been well supported throughout its history, with drivers enjoying close racing and forgiving handling.

The logical and correct decision was taken to keep running a separate Kent Festival. For four years from 1993 to 1996, the Brands Hatch crowd was treated to two Festivals in one. The first couple of years in particular were especially high quality as the Kent class was the one still adopted in many European series. The general consensus was that the Kents provided the better racing.

In 1993, there were still a multitude of thriving local, national and overseas FF1600 series and assembling a hefty Festival entry wasn't too much of a challenge. In total, just over 100 cars assembled to compete across six heats. This would be chopped down to form the grid for two semi-finals (just about half the field going home on Saturday) and then the final itself.

In 1993, it was almost business as usual compared to the old Kent Festivals, but with six heats feeding just two semi-finals there were plenty of banana skins ahead. Svend Hansen won a dull opening heat 12 seconds ahead of Robert d'Ercole and 30 seconds up on third-placed Simon Kinsey. The second heat was more exciting as future Australian touring car star Craig Lowndes prevailed, the scrap for second eventually headed by Chris Ward keeping the crowd entertained.

Louis di Resta and Andrew McAuley dominated the second heat, the latter looking set for a comfortable win until he took to the grass to avoid a spinning backmarker. Di Resta was duly promoted to take his first Festival race win. Ulster's Peter Duke was the comfortable winner of heat four, his margin of victory over Jan Eric Lofgren looking close on paper as he backed off late on. There was a good dice for third with plenty of place swapping – Hans Pfeuti earning a trip to the podium when the music stopped.

One of the pre-event favourites, Sami Lahokoski, made it no further than Druids before crashing out of heat five. The Finn was one of five leaders in what was the pick of the heats, Nicke Blom's tactical astuteness in taking the lead late on proving decisive. A close second went to Jakob Sund, with Richard Fores a fraction of a second further back. The final heat saw Team USA scholarship winner Jerry Nadeau put in a crushing performance to take the flag by 26 seconds from Jan Neumann – the sort of dominance rarely seen in a heat since the early 1980s.

A frustrated Simon Hill took part in the final heat: 'I'd qualified fifth which I was disappointed with as I thought circuit knowledge would count for a bit more. I made a great start, but went too hot into Druids. I flew up the inside, locked the brakes, hit someone and broke the suspension. That was my Festival over after two corners. I was close to tears, I'd had to really scrape the money together to be there, and just wanted to see how I would do against that strong a field.'

The racing got far more serious on Sunday with the semi-finals producing the close and gasp-inducing racing synonymous with the Festival. A timekeeper's dead heat was the outcome of the first encounter – Patrick Simon getting the nod following a phenomenal performance that cast into the shade his anonymous run to fourth a day earlier. Second went to McAuley who was the principal beneficiary of an early red flag, produced seconds after he'd spun down the order. Blom took third and was in contention throughout, finishing just three-tenths back from the leaders.

The smart thinking from Saturday's heats was that the second semi-final was the stronger, featuring Duke, Nadeau and Lowndes. It was this trio plus Chris Ward who were the principal protagonists in deciding the outcome. Once more, it was Formula Ford racing at its best with a close leading group ebbing and flowing over the 15 laps. Despite the closeness, Duke led nearly all the way, taking advantage of a first-lap error from Nadeau. The American remained on Duke's case. Every time it seemed as though a gap was opening, it was soon closed down. However, there was no way through, Duke taking the win by three-tenths. It was the same margin again back to third and Lowndes who had been with the leading pair and certainly had the pace.

The final promised to be spectacular, with at least six drivers legitimately staking a claim on victory. Unfortunately, it went awry at the first attempt. An uncharacteristically slow parade lap only served to ramp up the nerves before it all went wrong at Paddock – in mid-pack, Svend Hansen was tipped into a spin and was subsequently collected by all comers (the chaos immortalised on *Havoc 12*), leading to the red flag and precipitating a lengthy delay.

Once things got under way in earnest it was Simon who took the early lead, having squeezed out Duke on the run to Paddock, with McAuley, Nadeau and Blom chasing. The latter was the first to exit the fray after a spin at Clearways before his stranded car was hit by those following. Meanwhile, Duke was looking ever keener in his bid to move past Simon, the decisive moment coming on lap seven. Spying half a gap into Surtees, Duke committed to the pass, but Simon was already turning in. Contact followed as both cars, sporting realigned suspensions, careened over the grass and into retirement.

This elevated McAuley into the lead, but not a comfortable one, with a nine-car pack all disputing first place. The wildcard was Lofgren, who had found a new lease of life from his semi-final and was right in the mix. As McAuley astutely defended his lead, the dispute for second place was thrilling, with Nadeau, Lowndes and Lofgren all in the mix. It was partially settled in Lofgren's favour following a superb move at Paddock where he passed both Nadeau and Lowndes in one swoop, eliciting a huge cheer from the grandstand. A lap later, Nadeau was back past before a huge moment at Paddock enabled both Lofgren and Lowndes to secure the remaining podium places.

It was an impressive performance from McAuley in a high-calibre Kent Festival, which, despite the new second-class status, clearly showed why the category was so beloved.

Reduced to just four heats for 1994, the Kents still provided plenty of action with some of the closest and most dramatic racing of the weekend. The upsets started almost immediately. After a downpour delayed the start of the opening heat by half an hour, polesitter Mark Marchant immediately struggled with a chronic misfire, which meant he only just crept into the semi-finals from 12th. Instead, it was Adrian Cotterill who led all the way but under constant pressure from category perennial Rick Morris, who was campaigning a 1975 vintage Royale.

Graham Riley took the second heat on the road from Nigel Greensall, but a jump-start penalty dropped the latter to fifth, promoting Chris Paul to second. A fearless start from Michael Duke gave him the third heat ahead of German champion Nick Heidfeld – the latter's presence and subsequent progression to Formula 1 being an indication of just how competitive the Kent class remained. The concluding heat went to Nick Hart, who was comfortably clear of Damien Faulkner and Castle Combe favourite Gavin Wills. Remarkably, all four heat victories went to the Swift marque – an unlikely clean sweep.

Sunday morning started wet with a drying line, conditions that were far from ideal for drivers hoping to climb the order. Somewhat inevitably, the opening semi-final veered towards the chaotic with two red flags and a result being declared after ten laps. The main casualty of the first attempt was Heidfeld, pitched into retirement avoiding a spinning Michael Duke.

With cars off around the circuit, the race was halted to allow the marshals to safely clear the wreckage. At the restart, it was Mark O'Conner and Cotterill who were the class of the field, the former taking the lead decisively on lap eight, Morris holding a somewhat distant third. Duke rotated again, this time into the gravel at Paddock, bringing out a second and final red flag – the miscreant fortunate that the countback rules in place at the time enabled him to progress to the final – today, any car not running when a red flag is shown is considered retired.

The countback rules also came into play in the second semi-final. Spurred on by their peers' antics, the race was even more incident-strewn than its predecessor. Faulkner spent much of the race battling with Riley for the win. With a move at Paddock on lap eight, it seemed as if Riley had made the decisive pass, only for him to spin down to fourth at Clearways a lap later. Meanwhile, Hart and Paul tangled at Clearways early on, whilst Wills and Mads Gisselbaek disputed the remaining rostrum space. Wills had the advantage until Gisselbaek spun him following hefty contact along the Cooper Straight, leaving his nose cone in Wills' rear suspension. It got even worse for Wills a few corners later when Greensall went flying over him at Druids.

The race was stopped following a nasty incident at Paddock. The recovering Riley dived to the inside of Champion of Brands John Hayden to take third, but immediately spun into Hayden's path. This left the latter with nowhere to go as he hurtled head first into the tyre wall at near unabated speed. The race was immediately stopped, followed by a lengthy delay as Hayden was extricated from the car with back injuries. Despite facing a period of convalescence, the local favourite waved to the crowd from the stretcher as he was transferred to the waiting ambulance.

The result was declared after ten laps, with Faulkner the winner from Gisselbaek and Hayden third. Wills was the big winner of the chaos, being classified fifth and able to start the final provided that the two damaged corners to his Swift could be repaired in time.

Wills was there as the field formed up for the final. Starting from pole, Faulkner led the initial charge but was demoted by O'Connor before they reached Druids, with Cottrell slotting into third. The order wouldn't hold for long. Cottrell took Faulkner at Clearways on lap two before O'Connor spun away the lead at the same spot a lap later. Cottrell did his utmost to build up a lead but could never open a clear advantage. Behind, Wills was coming good, and was soon up to second before passing Cottrell at mid-distance.

Another strong recovery drive was under way. Marchant, who'd spent the day recovering from his disastrous heat, was up to third, pressuring Cottrell and suggesting he had the pace to fight Wills. It wasn't to be. Attempting to pass Cottrell at Druids, the pair locked wheels and Marchant was tipped into a barrel roll across the gravel trap. Fortunately uninjured, both drivers were out, although Marchant's Jamun upturned and the race was stopped.

The race restarted over seven laps, the result of which would be combined with the 11 classified laps from the first section to give an overall result over 18 laps. After all that had come before, the final few laps were relatively drama free, a euphoric Wills taking victory. Second went to Alistair Weston, who succeed in staying out of trouble, whilst almost unnoticed Jan Neumann completed the podium, with Morris a hugely popular fourth.

Interest in the Kent class remained high for 1995, with four heats worth of cars being assembled – a core of Champion of Brands and regional competitors being challenged by a strong cohort of Scandinavian and Irish runners.

Reflecting the high standards of preparation at the front of the field, the Apollo Motorsport Swifts would be the cars to beat, particularly those of Topi Serjala and Fredrik Sorlie. The squad, run by former heat winner Ken Bowes, were the match of many of the Zetecs in standards of preparation.

The first heat went the way of local favourite Mark Marchant, who, despite not racing much during the year, looked anything but race rusty. Second went to Oulton Park champion Mike Bennett, who was one of several beneficiaries of Mike Hardisty making a terrible start from the front row. The second effort was punctuated by two stoppages, the result being determined on aggregate. The first halt followed a multi-car pile-up at Graham Hill Bend before a litany of damaged cars surrounding the circuit forced a second stoppage. Converting pole position to victory was Mikko Lempinen, who led home Simon Hill.

Hill was confident of chances for the weekend: 'I was in the car Gavin (Wills) had won in the previous year, and the car was really good. It was a last-minute deal, and you could see the difference between us, and someone like Apollo who had the new cars and tested a lot. I also only had one engine, and really you needed another one you could bolt on for the business end of the Festival.'

Heat three was also carnage-strewn, with another opening-lap stoppage following a pile-up at Paddock Hill Bend. Norwegian Sorlie emerged as the winner, aided by fellow podium finishers Nicke Blom and Noel Dunne both having adventures of their own. The closing heat featured pre-event favourite Serjala. The Finn didn't have it all his own way, initially trailing compatriot Risto Virtanen until he made a sensational pass to the outside at Paddock on lap five, leading thereafter.

In heats largely dominated by the Scandinavians, only Marchant had proved a match. He and Sorlie shared the front row for the first semi-final, with the Jamun pilot leading for the first half of the race. Once through on lap eight, Sorlie never decisively broke clear, taking the win just three-tenths clear. A distant third went to Noel Dunne, who in turn had about a second's advantage over his pursuers. The second semi-final was even less of a contest with Serjala leading throughout, despite spinning up his tyres at the start. Runner-up Lempinen finished two and a half seconds back, with Virtanen making it an all-Finnish podium.

With a race time some seven seconds faster than Sorlie's, Serjala lined up in pole position for the final, with Lempinen and Marchant sharing the second row. Serjala led away from Sorlie into Paddock to form the order that would hold throughout. Despite the positions not changing, Sorlie maintained the pressure, forcing Serjala into an error at Surtees which dislodged his undertray with a consequently detrimental effect on handling. The second row, meanwhile, proved cursed. An obvious jump start from Marchant landed him a ten-second penalty before an overambitious move from Lempinen at Paddock on lap six eliminated both. Serjala took the flag a second clear of Sorlie, with Virtanen a distant but conclusive third, Chris Paul the first British competitor home in fourth albeit 15 seconds back from Serjala.

1996 followed the same format as the previous year. The big question was whether Mark Marchant could vanquish the bad luck of the past few years and claim the Kent Festival title. His weekend got off to a perfect start with a comfortable win from pole in the opening heat. The second heat was run over two legs following a red flag, but once under way properly it was a good race, with Scottish champion Jim Forsyth coming out on top following a close dice with Nick Hart. Castle Combe favourite Kevin Mills was a comfortable winner of the third heat, some three seconds clear of Janne Koistinen. The closing heat was the best of the day, a leading trio of Simon Hill, Stewart Roden and Raymond Knox separated in that order by just three-tenths of a second. Hill remembers, 'I was delighted as it was my first win in Formula Ford. For whatever reason, they didn't have the podium set up so there wasn't the opportunity to celebrate.'

Marchant and Mills were the class of the field in the first semi-final, the former taking the early lead. Marchant, a senior instructor at Brands Hatch, put all his knowledge to good use by ensuring his Jamun was able to thwart any challenge from Mills. Initially, Mills was content to settle for second, but soon started probing for a way past to no avail. Third went to the Eddie Irvine-mentored Jeff Wright.

Defensive driving remained the order of the day in the second semi-final. Hill claimed the lead into Paddock but couldn't pull away with a ten-car train rapidly forming behind the leader. Nick Hart came closest to overhauling Hill, but he suffered a suspension failure at the exact moment it appeared he'd made the decisive move at Druids. Forsyth also took his turn to challenge, but contact from behind eliminated him from the race. This gave second to Knox, with Allan Bernt rounding out the podium. Hill's performance was all the more impressive considering he set only the 23rd-fastest lap of the race out of 28 starters.

Hill had mixed memories of the race: 'I enjoyed this Festival the most. The thing I remember most vividly is racing against people I'd not raced with before. I got a good start for the semi-final, but the car felt sluggish. It was handling beautifully though, so I just had to brake impossibly late and make myself impossible to pass. I used all my instructor tricks to my advantage. It turned out the distributor cap had broken, so I was down to two or three cylinders for the race.'

The final was a near carbon copy of the first semi-final. The first half of the race and beyond saw Marchant and Mills well clear of the rest, with Mills trying every which way to dislodge Marchant. As it had been earlier in the day, there was no way through, Marchant driving around the Jamun's strengths to thwart Mills. Hill initially held third, but suffered from a deteriorating engine, enabling Wright to move through.

Hill remembered, 'Swift were running loads of cars that weekend, and my engineer was taken off my car at the last minute to help prepare one of the Zetecs for the final. In the panic, they may well have put the faulty distributor cap back on. I'm not sure I would have won it as Mark was so quick, but I would have finished on the podium.'

Once in clear air, Wright was able to reel in the leaders to make it a three-car chain. With each lap Mills was ever bolder in his attempts to snatch the lead, but there was no way through. The group was covered by just half a second as Marchant took the flag to score a popular victory.

The Kents then proved to be the primary victim of the Festival being rebranded as the World Finals for 1997. With no space on the timetable for a Kent Festival, the beloved cars would be relegated to a one-off trophy race.

The decision was far from popular with correspondence to *Autosport* reflecting that 'our Festival has been hijacked'. Depending on your perspective, since 1993 the Kents had either been the highlight of the weekend or a thorn in the side of the shiny new Zetec era. Always drawing more cars and frequently providing better racing, they were a constant reminder of why the original design and ethos of Formula Ford still worked. Hill recalled, 'That was a bolt from the blue, the Kents were still so strong, why would you take that away? It was very frustrating as we all loved the coverage that the Festival got, but it was an era where the manufacturers were stretching their legs so I can understand it.'

For a five-year period from 1997 to 2002, the Kents were dropped from the Festival, although standalone trophy races were held during the weekend along with championship rounds of the plethora of classic and historic series. For many, this took some of the soul out of the Festival, although the races remained entertaining and featured strong fields – the likes of Anthony Davidson taking victory in 1999 before graduating to the Zetec class.

From 2002 to 2012, the Kents got a Festival back running alongside the headlining Zetec and Duratec cars. Most years, the field had two full grids of cars totalling the mid-50s. This compared poorly to the Walter Hayes Trophy, launched in 2001 and run at Silverstone, which frequently boasted entries in excess of 100 cars and seemed to corner the market in eye-catching one-off appearances.

Dave Fricker and Matt Gilmore won the 2002 and 2003 editions, the final of the 2003 meeting eventually being run after the Zetec final, following two red flags and a stern telling-off from officials.

2004 drew 41 cars to Brands Hatch in what was a generally under-supported weekend. As always there was fierce competition at the front, evidenced by Morgan Dempsey taking an incredibly close opening heat by just three-thousandths of a second from Peter Dempsey. It was slightly easier for 1994 winner Gavin Wills later in the afternoon as he enjoyed a more comfortable win.

Wills maintained his form into the semi-finals, taking the flag just under a second ahead of Peter Dempsey. He would share the front row for the final with 2003 Zetec winner Joey Foster, who bested Morgan Dempsey by almost two seconds. In the main event, Foster duly made it back-to-back Zetec-Kent victories, edging out Morgan Dempsey by eight-tenths of a second, Darren Burke completing the podium.

A year later, the 53 car field was split over three heats, which offered varying entertainment value. Castle Combe stalwart Ed Moore was dominant in the opener, running home four and a half seconds clear of the rest. Peter Dempsey was also a reasonably comfortable winner in heat two, as Neville Smyth and Gavin Wills enjoyed a very close battle for second. The concluding heat was the best of the bunch, with Darren Burke making the decisive move on Morgan Dempsey at two-thirds distance, the pair separated by under a tenth of a second for much of the race.

Peter Dempsey had another relatively comfortable win in his semi-final, leading home Wills, whose move for second on Burke just as the safety car came out proved decisive. Smyth, meanwhile, dominated the second semi-final, driving away from Moore and Morgan Dempsey at ease in a race with little movement in the upper order. The final proved to be attritional, with Peter Dempsey retiring at the start of the second lap as he looked to overhaul early leader Smyth. Indeed, the final looked to be Smyth's until he hit trouble with just five laps to run. This elevated Wills to take his second Festival victory from Burke and Morgan Dempsey. Dave Collier finished second on the road, but a two-second penalty dropped him from podium.

2006 saw the field back down to 40, albeit with some excellent racing, the bulk of the frontrunners having made the trip over from Ireland. Irish competitors had always been huge supporters of the Festival, but the mid-noughties saw a particularly strong generation of drivers consistently fighting for Kent honours. The Irish enjoyed a clean sweep of the podium in the opening heat with 1.1s covering Morgan Dempsey, Mike Edgar and Neville Smyth. There was more to celebrate for the Emerald Isle in heat two as Noel Dunne edged out British interloper Matt Rivett.

Whilst Saturday was dry, Sunday's weather was wild – heavy showers interspersed with sunny spells before a downpour for the final. In these conditions experience was at a premium, and came to the fore as Gavin Wills claimed the first semi-final from Ivor McCullough and Dunne. Smyth prevailed on a drier track in the later race to claim pole position for the final. He was taken to the wire by Lee Mumford, with Rivett a close third in what was one of the races of the weekend.

The wet track made close racing in the final a precarious business, with both Smyth and Rivett falling victim. In amongst the gloom, Dunne delivered a superb performance to take the flag three seconds clear of Morgan Dempsey and Edgar, Wills a very distant fourth.

A year later and the Kents didn't even have heats to play with, qualifying directly into the semi-finals and just 38 cars in total. Once more, the anticipated frontrunners would come from the Irish Formula Ford scene. Stepping back from the Duratecs for the year, Peter Dempsey was clear winner of the first semi-final. Far more attention was paid to the second race, where newcomer 17-year-old Wayne Boyd scored a sensational victory from pole position.

The final was set to be a Dempsey–Boyd head to head, but instead turned into a classic final with a five- or six-car train all disputing the lead. Neville Smyth's run of wretched luck continued as he retired into the gravel. Meanwhile, Boyd was in a Dempsey sandwich, pressuring Peter, whilst older brother Keith was pushing him along.

It came to a head on lap 19, Boyd making a stunning move into Paddock to take the lead. Peter Dempsey, displaying the impetuosity that got him involved in more than a few incidents, looked to fight back immediately, going for a move that was never on into Druids. Inevitably, contact followed as he was launched over Boyd, both retiring into the gravel. With wrecked cars all over the circuit, there was no option but to stop the race. This gave the win to Keith Dempsey from Robert Barrable and Patrick McKenna – all three fully deserving of their place on the podium following a superb race.

The following year saw the Kent Festival step up a notch, a key component being the reintroduction of the Team USA Scholarship drivers. Overseen by journalist Jeremy Shaw with support from many key US motorsport figures, the Team USA scholarship was started in late 1990 as a programme to give up-and-coming US motorsport talents the opportunity to compete overseas.

The first entry at the Festival for Team USA was in 1990 where Jimmy Vasser made the trip over. Unfortunately, his weekend was short lived as he retired following a collision in his heat. This was far from the end of Vasser's motorsport story. He went on to be one of the top IndyCar drivers of the 1990s, winning the title in 1994. In one of those motorsport sliding-doors moments involving the Festival, also selected to take part in 1990 was sprint car driver Jeff Gordon. Gordon had clashing commitments so didn't make the trip. This did not hinder Gordon's career as he progressed to NASCAR and became arguably the best-known figure in US motorsport of the past 30 years – sadly, we can only imagine how he would have gone on a cold October day at Brands Hatch.

The decision of Shaw to re-enter the Team USA drivers into Formula Ford 1600 competition in 2008 proved a ringing endorsement of the category. The class of 2008, including Josef Newgarden and Conor Daly (son of 1976 winner Derek), was an exceptionally strong one. Both would be among the favourites in the 40-car entry.

The heat wins were split between Graham Carroll and Peter Barrable, Newgarden finishing fourth in his heat whilst Daly retired. The sharp end of the weekend really began with the semi-finals. Newgarden stunned the field in the first, taking the lead on the second lap before inexorably building his advantage to win by over four seconds. The second race was just decided in favour of Neville Smyth by under seven-hundredths of a second from Patrick McKenna, Daly an impressive sixth from the back of the grid.

McKenna took the charge to Newgarden in the final. Despite leading in the early stages, the American never had any daylight, McKenna's moment coming shortly after an early safety car. Newgarden wasn't behind for long, reclaiming the lead on lap 13 and pulling away thereafter to take a fine victory. It was a stunning performance that marked Newgarden as one to watch –

the following 13 years (at time of writing) being a story of talent fulfilled. McKenna maintained second, with Carroll rounding out the podium for the weekend.

The final brace of Kent Festival wins before the Kent cars returned to being the main Festival class, went to Ivor McCullough in 2011 and 2012. McCullough, a former British F3 hopeful, had endured a disastrous event in 2010 but was always very rapid, his two wins being richly deserved.

2012 saw an entry of 43 cars with considerable strength at the top of the field. With the heats focused on grid position for the semi-finals, the action really picked up on Sunday morning. Team USA driver Tristan Nunez won the opener by under two-tenths from 2011 winner Ivor McCullough, with Luke Cooper a close third. The second encounter went to 2006 Kent winner Noel Dunne, who romped home over eight and half seconds clear of the rest.

Nunez had pole, but was quickly demoted by Dunne and Graham Carroll. The pair closely disputed the lead until lap five when Carroll retired, followed by Dunne a lap later. Nunez also hit trouble and elevated McCullough into the lead. Thereafter, McCullough held the advantage over Stuart Gough and Luke Cooper until red flags brought proceedings to a premature close. The following year the Kents would, in the eyes of many, return to their rightful place after 20 years in the shadows.

If the Kent cars could always be relied upon for a full grid and spectacular racing, the same could not be said for the Zetecs. Despite running as the national Formula Ford class for over a decade and with a sufficiently large pool of machinery, the Zetecs never really trickled down to be a popular club-level car. There was briefly a club Zetec championship in the early 2000s, but by the middle of the decade it had largely disappeared.

From 2006 to 2014, Zetecs were welcomed to the Festival, either to fill out the Duratec class or as a standalone series of races. With Zetecs still being the primary class in Scandinavia in 2006, alongside a healthy class B in Britain, 21 cars ventured to Brands Hatch. The final, fought in atrocious conditions, was close, Benoit Perret winning by a quarter of a second from Takeshi Nagase, Zetec-stalwart Neil Tofts an impressive third.

After a tentatively promising 2006, the competition fell off a cliff in 2007. In what was a bizarre event for the Zetecs, just three cars entered. As a result, the Zetec final was run as part of an extended last-chance race. Incredibly, although well adrift of the rest, two of the cars collided, leaving Raphael Hubeau to take the Zetec victory, 41 seconds back from Duratec winner Johan Jokinen over 13 laps.

The following years saw ups and downs in interest, but rarely got close to providing a full grid of cars. Tofts was the best of the six cars in 2008, following a good dice with Antti Buri, before repeating the feat in 2009 (ten cars) after seeing off another Finn, this time Sebastian Nummi. Tofts was unable to make it a hat-trick in 2010 when a mechanical issue pitched him into the barriers early on. Julian Hoskins was left to take a very comfortable win from Lucy Wardrop, who became the second female to finish on the Festival podium.

The entry jumped to 15 for 2011, when Tofts was once more triumphant, heading the ever-durable Rick Morris. The latter was the crowd favourite, with almost everyone bar Tofts willing him on to that elusive Festival victory, but it wasn't to be.

For 2012, the Zetecs once more had a standalone final with a 12 car entry for the weekend. It proved to be one of the better events in terms of quality of racing, with Xavier Michel prevailing after a late safety car bunched the field. Until that point, Michel had enjoyed a comfortable lead, although there were some close battles behind. Just six Zetecs came out to play the following year as they were once more combined with the Duratecs. Julian Hoskins scored his second Festival win, finishing over nine seconds up on his nearest rival.

2014 was the final, somewhat desultory, Festival appearance for the Zetec formula, with just three cars entered in a combined five-car grid with the Duratecs. The racing was unsurprisingly far from inspiring as Hoskins took his third win, the best part of 15 seconds clear.

Whether victims of circumstances, or just not as satisfying to drive, the Zetecs were not overly loved, certainly not after they stopped being the contemporary class. Many of the chassis have enjoyed something of an afterlife, having been adapted to run to Kent specification, although there are still a handful of cars that occasionally appear in Monoposto competition. Otherwise the Zetec-era Formula Fords are largely forgotten, with little grassroots energy to revive the category.

Duratec cars seeded into club motorsport even less than Zetecs but limped on for a further two years after being dropped as the lead category. In 2013, eight cars, almost exclusively from Europe, kept the flag flying. Bart van Os emerged triumphant after early leader Frederick Schandorff hit trouble mid-race – the battle for the lead having been close up to that point. With interest in the Netherlands dropping in 2014, just two cars appeared at the Festival, Thomas Craincort winning in a race spoiled by his rival John Whitbourne picking up a ten-second penalty at the start.

From 2015 onwards, the Festival has once more solely focused on Kent specification cars. At the time of writing, it doesn't appear likely that either Duratec or Zetec cars will be making an imminent return.

Rebirth with Duratecs

AFTER 13 seasons, 2006 brought another new dawn for Formula Ford with the Duratec class. The lighter, punchier cars proved to be a success from the outset, with 16 Duratec-spec cars taking the grid for the season opener at Oulton Park, which grew to 20 or so by season's end.

Oulton Park set the tone for the season with some great dicing between Peter Dempsey, Nathan Freke and Nick Tandy. As the year progressed, it was Freke who emerged at the head of the field, taking the title. On his day, Dempsey arguably outpaced Freke but overstepped the line too often with his aggressive style. Meanwhile, Tandy emerged as the find of the season, becoming Freke's main challenger.

If it was just a changing of the guard among the drivers, there were fluctuating fortunes among the manufacturers too. Coming off a dominant 2005 season, Mygale seamlessly transitioned to the Duratec formula, taking Freke to the title. However, it was the Ray chassis in the hands of both Tandy and Dempsey that was the main rival to Mygale. Late-season, they were joined at the front of the field by the angular Australian-built Spectrum. Meanwhile, after largely dominating for the past decade, Van Diemen were nowhere – Richard Tannahill was normally fighting to round out the top five in the previously pre-eminent entry.

Crucially, the first year of the Duratec era of Formula Ford is remembered for superb racing from the high-quality field – not quite a return to the glory days, but certainly an improvement on the previous two seasons.

Memories of that first Duratec season, however, largely pivot around the Festival and the hugely dramatic Sunday played out in atrocious conditions. As seen in previous years, the late-October weather could be inclement, but the rainfall throughout the semi-finals and final was altogether something else – indeed, had it not been the Festival meeting, it is quite possible the plug would have been pulled on the event.

It was a healthy entry with just shy of 25 Duratecs predominantly drawn from the British Championship with a couple of Scandinavian visitors. For the purposes of the heats and semi-finals, they were pooled with a strong Zetec entry largely from the Benelux and Scandinavian championships

The form book suggested that Freke, Dempsey and Tandy would be the main contenders, with the latter pairing possibly more heavily favoured. The heats went the way of Freke and Tandy, and whilst Tandy led from lights to flag, Freke had to overhaul Dempsey en route to victory.

On the Sunday morning, faced with horrendous track conditions, events moved on a notch. Tandy took the first semi-final again from lights to flag, despite enduring a restart following a nasty incident involving journalist Emma Parker-Bowles, who spun off at Paddock Hill Bend only for her car to be hit by another competitor as she was climbing out, and a late-race safety car. Freke, meanwhile, won the second semi-final from Dempsey, the safety car coming out mid-race this time around. Behind the winners, the progress of the Van Diemens was not going unnoticed, with Tannahill, James Nash and Niall Doran all showing strongly.

This set the stage for a titanic final. The weather had remained atrocious, but the 20 remaining cars took the grid for the 25-lap race. The immediate battle was between Freke and Dempsey, the former naughtily running Tandy wide at Druids on the second lap, forcing him to spin to the rear of the field. The incident allowed Dempsey to take the lead, but before long Freke was back with Dempsey and then past him.

This order didn't last long as Freke was spun into the barriers following contact with Dempsey at Graham Hill Bend on lap six before, moments later Dempsey too was out, plunging into the gravel at Paddock. This promoted Tannahill into the lead from Jay Bridger, the pair spending the next ten laps never separated by more than half a second (albeit one of those behind the safety car). Meanwhile, Tandy was charging, despite a couple more spins; his pace was electrifying and by lap 15 he was up to sixth.

A further safety car on lap 16 bunched the field and provided the crucial moment of the race. Exiting Graham Hill Bend behind the safety car, Tandy spun again. Instead of slotting back into the queue, he passed those that had overtaken him while he rotated to regain sixth position. Racing resumed on lap 19 and by lap 22 Tandy was leading on the road. However, his safety car incident earned him a ten-second penalty. Nonetheless Tandy did his best to overcome it, taking the chequered flag three and a half seconds clear.

Once the penalty was applied, Tandy dropped to fifth and Tannahill became an unlikely winner for Van Diemen, with Bridger and Neil Doran completing the podium. It had been a truly spectacular final to inaugurate the Duratec era.

After the tumultuous end to 2006, Tandy returned to Formula Ford in 2007. He was not alone in coming back for more – Tannahill and Nash would also be on the grid. Their main rival would be newcomer Callum MacLeod in a Jamun-prepared Mygale.

Once more running at British Formula 3 events, the season turned into a feisty battle, with little love lost between MacLeod and Tandy. It was MacLeod who took the title, incidents stymying Tandy's shot at the crown. However, the personal animosity between the leading protagonists perfectly set the scene for the Festival.

In their second year, the Duratecs were proving their popularity with over 40 cars entered, the best turnout for several seasons, with just three Zetecs padding out the field. The format was still the same heats, semi-finals and final, but with the last-chance race once more reinstated.

MacLeod and Tandy were drawn together in the first heat, with the latter claiming a lights-to-flag victory, although MacLeod stayed within a second throughout. The second heat went to David Brown, who finished a comfortable three seconds ahead of Nash.

The main protagonists were split for the semi-finals. In his, MacLeod had a disastrous first lap dropping from second on the grid to eighth on lap one before fighting his way through to claim victory by 0.1s from Brown. Tandy had it far easier in the second semi-final, once more leading every lap to take a commanding win from Linton Stuteley. Crucially, the second semi-final also went the distance without a safety car interruption, giving Tandy the pole for the final.

In the event, the final proved to be a huge anti-climax. The early stages were initially thrilling as Tandy sought to hold off MacLeod, the pair of them weaving along the Brabham Straight. Once MacLeod was through, however, he was able to pull away with ease. His progress was stymied by a series of heavy incidents further down the field, prompting the intervention of the safety car and the moment on which the race turned.

Given the acrimony between the leading pair, the gamesmanship continued behind the safety car. Approaching the restart, as the pair jostled for position, Tandy struck MacLeod's car. Neither sustained any damage, but the loss of momentum enabled MacLeod to immediately build a decent advantage. Further incidents the following lap, and with one or two stunned drivers needing assistance, meant there was no option but to red-flag the race – which had just crept over the halfway mark, enabling a result to be declared.

MacLeod was initially the winners but Tandy protested his action behind the safety car. The result was a two-second penalty for MacLeod that elevated Tandy to victory – although this was not confirmed until some way into the evening as the wrangling continued. Stuteley quietly claimed third after a solid weekend.

It was an unsatisfying way for the result to be decided, in keeping with the tenor of the weekend, but ultimately depriving the crowd of the hoped-for, head-to-head battle. Nonetheless, Tandy was a popular winner, with many feeling that the victory was his just reward for the heroics of a year earlier.

Tandy's Formula Ford heroics marked him as a star of the future. Following some against-the-odds performances in Formula 3, including a 2009 win at Rockingham just days after his brother Joe passed away following a road accident, Tandy moved to sportscars, where, as a Porsche works driver, he won the 2015 24 Hours of Le Mans.

The Duratec category continued to produce superb racing throughout 2008 as the star of the Kent Festival from the previous year, Wayne Boyd, swept to the championship by winning 13 of the 25 races.

The Jamun team, once more running the Mygale chassis, was the class of the field, taking three of the top four places in the title races with Tim Blanchard and Victor Correa finishing second and fourth respectively. Van Diemen came on strong at the end of the season, with David Brown winning twice in the season finale at Donington Park.

Whilst the competition was tight at the front, the field wasn't enormous with just 15 regulars. Likewise, the Duratec category was only really gaining traction in Scandinavia and the Benelux countries meaning that the pool of cars for the Festival wasn't huge. In total, 37 cars entered to take their chances over the weekend, but this included a sprinkling of Zetecs, meaning that there were just 27 Duratecs in the hunt.

With a combined field throughout (albeit with the Zetecs starting separately at the back), the format was two heats setting the grid for the semi-finals and then a last-chance race to whittle out a few unfortunates who wouldn't progress to the final.

Bright and dry conditions were in store on Saturday as Correa and Blanchard stayed with the form book by locking out the front row for their heat. From pole position, Correa led every lap to take an unheeded victory from Rogier de Wit, a poor first lap from Blanchard relegating him to third.

Heat two was arguably the more interesting, featuring champion Boyd, 2007 Festival winner Nick Tandy and, making his Brands Hatch debut, Kevin Magnussen (son of 1992 winner, Jan). Pole position went to Chris Maliepaard, who'd finished third in the British Championship. In a desperately close session, he'd share the front row with Brown, with Tandy third and Boyd down in fifth.

It was Brown who got the better start, leading for the first couple of laps, before Maliepaard gained the advantage on lap four. Thereafter, the Dutchman romped clear to win by almost three and a half seconds from Brown, with Boyd and Tandy just behind.

Fortunately, the fine weather continued into Sunday morning, with Correa heading the grid for the first semi-final from Brown and Tandy. It was initially a superb race, with Brown and Tandy leapfrogging Correa at the start. It was close, perilously so, as matters came to a head at the start of lap six. Approaching Paddock, Tandy tagged Brown, the momentary loss of momentum allowing Correa to challenge to the outside. Incredibly, the trio conspired to exit the turn three abreast, Tandy to the inside from Brown and Correa.

On the run-in to Druids, Brown moved across to squeeze Tandy, pushing him on to the grass as the pair interlocked wheels. With Tandy half on the grass and fully interlocked with Brown, the accident was obvious several seconds before it occurred. Tandy was launched up over Brown's front right wheel, pirouetting in mid-air, before partially landing on the luckless and innocent Correa. Beached in the gravel and with damaged cars, Tandy and Brown were out on the spot, whilst Correa recovered to the midfield. Two of the favourites for the weekend would now have to take their chances through the last-chance race.

As the safety car was scrambled, Blanchard was promoted to the lead. Once racing was under way again, the remaining laps saw a thrilling battle between Blanchard, Nick Percat and James Cole, the latter pair rarely separated by more than a quarter of a second. Percat made the decisive move on lap 14 to lead his fellow Australia,n Blanchard, home.

The second semi-final would do well to match the first in the entertainment stakes. Maliepaard would start from pole with de Wit alongside him; Boyd, with ground still to make up following his difficult qualifying, would start third.

In fact, Boyd made it look easy, using a superb start to immediately clear de Wit, before taking advantage of Maliepaard's wider exit from Paddock to secure the lead up the hill to Druids – it was impressive, clinical driving. Thereafter, Boyd pulled away with each successive lap to score a commanding victory, and with no safety car period to interrupt the race, had the faster time, to give him pole for the final.

Meanwhile, Maliepaard was secure in second, the main upward movement coming from Adrian Campfield who took third from de Wit on the fourth lap. That settled the top positions, with the battle for second never quite being joined.

Attention now turned to the last-chance race, where both Brown and Tandy were looking to redeem their semi-final incident by at least making the grid for the big race. Despite starting on the third and fourth row respectively, they carved up the order, with Tandy winning the five-lapper by seven-tenths from Brown. They would share the tenth row for the final, from where a podium was highly unlikely but not totally impossible over the 25 laps.

The front row, meanwhile, was formed of Boyd and Percat, with Maliepaard and Blanchard next along – the leading quartet's task definitely made easier by Tandy and Brown starting far further down the order.

Hopes of a close final were obliterated by a crushing series of opening laps from Boyd. Leading by 1.4s at the end of the first tour, and extending the buffer by a further second next time around, he was in full control of the race. Never under pressure, Boyd would take the flag 4.3s up on the rest, with the sense it could have been more if he'd really pushed.

Percat was initially in second before steadily dropping down the order, leaving Maliepaard to head the rest. Taking a leaf out of Boyd's book, he also built a four-second buffer over his nearest challenger to enjoy a reasonably comfortable run to second. It was a race without much in the way of upper order movement or a safety car to bunch them up. Third was settled by lap five, with Blanchard again reasonably comfortable. He led home Campfield with almost two seconds to spare. Meanwhile, Tandy was arguably the standout performer, racing up to fifth by the tenth lap but being unable to make progress from there. Meanwhile, Magnussen would finish an impressive seventh, marking himself as one to watch.

Having been the star of the season, Boyd was a deserving Festival winner, after driving magnificently in both the semi-final and final. A move to Formula 3 the following year yielded one win before he looked to the USA to further his career. A return to Formula Ford 1600 once more demonstrated his pace, before going on to enjoy considerable sportscar success with the United Autosport team.

The star graduate from the class of 2008 would prove to be Magnussen, who got his Formula 1 break with McLaren in 2014. Unfortunately, his debut second-place finish would prove to be something of a highlight, the Dane never really having the machinery to show off his talent

2009 saw a slight resurgence in popularity for Formula Ford, with grids regularly topping 20 cars and a superb battle for the title between James Cole and Josef Newgarden. Formidable consistency would ultimately give Cole the nod in the championship battle, but it was Newgarden who was turning heads. The American outscored his British rival by nine wins to seven and had a devastating turn of pace. Third in the championship went to Gary Findlay, whilst Chrissy Palmer had shown a fine late-season turn of form, winning the two final rounds of the championship.

The British title contenders would be joined by an influx from the Benelux championship to give an entry of 41 cars (once more including a smattering of Zetecs), a slight increase from the previous year.

It was the European challengers who were the talk of qualifying, with Rogier de Wit claiming pole for the opening heat ahead of Cole. More surprisingly (although not to Benelux paddock insiders), Melroy Heemskerk was fastest in qualifying for the second heat to head Findlay and Newgarden. This certainly boded well for some lively racing.

The opening heat proved to be closely fought, with the leading trio of cars separated by under one and half seconds for almost the entire race. A poor first lap for de Wit saw him drop down to third, with Cole leading the way from Sepp Koster. As Cole led throughout, albeit not by much, it took de Wit until the sixth lap to find a way past Koster. A lap later, Maliepaard also demoted Koster and set about pressurising de Wit for second, but was unable to find a way through.

The second heat was even closer. Heemskerk led throughout but under immense pressure from Palmer who was only a few hundredths adrift for the entire race – it was Formula Ford racing at its best. There wasn't much of a gap to third as another Dutch competitor, Leroy Stuart, completed the podium from Findlay. Newgarden, meanwhile, had a tough time of it, finishing down in seventh after a frustrating race.

With the pack jumbled for the semi-finals, the first would see Cole on pole from Palmer, then Maliepaard and Findlay. In what was shaping up to be a superb Festival, this was another thrillingly close race, with Cole and Palmer disputing the win with a margin of hundredths of seconds throughout. Cole led for the first half of the race under sustained pressure from Palmer, before the order switched on the ninth lap. Despite taking the lead, Palmer couldn't break clear, leading Cole home by just under two-tenths of a second. Findlay enjoyed a far less eventful run for third, never quite getting on to terms with the leaders, but being over four seconds clear of the rest.

After his starring role in the heats, Heemskerk would head the grid for the second semi-final ahead of de Wit and Stuart. It was this trio who immediately broke clear of the rest to fight for the lead. Stuart had the early advantage from Heemskerk, the pair rarely separated by more than two-tenths of a second for the first 14 laps. The pivotal moment came at Druids on lap 15 when Heemskerk tagged Stuart and was launched into the gravel. With the Zetecs having a separate final, Heemskerk would start the final but from a lowly 27th – any chance of victory was effectively over.

The incident was also enough to delay Stuart, allowing de Wit to sneak through and snatch victory. Third would go to Ben Barker, who once past Koster was able to quickly close on to the leading pair but didn't have enough laps to do any more than that. Meanwhile, Newgarden had another rotten race, hitting trouble on lap seven that put him to the tail of the field – he recovered to 14th, but with likely too much to do in the final, particularly as he'd not been on the pace all weekend.

By virtue of his semi-final being the faster, de Wit would start from pole, but alongside him Palmer would be a potent threat. Likewise, from the second row, Stuart had looked on course for victory in the semi-final before his clash with Heemskerk, and Cole had won the British title. Based on the weekend so far, it certainly promised to be a closer final than 2008.

Once again, Stuart was able to jump the front row in the opening exchanges to lead at the end of the first lap from Palmer and de Wit. De Wit's tenure in third only lasted for a lap before Cole was through to third, with Barker also in close attention, broadly making it a quintet for the win. The first big sort-out came on lap eight as de Wit departed into retirement and Barker took advantage to climb to third ahead of Cole.

This gave Palmer the smallest of windows to ramp up the pressure on Stuart without having to overly check his mirrors. The pressure paid off and a small error from Stuart at Graham Hill Bend on the 13th lap was enough for Palmer to leap through. Thereafter, Palmer was able to gradually open up the lead to about a second, which was enough to give him victory. He was somewhat aided in this by Cole and Stuart disputing second, but the Dutchman didn't make another error, taking a well-deserved runners-up spot from Cole. Neither Heemskerk nor Newgarden were able to make much of a dent – the former finishing at the tail of the field following a spin, whilst the latter was an opening-lap retirement.

Four years in and it was clear the introduction of the Duratecs in 2006 had given Formula Ford the boost it needed – the cars were more enjoyable to drive and the racing was almost uniformly superb. Whilst the entry levels never got close to the Kent era, or indeed the peak of the Zetecs, there was always strong and evenly matched competition.

I broke into motorsport commentary around this time, interviewing both Newgarden and Magnussen. The two of them, along with Daniel Ricciardo, still stand out with an impressive combination of total focus and assurance (but not arrogance) concerning their own ability.

At the turn of the decade the Duratec era of Formula Ford was at its peak, with entries at close to 20 cars for most rounds, but crucially comprising a high-quality entry. This was headed by Australian Scott Pye, but also included rising star Scott Malvern, Josh Hill (son of 1996 World Champion Damon Hill), Grand Prix Shootout winner Tio Ellinas and future BTCC star Dan Cammish.

The title came down to a battle of the Scotts, with Pye eventually edging out Malvern following a strong final weekend of the campaign. Malvern actually scored more points than Pye, but consistency worked against him as dropped scores came into play. The season had been characterised by frantic battling as the evenly matched field spent most encounters glued together as a large pack.

Six drivers had taken victories throughout the season, and as eyes turned towards the Festival it was clear that, although Pye was the favourite, the competition was wide open. As ever, one-offs and to-the-wire deals bolstered the entry to a single-grid capacity 28 cars. A late entry of note included Danish early-season race winner Dennis Lind, who scraped together the money to get on the grid with Van Diemen – this went as far as family members electing to get refunds on their flights to the UK in order to fund tyres. Also appearing as a one-off was prize-drive-winning South African Robert Wolk who would be at the wheel of one of the pace-setting Jamun Mygales.

Two format changes from the previous year added to the fun – the Duratec contenders would have heats, quarter-finals and semi-finals to set the grid for the final and they wouldn't have to share the grid with the Zetecs.

With elimination only through vehicular destruction and disqualification, the gloves were truly off throughout the qualification races. Prior to the semi-finals, almost all the expected frontrunners hit trouble – Josh Hill suffering gearbox trouble in qualifying, Scott Malvern experiencing driveshaft failure on the formation lap of his heat and Scott Pye being drop-kicked out of the quarter-finals by Rogier de Wit. Through all the early drama, it was Dennis Lind who caught the eye, impressively winning both his heat and quarter-final.

This set the scene for two frantic semi-finals. The first was memorable for the gigantic incident that befell Robert Wolk at Paddock Hill Bend. Breaking out of sync with the car of Thomas McGregor ahead of him, Wolk was launched into a terrifying series of cartwheels, the Mygale flying almost 15 metres above the circuit before landing upside-down in the gravel trap. It was one of those moments which bestows instant silence on everyone present. Miraculously, Wolk escaped serious injury and the race continued behind the safety car. At the front, Lind withstood pressure from Malvern to continue his perfect record for the weekend as only eight cars made it to the chequered flag.

In the second semi-final it was the turn of disqualification to shake up the order. Josh Hill took victory on the road following a feisty drive and some ferocious dicing. Unfortunately, Hill had been judged to have jumped the start and was ordered to serve a drive-through penalty but he didn't see the flag and pressed on regardless. The drive-through was upgraded to a black flag (meaning disqualification from the race), but Hill still continued. Not unsurprisingly, his on-the-road victory was expunged and Hill could count himself extremely fortunate not to be expelled from the meeting, although he would start the final from the back. Tio Ellinas was awarded the victory from Pye, who had started from the rear of the grid.

The final itself was both an excellent race but also somewhat anticlimactic, as 24 cars survived to take the start. At the head of the field, Dennis Lind enjoyed a lights-to-flag run to become the 38th winner of the Formula Ford Festival, whilst behind there was a superb scrap for the remaining podium positions. Having raced through from the back of his semi-final, Pye emerged at the head of a titanic race-long tussle for second, edging out Tio Ellinas into third by just a quarter of a second. Unrewarded with a podium but with the pace to win all weekend, Josh Hill finished an eventful seventh, having climbed from last on the grid.

Victory in the Festival didn't lead to F1 stardom for Lind, but he went on to carve out a successful career in sportscars, claiming the victory in the Lamborghini Super Trofeo World Finals in 2016.

With its 40th anniversary, the 2011 Festival should have been celebratory. In reality, the event had bittersweet undertones from start to finish. The Duratecs had enough cars but didn't have the strength in depth of previous years, whilst the Kent entry was under capacity. Most poignantly of all, at the celebratory dinner on the Saturday evening, Dan Wheldon was one of many drivers mentioned in the roll call of Festival alumni who'd gone on to stardom. Tragically, within hours of Sunday's final chequered flag, he would be killed in an IndyCar race in Las Vegas.

In truth, anniversary aside, there wasn't the same anticipation for the Festival as in previous years. The 2011 British Formula Ford season had seen a dip in entries with only ten ever-presents and grids only topping 20 cars when the pack was joined by entries from overseas, most notably the Netherlands.

That's not to say there weren't quick drivers on the grid – champion Scott Malvern has gone on to a respectable career, as did rivals Antti Buri and Jeroen Slaghekke – but unlike previous years there wasn't anyone who seemed to be on the fast track to the elite. Domestically, the top talent was in Formula Renault where both champion Alex Lynn and runner-up Oliver Rowland are, at the time of writing, Formula E frontrunners.

Above all, looming over the Festival was the knowledge that this was the penultimate season for the Duratecs. Having only been introduced in 2006 and proving popular with teams and drivers alike, many felt it was too soon for such a big technical change. The Duratec class, whilst not offering the glamour of rivals Formula Renault and Formula BMW, had proved affordable, encouraged engineering innovation and given spectators some great racing. Most importantly, the Duratecs had taught racecraft to a generation. Over time, it would become clear the 2006–2012 era of Formula Ford had a great hit-rate for launching drivers into successful careers.

Arriving for 2012 would be the Ecoboost car based around the turbocharged Ford Ecoboost engine, which would be more powerful. The new formula would also represent an upgrade in safety, with chassis required to be compliant with Formula 3 safety standards. Whilst representing a technical step forward, the cars would be more expensive and complex to run. Demonstration laps at the 2011 Festival received a lukewarm response. At the time it wasn't said so explicitly, but 2011 would be the final running of the Formula Ford Festival for cars on the contemporary single-seater ladder. Already it was clear that interest in the Ecoboost formula would give a grid of 12 to 15 cars at best, and in the UK only – certainly not enough to justify a Festival format. In addition, rendering the Duratec cars obsolete so soon after their launch ensured they would receive limited support at club level.

When assessing the favourites for the Festival, it was hard to look past Scott Malvern. The 22-year-old had swept aside all comers, winning 18 of the 24 races during the campaign. Only Jeroen Slaghekke from the Netherlands and the Australians Nick McBride and Geoff Uhrane had also won during the year.

The 20-lap final went the way of much of the year, and although close, was comparatively sedate for the podium places. Malvern led from lights to flag, heading home Steijn Schothorst and McBride. Aside from Schothorst passing McBride on the opening lap, the order remained the same throughout the race.

In the context of the year, it was a fitting result – Malvern had been dominant – but it wasn't a final to rival the majority of its predecessors. Thus it was on a muted note that the Festival's 40-year run of being a fixture on the ladder to F1 came to an end. The Festival talent pool had started to dilute a decade earlier as tipped drivers from karting chose other entry-level formulae, but the Duratec era still propelled drivers up the ladder: Kevin Magnussen to Formula 1, Nick Tandy to Le Mans victory in 2015 and Josef Newgarden to the IndyCar title in 2017 and 2019.

If the prestige of the Festival had been on a gentle downward glide for much of the previous decade, in 2012 it definitively dropped into the realm of the club event. With the Ecoboost cars filling the main class of the British Championship, just 13 Duratecs were mustered. The quality of the field wasn't close to matching the pack of even two years earlier. Antti Buri took the victory in a dull final where he, Eric Lichtenstein and Bart van Os drove away from the rest of the field and each other. For the second year in succession, the podium positions were unchanged by the end of the first lap.

It was a sad end to an era which had started so brightly. For six years, the Duratec class continued Formula Ford's lineage, providing a relatively affordable start in professional motorsport. The racing was frequently brilliant and a handful of stars were unearthed. With Ford's promotion of the Ecoboost driving a new version of Formula Ford that was a further departure from the category's founding principles, the Festival could no long stake a claim to being the event it once was. Forty years since taking its bow, the Festival was no longer part of the road to Formula 1.

Return to club roots

THE 2013 season once more saw a shake up to the established order of the British single-seater ladder. The British Formula Ford championship decisively broke from the formula's roots, sacrilegiously appending front and rear wings to the cars and hitching back on to the BTCC package in a bid to boost entries. With most grids hovering at around the 12-car mark, it was only partially successful, but in runaway champion Dan Cammish (who won every race he started) and runner-up Harrison Scott, the series propelled two more graduates on to further success, with the former a now established BTCC frontrunner.

Once more, it was the proprietors of Brands Hatch (the Jonathan Palmer-led MSV) who challenged the established order of things. Pre-empting the FIA (who later had to reacquire the name from MSV), the newly launched BRDC Formula 4 championship was a contemporary twist on the Formula Ford philosophy. Although running to controlled chassis and engine regulations, the cars were (in motorsport terms) affordable to run, enabling privateers and drivers with smaller teams to be competitive.

Among the winners in its debut season was Pietro Fittipaldi, nephew of 1972 and 1974 Formula 1 champion Emerson, who replaced Romain Grosjean at Haas for the final two races of the 2020 Formula 1 season. In 2014, the series had an even greater find in George Russell, whose run to the title caught the eye of Mercedes, and with backing from the German marque progressed to Formula 1 where he currently partners Lewis Hamilton.

With a full field from day one and cars that were not overly aerodynamically dependent, the three years of the BRDC Formula 4 championship provided close, entertaining racing on a budget that was a fraction of the cost of comparable categories. Motorsport politics eventually intervened and the series morphed into the BRDC British Formula 3 championship, which has been a success, but without the same energy of that initial three-year burst.

For drivers on the F1 ladder, this was happening in a stratosphere well beyond the Festival, but after a trying 2012, the event bounced back in 2013. Although 15 or so Duratecs and Zetecs raced, the headline event for the first time since 1992 was the Kents. The introduction of an historic class and final lured some lesser-seen cars out of garages, and whilst the field was still just shy of 50 cars, it was phenomenally competitive.

Formula Ford 1600 was now a national club-level category underpinned by a strong championship promoted by the BRSCC. With few other viable and even semi-affordable entry-level routes into single-seaters, a number of karting graduates were dipping their toe in Formula Ford before moving on to higher-stakes categories. The Festival, together with Silverstone's Walter Hayes Trophy a week later, have remained solid end-of-season favourites. Throughout much of the 2010s, it was the Hayes that had the edge in terms of support and one-off special entries. Whilst the Festival was typically limited to three heats of cars, sometimes double that number made the trip to Silverstone.

Nonetheless, there was still some fantastic racing to be found at Brands Hatch, where established names such as Niall Murray and Joey Foster would take on the best of the Team USA scholarship runners and other newcomers using Formula Ford as an initial step on the motorsport ladder.

Continuing the lull from 2012, 2013 proved to be one of the Festival's difficult years with just 46 cars entering – resulting in two less-than-capacity heats. As ever, the quality at the front was good, with less than a second separating the top ten and nine respectively in qualifying for the heats. Foster and more surprisingly Team USA scholar Jake Eidson split the victories, with anticipated frontrunners Murray and Wayne Boyd finishing their respective races in the lower reaches of the top six. Foster continued his winning streak into the first semi-final, taking the flag just under two seconds clear of Boyd. Noel Dunne, meanwhile, won an exciting second encounter just a couple of tenths up on Oliver White.

With his race uninterrupted by the safety car, it was Dunne who took pole position for the final. He initially used this to his advantage, leading from White and Boyd. An early safety car served to bunch the field up before Dunne tried to break clear. On lap nine, Murray started his forward progress, moving to third ahead of Boyd before clearing White a lap later. After just one lap behind Dunne, Murray was through into an unheaded lead, a couple of poor laps seeing Dunne drop to the lower reaches of the top ten.

Murray immediately came under sustained pressure from Boyd, who spent five or so laps glued to his gearbox. A moment on lap 18 dropped Boyd to third behind White, the pair of them engaging in battle to allow Murray a decisive escape. Boyd regained second on the final lap, with Champion of Brands frontrunner White taking a deserved third. For front-row men Dunne and Foster, it was a race to forget, the pair finishing seventh and tenth respectively.

The 2013 action brought a few more out to play a year later, with the pair of heats featuring 55 drivers. The returning Dunne and Boyd were among the pre-event favourites, with Ciaran Haggerty and the Team USA scholarship driver Aaron Telitz expected to challenge.

Telitz took an impressive pole position and win in the opening heat as Dunne was a mid-race retirement. Boyd, meanwhile, claimed the second heat, albeit under pressure from Chris Middlehurst, in a race punctuated by two safety cars. The semi-finals would see the field jumbled, but Telitz continued his perfect record, winning by just over a second from Middlehurst and an ever-improving James Raven. There was more drama in the second race where Boyd was a second-lap retirement. This gave way to another thrillingly close race, claimed by Jonathan McMullen, who finished just a couple of hundredths clear of Stuart Gough in his comparatively elderly RF92.

Again it was a quantum of safety car laps rather than outright pace which determined pole position for the final, McMullen the beneficiary of just a brief interruption in his race. As 12 months earlier, the polesitter gained the initial advantage, McMullen taking an early lead from Telitz, Raven slotting into third and Middlehurst in the mix. The first moment of drama came on lap four when Telitz and Middlehurst collided, ending hitherto promising weekends for both drivers. This brought out the safety car for a couple laps.

Once released, Raven immediately applied pressure to McMullen, before moving into the lead on lap seven. After trouble in qualifying, Raven had started his heat down in tenth, and now with solid racecraft throughout the weekend he was out front. As McMullen and Gough engaged in battle, he was able to establish a sizeable lead. Continuing to press, Raven took the chequered flag over five seconds clear of the rest, recording a highly impressive victory. A superlative defensive drive from McMullen gave him second, with Gough a fine third, the pair both pressured late on by Noel Robinson. It was a good final, albeit tinged with anti-climax as Telitz and Middlehurst's early retirement deprived the race of a closer battle for the lead.

2015 saw the field initially spread across three heats, with 68 cars making the pilgrimage to Brands Hatch, an impressively strong entry with a good ten drivers in the hunt for overall honours.

Still smarting from his 2014 disappointment, Boyd laid down an early marker by winning a wet first heat, a race including Niall Murray and Chris Middlehurst, by over four seconds. Stephen Daly, meanwhile, took the second, clear of Joey Foster, with Stuart Gough down in fifth. Michael Adams took the last of the heats as reigning champion. Raven finished down in eighth – signalling the start of a difficult weekend.

Fortunately, Sunday saw much improved weather, but no immediate change to the form book, with Boyd taking the first semi-final from Joey Foster. The gap between the leading pair had continually opened as the race progressed, once more signposting Boyd as the driver to beat. A lengthy safety car ate up the middle third of the second semi-final as Daly took the win, just under a second up on Luke Williams. Raven was the race's big casualty, spinning out late on, a further retirement during the last-chance race emphatically ending his weekend.

For the first time since the 1970s, there was a third semi-final and this was the best of the bunch. Murray, having missed the previous year, proved he was back with a vengeance, taking a thrillingly close race that saw the leading quintet covered by under a second.

With only the top eight from each semi-final advancing automatically to the final, the remaining six spots on the grid would be filled with the top six finishers from the last-chance race. Historically, this race had given some of the slower drivers a final run-out, with any favourites hitting trouble in the semi-finals normally able to progress without too much drama. Not this time – a full 30-car grid of considerable quality would vie for progression. The previous year's runner-up McMullen prevailed, with the last spot on the grid for the final going to 2013 podium finisher White.

Boyd deservedly had pole position, having consistently been the fastest driver throughout the weekend. Daly lined up alongside him, with Murray in third. The final proved to be a frustrating affair after a mid-race red flag (Murray, White and Foster among those in the scenery) sapped the momentum. On the restart, Boyd was once more imperious, romping clear of a stunning dice for second. As Boyd took his second Festival win, over four seconds clear of the rest, the second- to eleventh-placed cars were running largely nose to tail. It was Barrable who emerged to finish runner-up, Gough once more steering his trusty Van Diemen to third.

A year later, the entry once more remained well over 60 cars, but with a slightly tweaked format; the three heats would filter down to the more traditional pair of semi-finals. Stuart Gough, newly upgraded to a 2008 specification Van Diemen, took the first heat, after Canadian scholarship driver Parker Thompson took a sensational pole before dropping down to sixth. Niall Murray took an impressive lights-to-flag win in heat two despite Luke Williams being with him throughout, the pair well clear of the rest. Returning to the Festival, 2011 winner Scott Malvern took a keenly contested third heat with Luke Cooper, Neil MacLennan and Jake Byrne all finishing within a second of the winner.

The sorting of the field produced a Murray and Gough front row for the first semi-final. After the first third of the race was lost to a lengthy safety car period, Murray quickly asserted his pace and was never heeded as he took the win by four seconds. Second went to impressive Team USA scholarship driver Oliver Askew, who would graduate to IndyCar in 2020, and Gough. The real fight was for the rest of the top ten, with fourth through to eighth separated by just over half a second.

Another opening-lap safety car also sapped the initial excitement of the second semi-final. Among others, the early incident eliminated Thompson and the hugely experienced Andy Charsley, who had both had podium finishes in the heats. Once properly under way it was a good race, with Malvern and Williams running in close contention. Williams took the advantage on lap ten before Malvern retaliated late on, Williams being pushed down to third behind Finnish teenager Patrick Pasma.

The final was all about the two previous winners sharing the front row: Malvern and Murray. It proved to be a one-sided affair. After leading the first lap from pole position, Malvern was demoted on the second tour and, thereafter, Murray inexorably pulled clear. Finishing over three and a half seconds up on the field, Murray had never looked troubled. It wasn't a classic final as multiple incidents served to split the field, cars tending to pair up rather than form long trains. Malvern took second, clear of Chris Middlehurst who'd never quite got on to terms, not least because Williams was snapping at his heels for the final podium position. Whilst Murray was an impressive and deserving winner, the 2016 event, after building nicely throughout the weekend, didn't have the pay-off of a thrilling final that the earlier races had hinted at.

By 2017, the Festival appeared to have reasserted its place within the contemporary Formula Ford calendar. The 75-car entry was the highest seen for over a decade and truly gave the heats teeth, with a good 15 cars failing to progress beyond Saturday.

That jeopardy came to the fore in the first heat as Joey Foster took a comparatively comfortable win from Neil MacLennan. Luke Williams, who'd finished fourth the previous year, retired with mechanical troubles and was out of the event. There were no significant casualties in the second heat as Chris Middlehurst took the honours, having deposed early leader Jamie Thorburn just before half-distance. The final heat claimed another competitive victim. Polesitter and long-time race leader Jake Byrne crashed out as he came under pressure from Matt Cowley. The latter duly proceeded to take victory from Matt Round-Garrido.

Cowley and Foster had the front row for the opening semi-final in what proved to be a close battle. Once the early safety car had been seen off, the front-row pair were joined by the impressive Keith Donegan, with Luke Cooper never far behind.

Cowley was able to hold off Foster until the tenth lap, before he conceded to the Cornishman. Thereafter, Cowley was glued to Foster's gearbox, but couldn't find a way through, the pair covered by just over a quarter of a second.

A late change of lead also decided the outcome of the second semi-final, with MacLennan's 12th lap move on Middlehurst proving decisive. A close third went to Matt Round-Garrido before the gap opened out to the rest of the field. With no safety car to punctuate proceedings, this would also give MacLennan pole for the final.

After the damp squib of the year before, this was a truly excellent final with a train of cars in contention for much of the race. MacLennan led away from pole position, with Foster tucked in right behind him, Middlehurst and Cowley not far adrift. An early safety car gave MacLennan a brief respite before Foster dialled up the pressure. On the ninth lap Foster made his move, giving him the advantage and a second Festival victory. Late on, he was forced to work for it, but not by MacLennan. Down in fifth early on, and still fourth by lap 12, Donegan flew late on, moving past MacLennan and Cowley (the latter second by this point), before challenging Foster. He only missed out by just over a tenth of a second, but still took a hugely impressive second, with MacLennan rounding out the podium after a moment for Cowley with a couple of laps to run.

2018 served up more of the same, with just shy of 70 cars to be whittled down through the trio of heats. Television coverage (particularly with the demise of Motors TV) had given way to live streaming, bringing the event online for those that couldn't make it on the day. Joshua Smith took an impressive pole position for the first heat, qualifying ahead of both Niall Murray and

Keith Donegan. The race was a different matter, with Murray taking the flag over seven seconds up from Donegan, Smith an even more distant third, heading a four-car train.

Qualifying for the second heat was extraordinarily close, with Neil MacLennan pipping Matt Cowley by nine-hundredths of a second, with Jake Craig just a further eleven-thousandths of a second slower. Now past the 50-year mark as a category, Formula Ford was still showing just how close it could be. The trio plus Chris Middlehurst retained that closeness throughout the race – the four cars covered by under a second for each of the final eight laps. Cowley ran out the winner, taking the lead from MacLennan on the penultimate lap, with Middlehurst rounding out the podium.

Heat three was more straightforward, with Michael Eastwell taking an untroubled victory from pole position. Winning by just under three seconds, Eastwell's performance was all the more impressive given that the first third of the race had been lost to the safety car. Oliver White took second by the slenderest of margins from Joey Foster.

Sunday morning and the semi-finals saw Murray and Eastwell sharing the front row for the opener. Both would experience wildly contrasting fortunes. Murray took yet another Festival race victory, leading throughout. The first half of the race saw him under constant pressure from Eastwell and Smith, but Murray was able to open up a slight advantage as the race wore on. Meanwhile Smith passed Eastwell on lap 11, before the latter hit engine trouble and was forced into retirement – the first of the weekend's favourites to drop out of contention. MacLennan was duly promoted to third after fending off a train of cars headed by Foster.

The second semi-final saw Cowley and Donegan on the front row. Once more, there were mixed fortunes as an early spin for Donegan found him needing to piece together a recovery drive to finish an eventual sixth. Also in the wars was Middlehurst, who became another of the weekend's favourites not to advance to the final. Meanwhile, having spent the first half of the race shadowing Cowley, White made his move on the ninth lap, before gradually pulling away to victory, Peter Dempsey taking third after impressively moving through the field.

Once it got going, the final was a thriller, but it did take a couple of attempts with two red flags meaning that the matter was eventually decided over eight laps. Taking advantage of good starts, Smith was able to go toe to toe with hot favourite Murray. After initially leading, Smith was deposed by Murray, but in a reversal of the earlier form book, Murray was unable to pull clear. Smith left it late, but a move at Paddock on the last lap forced Murray on the defensive for Druids, which in turn enabled Smith to move into the lead approaching Graham Hill Bend. It had been an impressive weekend from Smith, his defeat of Murray in the final a true upset for the formbook

2019 saw a slight decline in fortunes, with lower levels of support than the preceding years. The meeting evolved into a head to head between the two Irish drivers Jonathan Browne and Niall Murray. Once more, the experienced Murray had to settle for second as Browne enjoyed an imperious weekend, leading every lap of the final whilst building up a margin over Murray.

Perhaps against the odds, the 49th running of the Formula Ford Festival did go ahead in front of spectators on the weekend of 24-25 October 2020, just days ahead of a month-long national lockdown announced by the government the following week in response to Covid-19. Furthermore, the event was deemed sufficiently elite to enable overseas competitors to travel to Kent and compete.

As with everything during the Covid pandemic, motorsport experienced a strange 2020. In April, the question had been whether there would be a 2020 season at all, but once the circuits reopened in June, events across the board were well subscribed with large fields. As the autumn crept in, however, most series organisers were in a race against time to get their schedules completed and some meetings were pushed back into December in order to enable championships to be decided.

Entries for the Festival were largely in line with previous years, with just over 50 cars giving two full grids. The pick of the frontrunners were all drawn from the UK series, although several Irish competitors, the Team USA scholarship drivers and some European competitors were found throughout the entry. It wasn't a classic Festival, the usual intensity only really picking up in the final, with both the heats and semi-finals fairly pedestrian in comparison with some of their predecessors.

The final itself was a good race, with the pace and risk taking notably stepped up from the earlier races. Rory Smith added his name to the Kentagon roll of honour, leading Jonathan Browne home by just over half a second. A super battle for third saw a three-car train covered by a just a few tenths, Matt Cowley coming out on top, edging out Chris Middlehurst and Team USA's Bryce Aron.

The Festival's 50th anniversary weekend was a superb celebration of the Festival and Formula Ford. Whilst still very much a club event, such luminaries as Eddie Irvine were to be found in the Paddock grandstand during the weekend, the hallowed seating being something of a who's who of Formula Ford past. Former winners Roberto Moreno and Jan Magnussen were tempted to come out and play – Moreno reunited with an RF80 bearing an identical livery to his 1980 challenger RF80.

If the weekend ticked all the nostalgia boxes, the current generation of drivers also put on a thrilling show at the front of the field. The clouds served up classic Festival weather too, with Sunday's action delayed at some points due to standing water before conditions cleared for a largely dry final.

The final was truly fitting for a 50th anniversary race, the only thing missing being a true grandstand finish. Otherwise, the merits of the category were to the fore, with a leading pack of cars running wince-inducingly close to each other throughout. 2003 and 2017 winner Joey Foster started from pole and, for the first half of the race, seemed set for his hat-trick. Foster's lead was never comfortable and the Ray was far from the quickest car around much of the track, but tactical wiles seemed to be enough.

The early laps were too intense to last, the cars running impossibly close with no margin for error. The inevitable accident occurred on the run to Druids on lap four as Niall Murray and Oliver White touched, the ensuing pinball of cars eliminating Thomas Mills. The resultant safety car meant there was no hope of early escape for Foster.

When the safety car retreated, Foster was under sustained pressure from Jamie Sharp, who remained within a couple of tenths of a second. On lap ten, Foster ran wide at Clearways, elevating Sharp. Sharp and Neil MacLennan then enjoyed a ferocious fight for the lead, with the honours moving back and forth before Sharp took a decisive advantage on lap 17. He was chased all the way by MacLennan, taking the flag just

0.077s clear, with Max Esterson a very close third. Post-race, MacLennan lost his second place to a yellow-flag infringement, with Andre Castro elevated to complete the podium.

It had been a hugely impressive performance from Sharp, who now faced the challenge of five decades worth of winners before him in trying to pick his way upward through the motorsport ranks. Meanwhile, 50 years on from the first Festival, Formula Ford once more showcased its ability to provide thrilling racing.

Afterword

FOR A motorsport series or event to last ten years is an achievement. That the Formula Ford Festival is still going strong 50 years since its launch is an incredible feat, especially given the shifting sands of motorsport politics – some of which have been covered in this book. It has been an ever-present and source of enjoyment for so many during this time.

Hopefully this book has captured some of the flavour of the Festival and revisited a few of the great races and dramatic moments. However, it will only ever be the second-best (if that) option – do yourself a favour next October and spend Festival Sunday in the Paddock grandstand. I promise you won't regret it.

obil 1
Ford
Cars with a future
GEMINI OIL
DUCKHAMS
47